JURA REILLY

CIRCLE OF AMBER

PO Box 6415, Highton Victoria 3216 Australia

Email: jurareilly@hotmail.com

This book has been published under the auspices of Geelong Writers inc., PO Box 1306 Geelong Victoria 3220 Australia, in association with Beach Shack Publications & with seed funding from the Australian Lithuanian Foundation. The contents of this book do not necessarily represent the views or policies of these organisations.

ISBN: 978-0-9953868-0-8

eISBN: 978-0-9953868-1-5

Acknowledgements

To all members of my U3A Life Matters Class, not only for their constructive criticism about some of the parts of this novel that were read out as short pieces, but also for their friendship.

My thanks also go to Birutė Mašanauskas, John Mašanauskas and Dana Kendall-Sanders for their valued input, and to Ann & Geoff Usher for their hospitality and showing me the sights of Sydney.

For financial support, I am grateful to the Australian Lithuanian Foundation, with a special thanks to Algis Šimkus OAM for his encouragement in this project.

Technical and editing support was provided by Dr. Martin Hooper, and by staff at IngramSpark & BookPod.

Many thanks to my husband for the cover illustration depicting the village of Ventuva, and for his editing, encouragement and patience.

Foreword

This novel is dedicated to my children and grandchildren, so that they may discover more about their Lithuanian heritage. The recipe section at the back of the book is for those who want to learn to prepare food from Lithuania, Latvia & Estonia.

If readers want to learn more about Baltic traditions and culture, I invite them to join the Facebook group *Baltica: https://www.facebook.com/groups/291014531051707/*

The author's short stories & poetry in English have been published and are noted in www.austlit.edu.au.

The author may be contacted by e-mail at jurasamber@gmail.com.

Contents

Contents

KRISTINA

Winter had crept upon Samogitia and a light snow was falling in the remote village of Ventuva. Tucked away in the north west of Lithuania, it nestled comfortably on the banks of the Venta River. In her simple wooden cottage, Kristina shivered as she took off her long woollen shawl and put on an apron, hoping that the stack of birch logs would last the coming winter. People usually described her as a pretty, slightly built woman, with long, blonde hair that she sometimes wore plaited and pinned up on top of her head. The intensity of her topaz blue eyes startled everyone who met her for the first time. She started to grate potatoes for the big meat dumplings, which the Samogitians called *kleckai* that her family would enjoy for dinner. Humming to herself, she fashioned them into smooth oval shapes, filling them with minced pork. Setting them to one side, Kristina looked out the kitchen window waiting for her husband's horse and wagon to appear. In the meantime she observed the village women. They reminded her of a colony of ants, as they scurried back to their cottages, cocooned in their thick winter cloaks and headscarves. Everyone knew that once the sun had set, witches would start to lurk about dark corners, even in summer when the sun shone brightly for most of the night. Stealthily nipping across the river, they could create all sorts of havoc for those foolish enough to be outside. Kristina spied her big black cat Murk at the windowsill and knew it would be a long cold winter, for he'd grown a layer of fur so thick, that she could not even feel his ribs. Sarga, her faithful wolfdog, was already stretched out by the fire, her bushy grey tail covering her eyes. Her paws trembled slightly, as she dreamt of the rabbits that had escaped her iron jaws that morning.

Suddenly, an uneasy feeling ran through Kristina. Instinctively she began to fight the eerie forces that she could feel swirling about her home. She knew what had to be done and began to grind up the wild herbs that she'd collected previously in the forest. Taking off her circular amber pendant, she held it high above her big cooking pot and called upon Vėjas, the Lord of the Wind, and Zvoruna, the Forest Goddess, for their assistance. She then chanted the magic words as she threw the herbs into the boiling water.

'Turn circle turn, turn to the East. Turn circle turn, turn to the West. Turn circle turn, turn to the North. Turn circle turn, turn to the South.'

The pendant swung towards the east and there was a rumbling as a flash of lightning zigzagged across the evening sky and lit up her home. From deep inside the misty pine forests, The Ancient Ones answered.

'Beware! Take care! Three revolutions are in the air!' howled Vėjas and Zvoruna, as Kristina felt an artic chill descend upon the room.

'Call upon us in your hour of need,' they shrieked as they swirled out of Kristina's cottage and back into the pine forests. Although Kristina was somewhat puzzled about what three revolutions could possibly occur in Ventuva, she stretched out her arms to give thanks to the Ancient Ones. She then shook her head to clear her fuzzy brain as she came back to herself. Time was the essence. The time would surely come when she would need all her spiritual and physical strength to do battle. Kristina would summon the ancient gods to help her, for the number three was more powerful than one. Whilst she was pondering whether to start boiling the water to cook the potato dumplings, she heard a frantic knocking. On the frozen doorstep stood Maria, her sister-in-law's neighbour.

'Kristina! Thank goodness you're home! Asta's screaming like a pig being led to slaughter!'

'Jėrgotėliau, kon dabā dėrbtė? - Oh what shall we do? Romas isn't back yet!' Kristina replied in Samogitian.

'Quick! You have to come with me this very minute! You know what happened last time!'

Asta had been in labour for two days, and Kristina had been run off her feet checking on her sister-in-law's progress, then rushing back to her mother's cottage to collect her two little girls. She gathered her herbs and oils and trudged along the muddy path to Asta's cottage. It had seen better days, since it had been inherited from her husband's uncle, who'd been the village blacksmith. Unlike his uncle, Tadas wasn't a diligent bookkeeper and the villagers had run up countless debts after he took over the smithy. Still, he was the only blacksmith in Ventuva and although he had some outstanding bills, he was sure that the villagers would pay up sooner or later. Kristina could hear Asta screaming, as she twisted and panted on her bed.

'Oh my God! Make the pains go away, just make them go away. Kristina, I beg you!'

Asta was delicately built and Kristina worried whether this baby would be able to be born. Asta had lost two babies in two years, unable to carry them to full term. She then asked Maria to walk Asta around the cottage, to ease her pain and to hasten the baby's birth. Then they helped her sit up in bed, propped up by four pillows.

'It won't be long now,' Kristina reassured Asta, as she wrung out the wet cloth again and placed it on her forehead. 'You must conserve your strength for the last stage.'

'What do you want me to do?' asked Maria.

'Why don't you boil the water to make Asta a cup of raspberry leaf tea hurry along her labour?'

Getting out her lavender and sage oil, Kristina started to massage Asta's belly, singing to the unborn babe the songs of the forest, which had protected her people for centuries. Asta's screams intensified as she cursed Tadas, Maria and Kristina. From experience, Kristina knew it was the last stage of her labour.

'Bear down, bear down now, just one more big push,' she instructed Asta, who had started screaming for God to take her.

'Oh my, look at that, it's a healthy little girl,' whispered Maria, after the tiny babe finally slithered out from Asta, who felt dizzy with relief. She fell back exhausted against the feather pillows and closed her eyes. Kristina tied the umbilical cord and cut it at her forefinger's mark, then rubbed the new born all over with salt. Afterwards she wiped the babe with warm water and a clean cloth. Like her mother had taught her, Kristina gently cleansed the baby's gums with honey, to increase her appetite. Last of all, she was wrapped tightly in swaddling clothes and put to her mother's breast.

'Poor Asta. She's totally exhausted,' said Kristina to Maria.

'We women were born to suffer. Praise God that Asta was able to give birth to a live baby this time,' replied Maria. She then turned to Tadas who was smoking his pipe in the kitchen.

'You can go in now to see your beautiful little daughter.'

Instead of going to see his wife and congratulate her on the birth of their baby girl, Tadas went straight to the cupboard and pulled out a bottle of *samagonas*.

'Blast her! She should have given me a son!' Ignoring their raised eyebrows, he held the bottle to his lips and took a few long gulps of moonshine.

'What? Don't give me any of your filthy looks! A man's got to toast his daughter, doesn't he?' he snarled in response to the reproachful glances from Maria and Kristina.

Kristina ignored him and went outside to bury the afterbirth under the oak tree and chanted the magic words to keep Asta and her baby girl safe from harm. She promised to return the next morning to check on both of them. Only then did she return home. Thank goodness that Elena would look after her daughters whenever she was called upon to deliver a baby in their village. Sarga looked up hopefully at Kristina from the fireside that she shared with Murk. The wolf dog was a flash of silver grey with black markings on either side of her chest, the result of Ventuva's village dogs interbreeding with the timber wolves over many decades. She'd been hand raised by Kristina from a tiny pup, after Romas had found her curled up, cold and shivering beside her dead mother, whilst he was out cutting timber in the forest. He'd bundled her inside his fur lined jacket next to his heart and brought the puppy home, much to the delight of his two daughters. Until Sarga was six months old she slept on Virginia and Renata's bed, and more often than not, had shared their food. Sarga had repaid their family by turning out to be an excellent watchdog in return for saving her from starvation. She'd chased many foxes out of the henhouse and slept beside the calves in the barn. Usually, Murk and Sarga slept in the barn during winter, but from time to time Kristina relented and let them into the cottage. Wearily, she took off her apron encrusted with blood and placed it into the wooden washing pail to soak overnight. Carefully washing her hands and face in the basin, she then crept into bed beside Romas, thankful for the warmth of his body and their feather duvet.

'We have a little niece,' she whispered and kissed his cheek. He mumbled something and wrapped his strong arms around her, gathering her to his chest. Lulled by his steady heartbeat, she fell asleep instantly. That night, she dreamt that Asta was screaming for her to remove the three grass snakes that had coiled themselves into her matted hair. The next morning, Kristina recounted her unusual dream to Romas.

'Sweetheart, it was only a dream. You're just overwrought with helping Asta give birth, that's all,' he reassured her. 'Come on, let's have some breakfast and you'll feel a lot better.'

'Typical,' thought Kristina, 'men and their stomachs. Food's their answer to everything!' However, she was secretly pleased when the whole family tucked into her fragrant home-made rye bread spread thickly with freshly churned butter and cottage cheese. Whistling cheerfully, Romas kissed Kristina goodbye, hitched his wagon to his trusty horse and set off to work at a Latvian farm across the river, where he and his men were going to build a barn. Once he had gone, Kristina checked her cauldron. Her potion had cooled, but as she began to bottle it, she felt that it lacked something. Later, she would have to consult her little book of herbs. She was certain that the Ancient Ones would give her a sign to guide her to the missing ingredient. Quickly, she dressed herself and her two little daughters in their warm winter coats, then gathered her herbs and set off to check on Asta. It felt unusually quiet in her house and no smoke rose from the chimney. Nervously, Kristina knocked then pushed open the door.

'Hello! Asta where are you?' Kristina called out, but there was no answer. Kristina made her way towards the bedroom. There lay Asta, as white as the linen sheet which covered her, the newborn babe at her side. Tadas was snoring like a train with his head on the kitchen table. Shocked to her core, Kristina recoiled from the pale body, although she sensed that her sister-in-law was already dead. She tried to shake Tadas awake, but he was a giant bear of a man, well over six feet. Nothing she tried was going to wake him.

'Tadas! Come on, for God's sake wake up! Your wife's dead!' Kristina shouted in a panic.

'Did you hear what I just said? Asta's dead!' She then gave his legs a few, hard, swift kicks in desperation.

'Wha, wha, what?' slurred Tadas in a drunken stupor, not comprehending what she was telling him.

'How could you? How could you get so blind drunk, and not realise your wife was dying?' Kristina screamed at him. Tadas snored loudly and slept on.

'You worthless piece of shit! Get up! Get up right now!' Kristina administered three more fierce kicks to his legs.

She couldn't remember being so angry in all her life. She snatched up the baby and was relieved to find that at least she was still alive. She set down eighteen month old Virginia into a corner and told Renata to keep an eye on her. Pacing the floor she wondered what she should do. She was still breast-feeding Virginia to comfort her now and then, so she put the new baby to her breast. She could always give her a top up with goat's milk if she didn't have enough. All she knew was that she certainly couldn't leave the poor little mite there. Rewrapping the baby up in her swaddling clothes, Kristina picked her up carefully and then took Virginia's hand and placed it into Renata's.

'Be good girls for me. Now, hold hands, so you don't slip in the snow. We're going to see Aunty Maria.'

A few doors away, Maria saw Kristina trudging up the snow covered path with her two little girls and a bundle in her arms.

'What have you got there Kristina? A cabbage from your garden for me?' she said jokingly. Choking back her sobs, Kristina told her the sorry tale.

'Oh Maria, It's awful. I think that Asta must have haemorrhaged to death whilst Tadas, that drunken, good for nothing husband of hers snored on and on. What am I going to do? Everyone will blame me, I just know they will!'

'Shhh, my dear, don't blame yourself,' Maria tried to reassure her friend.

'They will, you know they will. They'll call me a witch. If only I'd stayed with Asta a bit longer, all this may not have happened. Maybe there was something wrong with her inside, you know, something I didn't know about?' Kristina kept on babbling.

Maria hugged her. 'Who knows? Who knows what happened,' she soothed. 'I can't blame you. I was there too. It's God's will.' She crossed herself. 'You're in shock Kristina. Sit down and I will make you some strong black tea, and I still might have a few pieces of my poppy seed cake in the cupboard.'

'Virginia and me want some cake too,' demanded Renata from the corner of the room.

'Asta's in God's hands now. You and Romas will have to help Tadas to bring up his baby.'

'Of course, of course, you're right,' replied Kristina, dabbing her eyes with her handkerchief as she sipped on her tea. 'As soon as he comes home tonight, I'll ask him what to do.'

'Romas is that poor mite's uncle. He won't object to helping out his brother for a while in these circumstances, now will he?'

Kristina finished her tea and thanked Maria, who reassured her that she'd go back to Asta's cottage, tend to her body and then bring over the baby clothes and nappies.

'Now don't you worry and keep blaming yourself. I'll drop them over as soon as I've fed my hens.' As they walked back to their cottage, Kristina asked Renata what they should name her new cousin.

'How about Julia or Edita?' replied Renata, thinking of her two best friends in the village.

'Dita, Dita,' lisped Virginia.

'Let's ask papa when he gets home tonight.'

Kristina put some thick borscht on the stove for their lunch, then opened her chest of drawers and removed one to lay the baby in. Gathering up a woollen shawl, she nestled the baby in the folds.

After lunch, Maria came over with all the baby things, informing Kristina that when she'd gone back to Asta's cottage, Tadas was nowhere to be seen.

'He's probably staggered off to Vlad's place to buy more of his *samagonas*.' Maria spat on the floor. 'That Tadas is as useless as tits on a bull.'

After feeding and settling her niece, Kristina went out to the well near the stable to fetch more water to wash her apron. It was still encrusted with blood from last night's birthing. As she cranked the bucket up, she thought she saw an image of Romas' face, contorted with pain. She quickly crossed herself three times, dismissed the image she'd seen, and hurried back to her washing. She touched her amber pendant nervously. Before long, they heard Sarga barking excitedly as Romas came up whistling up the path.

'How are all my gorgeous girls this afternoon?'

'Papa! Papa! Mama's got a new baby,' Renata informed him as she tugged at his coat, dragging him inside. 'And we're going to call her Julia!' She hopped from one foot to another. Virginia toddled towards him and clung to his legs. Romas laughed and swooped up both of his daughters.

'All right my beauties! Let's go and see what sort of baby your mama's got.'

To his amazement, there was Kristina sitting on their bed, rocking a newborn.

'Hello sweetheart,' he said, bending down to kiss his wife on her cheek.

'So when were you going to tell me that we have a new baby?' he teased. His wife looked up with tears in her eyes.

'Meet our little niece,' she said as she returned her husband's kiss.

'Shouldn't she be home with Asta and Tadas?' Romas glanced nervously around the room, expecting them to be sitting somewhere.

'Oh God, I feel so guilty! Asta died last night and no one can find Tadas.' Kristina dissolved into a flurry of tears.

'Heaven preserve us! What a terrible tragedy!' Romas ran his fingers through his hair.

'What are we going to do?'

'First we'll have to bury Asta, and then it looks like we'll have to look after the baby until we can find Tadas.'

'Some of the village men are searching for him and the women have gone to prepare Asta's body for burial,' Kristina blurted out in a rush.

'Good, at least we're trying to get things organized.'

'Can you climb up and get the cradle from the loft until we can get the one from Asta's house?' she whispered. 'We can't let her sleep in this drawer forever.'

Slowly Romas climbed the ladder up to the loft. He tried not to let his worry show as he indicated to Renata and Virginia where the baby was going to sleep.

'Does this mean that we get to keep her?' asked Renata hopefully.

'Baba,' said Virginia proud of her new word. The family gathered around Asta's baby.

'Let's call her Julia,' Kristina said. Renata danced around the table pleased that they had chosen the name she wanted.

'Julia, Julia, we've just got a new baby called Julia,' she sang excitedly.

After a quick dinner of *koldūnai* and once the three girls had been settled into their bed, Kristina and Romas talked long into the night about what they were going to do once Tadas was found.

'Perhaps I could look after Julia during the day and then Tadas could have her at night? But I think we will need to baptise her as soon as possible, don't you?' suggested Kristina.

As much as Romas loved his brother, he was well aware of all his faults and somehow he couldn't see Tadas looking after a newborn baby.

'Good idea sweetheart, I will ask Father Casimir when he can baptize Julia. Then Tadas could hire a wet nurse from the village. Anyway, let's just see what happens,' he said cautiously.

Privately he wondered whether Tadas had fled Ventuva and his responsibilities. Some of the men in Ventuva had upped and left their families in search of a better life in a land called America. Romas wondered what his life would be like in that mythical country he'd heard so much about. Someone had told him that the streets were paved with gold, and that they had running water and lights that miraculously turned on with the flick of a switch.

After the customary three-day vigil by the coffin, Asta was buried in the little cemetery next to her parents. There was no big wake, just Kristina's and Romas' families sharing a meal of *kugelis* and cabbage rolls. Romas' parents kept moaning on and on about the shame Tadas had brought upon their family since he had still not shown up. The villagers had begun to gossip that maybe he'd met with foul play, or perhaps a wolf pack had torn him to pieces. Others intimated that he might have a mistress in a neighbouring village or across the river in Latvia.

After a hasty baptism performed in their little church of St. Lawrence and nourished by Kristina's milk and some extra from their cow, Julia continued to thrive. At eight months she had a mop of blonde curly hair, big brown eyes and was crawling after Renata and Virginia. Then at ten months, she was toddling about in her circular wooden walker that Romas had made previously for his two daughters. At twelve months, Julia walked by herself. In time, the villagers accepted the fact that Tadas wasn't coming back and came to accept Julia as Kristina's own child. In the meantime, Kristina struggled to cope with three children less than five years of age. First, milking the cow and goat every morning, then scraping the messes off Julia's nappies into a wooden bucket, then emptying the contents into the hole in the toilet hut outside. Feeding Julia. Feeding Virginia and Renata. Making sure that Romas had some meat each day for his dinner. Trying to dry nappies in winter was no small feat either. After Kristina had washed them on her scrubbing board and wrung them out, she'd drape them around the stove to dry on the wooden rail that Romas had made. He often joked about coming home to a mass of white clouds. He saw his wife's exhausted face and would often ask Kristina if they'd done the right thing in keeping his brother's child.

'*Nu va*, well then. What else could we have done?' Kristina would reply, even though every muscle in her body ached.

'Who else in the Ventuva could have looked after her? Families have to stick together.'

Kristina considered herself lucky to have a married a strong and stoic man, who had surprised her by his wicked sense of humour as she got to know him better. Romas was the complete opposite to his brother Tadas who was a morose, sneaky, spineless creature. It was the unspoken, painful truth that she and Romas knew only too well. Luckily they had plenty to spare because Romas had a lot of work in and around Ventuva and was a highly regarded builder.

That year, Christmas wasn't the happy occasion it usually was at her mother's house. Still grieving for her sister-in-law, Kristina thought back to happier times when her mother Elena had followed all the traditional Christmas Eve customs. Although they had a Christmas tree, this year there weren't that many presents. Her sisters would egg her on and Kristina watched in awe, as her aunts on the stroke of midnight would put two candles on a table, then place between them a glass filled with water, a small handful of birch tree ashes and then drop one of their wedding rings inside. They would urge Kristina to look through the glass. She didn't recall ever seeing anything, but Elena would insist that surely she could see the image of her future husband. After everyone had left, Kristina's mother would go out to the barn and scatter a handful of wheat and peas on the ground. She was convinced that if she performed this task, the following year she would have healthy baby animals.

These childhood memories must have had some impact on Kristina, because on that Christmas Eve, she wouldn't let Romas lock their barn door.

'Please, please, can you nail a small wooden cross onto the door,' she begged her husband. Romas agreed good-naturedly, knowing that his wife firmly believed that any harmful spirits lurking about in Ventuva would be not be able to cause any mischief.

'Perhaps our animals will speak to us tonight,' he said, smiling broadly.

Spring announced itself when the first violets appeared in their garden. Renata, Virginia and Julia were making a huge racket, jumping up and down with excitement. They knew Easter was coming when their father went into the forest and came back with small branches of pussywillow to help their mother to make the traditional flower arrangements called *verbos*. Romas helped them secure the decorations with intricate coils of rope. Since Kristina had an eye for colour, her arrangements were much admired. If made carefully, some *verbos* could last a long time. Her mother would often remind everyone that she still had four of them in her loft that were at least twenty years old. On Palm Sunday, they took their floral arrangements to be blessed and then the traditional hitting with the *verbos* took place.

'Ouch, ouch! Stop hitting me!' cried Virginia in mock terror.

'It's not me silly! That was the *verbos*' fault, not mine!' chortled Renata.

At that point Elena decided to teach both granddaughters a lesson, so she gave them a good whack with her *verbos*. 'Now it's my turn to drive the devil out of you two!'

Julia said nothing. She had learnt to be quiet and docile and not attract any attention to herself. She hated violence of any kind, whether real or in jest.

The night before Ash Wednesday, the long awaited Shrovetide festival was about to take place. People had been busy constructing a huge papier-maché effigy of Morė, the female symbol of Winter, which was going to be burnt in their market place in the centre of Ventuva. All week Kristina had been helping her girls make masks to take part in the parade. Julia had been working on a dog mask, Virginia wanted a goat mask, whereas Renata insisted that she should have a bear mask. Kristina and Romas were going as a witch and a devil. Someone was going to dress up as the Fat Man in a pig costume and the girls had heard that he was going to have a huge battle with a villager dressed up as the Hemp Man.

'Why are they going to do that? They'll hurt themselves.' said Julia.

'Sweetheart, it's just an old tradition. It means that Spring is finally here and Winter is going to be defeated,' explained her father patiently.

How they all longed for a touch of the sun's rays and to see all the flowers budding, and to see the storks building their nests. Their summer stocks of preserved vegetables and fruit were running low, and Romas wanted to catch some fresh fish for his family.

'They're really excited, aren't they?' Kristina remarked to her husband as they walked arm in arm to the festival, pushing Julia in a wooden pram that he'd had made. Virginia and Renata skipped ahead, shrieking with laughter for being allowed to stay up so late. They joined their friends in the procession admiring each other's masks. Some wore tall witches' hats and had rubbed their faces with flour to give them a deathly pale appearance. Others took on the personalities of the masks they wore. As the procession passed the church, Elena noticed a young boy in front her, who was wearing a dog mask. As he walked along, from time to time, he would cock his leg up against Julia, who kept pushing him away.

'What in heaven's name is he doing?' yelled Elena to no one in particular.

'Calm down Elena,' said Romas. 'That little boy's wearing a dog mask just like Julia, so he's just imitating the village dogs he's seen. Haven't you ever noticed dogs peeing up against fences or posts?' Satisfied with Romas' explanation, Elena waved in a royal fashion to the villagers who were unable to take part in the parade.

'So, my sweetheart, are you excited like our girls?' Kristina teased Romas, once the procession ended.

'You bet I am, seeing you dressed up as my little witch,' he replied saucily as he playfully slapped her on the bottom. He didn't care what anyone thought when he saw a few of the village women giving him disapproving looks. In fact he decided to blow them a kiss.

'You'll pay for this!' shrieked Kristina as she slapped him back. People's laughter and the smell of pancakes added to the carnival atmosphere. They joined in the procession and sang traditional songs to mark the end of winter, finishing off with an impromptu folk dance to beat the cold. Across the Venta River, the Latvians were also celebrating Shrovetide and their melodious songs carried across the water.

'I wonder if they make masks and have a procession like us?' asked Virginia.

'I am sure they do, by the sound of that noise,' replied Romas.

'Winter, winter, get out of our yard!' sang their three girls over and over again until they were hoarse. Pancakes topped with cottage cheese mixed with cream and dried cranberries were among the crowd's favourites. Kristina had made some *spurgos*, those delectable jam donuts earlier that day, but they had all been gobbled up by lunchtime. After being in the procession, watching the traditional fight between Winter and Spring and the ritual burning of the winter effigy, the girls were totally exhausted. Romas helped Renata and Virginia climb into the pram with Julia and wheeled them home. As he lay them on the bed they shared, he felt blessed to have three healthy daughters and wife who grew more beautiful each year. As Kristina climbed into their bed, she rubbed her cold feet on Romas' calves. She started to think about about Easter and all the dishes she would make for her family, but there was seven weeks of Lent before that.

'Whose cold feet can I feel in my bed?' Romas demanded and began to tickle Kristina, who laughed and playfully pulled his ears. Nothing was sweeter than payback time.

At midnight, on Holy Wednesday, Romas went to the Ventuva communal bathhouse with all the other men for their ritual cleansing before Easter. They shared jokes and talked about all the work their wives would force them to do. The next day it would be the women's turn.

'I just can't wait to go and see to the dragging of the herrings around the church,' announced Virginia.

'Oh that's so cruel!' replied Julia, who was growing up to be a thoughtful little girl who hated cruelty of any kind.

'Well they won't be real ones! Don't you know anything?' said Renata scornfully to her youngest sister, whom she thought was quite silly.

Like their friends, Renata and Virginia had drawn a picture of a herring on a piece of wood and were pretending to drag them around the church and into the churchyard. They shrieked with laughter as they were followed by others, hitting the wooden fish. The next morning Kristina took her daughters to join the women at the bathhouse. She liked to gossip with her best friend Laima and the other women who had been her bridesmaids. Now they too had children and they compared what their offspring were doing or saying. Older women would interrupt and give them advice, mostly that naughty children needed a good clip around the ears to make them behave. After washing her daughter's long hair, Kristina combed it thoroughly so that there wouldn't be any fleas. The women were glad that Holy Wednesday had passed since it had been a day of fasting. Mind you, most women still gave their small children a drink of milk, or a piece of meat and let them have a bit of butter on their bread.

'Come along girls, today's Easter Thursday, which means that you have to give me a hand with the housecleaning,' said Kristina gaily as they walked home from the bathhouse.

'Oh mama, do we have to?' pouted Renata who wanted to play with her wooden dolls.

'Come on, if we split up the jobs, we'll get them done quickly and then we can have some of my special yeast pancakes with jam.' Kristina knew that bribery always worked wonders.

'How about you and Virginia wash the windows and sweep the floor? Here's some cold tea, get a rag and make a start!'

'Tea? What are we going to do with this tea?' cried Renata.

'Look, I'll pour the cold tea into this basin. Dip this rag into it then wash the glass in the window. Virginia can dry the glass off with another rag. Julia can sweep the floors.'

'Well, what jobs are you and papa going to do?' asked Renata with her hands on her hips.

'Papa will whiten the walls and the stove and I will wash the clothes,' Kristina continued.

'We don't want any dirty cobwebs in the barn, so I'll take care of that,' added Romas.

'And Papa, afterwards, we're going to fill our aprons with wood chips. Then we're going to scatter them in all the corners of our cottage,' added Renata.

'Yes, that's what we're going to do, because then we'll find a duck, sitting on some eggs,' said Julia solemnly.

'Oh, you girls are so funny,' chuckled Romas. 'Whoever told you that old wives' tale?'

'But it's really, really true Papa. Grandma Elena said so.'

'I'm sure it is,' replied Kristina. 'I also remember my aunts telling me to go over to our next door neighbour's house and steal a handful of firewood, because it would mean that I would find lots of birds' nests in summer.'

'And did you, you naughty girl?' asked Romas his sides splitting with laughter.

'No, not at all. Instead, the neighbour's wife chased me out of their house with her broom. I was so scared that I wet myself,' said Kristina with a smile. Her daughters' eyes were as wide as saucers at that image of their mother.

'Then I got into big trouble with Mama because my skirt was wet.' Kristina didn't want her daughters stealing anything. That night, once they were asleep, Kristina lit a candle, blew it out and put it into the corner of the kitchen. She then held up her amber amulet and chanted thrice, 'As this candle extinguishes, let our eyes close and disappear from our enemies forever.' Kristina hoped that this spell would keep the evil forces away. She then placed a handful of salt in a piece of cloth, tied it and hid it under their bed, so that no one would find it. This would protect her daughters and animals as well.

'I still don't understand how you can go to church and still follow the pagan ways,' remarked Romas, as he watched her.

'Well, that's just me. I believe in God, but I also believe in the Ancient Ones too. It's called Life!'

Romas just shrugged his shoulders and walked away. He hated it when villagers would nudge him and ask him how his wife the witch was faring.

When Kristina woke up on Good Friday, she was pleased that her cottage was spick and span. Now their flax harvest would be plentiful. Just for good measure, she heated up the stove with artemisia and scooped up any insects she could find and threw them into the fire. Then she asked Romas to take away the ashes and dig them under her big oak tree at the front of their cottage.

'Come on you lazy bones!' she called to her girls. 'Time to start baking the bread and decorating our Easter eggs.'

Renata, Julia and Valerija stumbled into the kitchen rubbing their eyes. 'Is it Easter today?' asked Julia. 'Has the Easter Granny left us any eggs?'

'I'm sure she will, but only if you do not speak with anyone, from midnight till noon tomorrow.'

'Mama you're joking, that can't be true,' pouted Renata.

'Of course it is,' replied Kristina solemnly. 'Grandma Elena says so.'

Two can play this game she thought.

'And as you know, Grandma Elena is always right,' added Romas.

'My grandma also used to tell me that on Good Friday everyone has to go and wash outside, because Spring has come and the water is warm.'

'Just don't smash any of my pots,' warned Kristina. 'That superstition's only for rich people.'

The family continued their good-natured banter about all the old traditions they knew throughout the day, whilst the bread was rising and the smell of it baking filled the cottage. Romas went out to milk the cow and check on his animals. He then went and got his fishing gear, dug up some big fat worms and set off for the Venta River nearby. As he reached his favourite spot, he saw Jonas Malkas, one of his co-workers, fishing there as well. Jonas was a mild mannered man, whose wife had died the previous spring. He was known for his fishing prowess and always managed to hook a good-sized pike at any time of the year. They both sat down on the riverbank. Romas lit his pipe and both of them chatted away about the next big building project they had to rebuild a barn.

'I wonder how that barn burnt down?' remarked Jonas casually.

'Who knows? The old fellow told me that lightning struck it,' replied Romas. They continued to muse for an hour or so about the many ways that fires started, until Romas felt a huge tug on his fishing rod. He played the line, walking along the riverbank, reeling in the fish.

'It looks like it's a big one,' remarked Jonas casually, even though he was a bit jealous that he hadn't got a bite first.

'Sure is, he's fighting me with all he's got,' replied Romas, desperately hoping that he wouldn't lose that night's dinner. Kristina had insisted that they must have the traditional fish dinner for Good Friday, come hell or high water. When Romas finally finished landing his catch, it was a huge pike, enough for dozens of meals.

'My goodness! It's a huge monster! He must be the old grandfather pike which everyone's been talking about for years!' shouted Romas.

'Haven't seen anything this big in all my life!' yelled Jonas, as he helped his friend pull the pike onto the riverbank.

'Look, why don't I give you some?' offered Romas. 'It's getting late and I'm sure that you and your boys wouldn't mind having a few bites of this big fellow.'

'That would be wonderful,' replied Jonas, 'It would sure save me a few hours trying to catch my fish for the day. Thanks, I really appreciate it.'

'Don't mention it. I'll need your help to carry him back to my house. Then we can gut him and cut him up.'

The two men hauled the fish onto their shoulders and walked slowly back to Romas' house. Along the way, they got quite a few admiring glances and numerous slaps on their backs. Young village lads began to follow them, poking at the fish and yelling out excitedly to Romas and each other. 'Mr Kirvis, Mr Kirvis! Let me touch it! Please!'

The word spread quickly that a huge monster had been caught.

When the two men got back to the cottage Kristina couldn't believe her eyes. A crowd had gathered outside her barn door, eager to see the enormous pike that everyone was talking about and would without any doubt, talk about for years to come. Her three girls crowded around their father and watched him haul it over to the barn. Fascinated, they watched as the pike was gutted and scaled and cut up into pieces. Sarga watched as well, knowing that when her master was finished, she would get the insides of the fish. She wasn't a fussy eater. That night, as Kristina fried the pieces of pike in butter, she gave a silent thanks to the Venta River for providing her family with such a delicious fish. Afterwards, she placed a dozen eggs on the table, ready to be decorated the next day.

'Don't anyone of you girls touch those eggs or there'll be hell to pay!' she warned her daughters.

The next day being Easter Saturday, Father Casimir blessed the water for people to take home. Afterwards, the men set to building a bonfire made of old crosses in the churchyard. The fire was lit and then everyone rushed to snatch some of the sacred Easter fire and hurry home with it.

'Can we come too? Can we? Please papa,' Virginia begged. Romas had always gone by himself. He would say, 'When you are bigger, I'll take you.'

'That's not fair!' complained Renata. 'You'd take us with you if we were boys.'

'Why don't you help mama dye and decorate the Easter eggs? She's been saving all our onion skins for ages!' Both Romas and Kristina had learnt over time that the key to managing their three daughters was to distract them with other things.

In order to carry the sacred fire back home, some people had brought along pieces of dried birch fungus, others had little coils of rope. Romas took a small metal can with a piece of rope inside, because from previous years, he knew what a huge effort was needed to keep the Easter fire burning, whilst everyone was hurrying home. Those who had it on a bit of rope would have to continuously twist it about and be very careful that they didn't burn themselves. Only three years ago, fire had blown into two little boys' faces and hair, scarring them for life. When Romas passed the sacred fire to Kristina, she put out the old fire in her stove and then she lit a new fire with the Easter flame. Their neighbour Rasa usually kept the Easter fire burning in the stove till next Easter, because like others, she believed that it would bring luck and peace to her family. Who would ever disagree with that? When building a new house, Romas always placed some coal from the Easter fires into the corners of the new home. He was never short of work as a builder, because people knew that he respected the ancient traditions and in turn the villagers respected him. That afternoon, Julia, Virginia and Renata made little paper egg nests and helped their mother dye the eggs with onion skins in a big pot. Romas took out his sharp knife and scratched a variety of traditional patterns on the eggs, showing his daughters how not break them. When the family had finished, Kristina got out a lace-edged linen serviette and placed the decorated eggs in a straw breadbasket in the middle of the table. After the girls had finally fallen asleep, she hid the eggs she'd dyed in bright colours beforehand. On Easter Sunday morning the girls were wide awake at five, and straight away began searching for their Easter eggs.

'Easter Granny left me two eggs in my clogs!' Virginia announced to everyone.

'Mine were in those baskets I made! Easter Granny liked them the best!' Renata informed her sisters.

'I found two under my bed in my dolls' box,' Julia told her mother shyly when asked where she had found her eggs.

'Mama, why are our Easter eggs different from the ones we've got for lunch?' asked Renata slyly. Some older children at school had told her that there was no such person as the Easter Granny. Kristina wasn't going to shatter the illusion and tell her girls that she secretly used different dyes. Even though she was barely awake, she put a leg of pork to cook slowly in the oven for lunch. Some people had begun to roast lamb on outside spits and the delicious smell of meat wafted across the village. Since they didn't have any lambs, she began to show her daughters how to construct one from a block of cold butter. It was going to have the pride of place in the middle of their Easter lunch on the top of some sprouted oat greens for grass.

When it was time to walk to St. Lawrence's Church, Kristina made sure everyone was warmly dressed even though it was spring. It was always freezing in church and Julia got colds so easily. They took some bread and cheese to place near the Virgin Mary's altar to be blessed by Father Casimir. After the service they wished their friends a Happy Easter and took Grandma Elena home with them for Easter lunch. Before the meal began, everyone stood around the table, whilst Romas prayed that their home be a peaceful one. Grandma Elena began the tradition of cracking eggs with everyone.

'You know, she said to her granddaughters, 'If your eggshell is stronger, you are going to live longer.' Everyone laughed as they cracked their eggs and wished each other a happy Easter.

'I win!' shouted Renata, 'Ha, ha, my eggshell is the strongest! Ha, ha! Now I'm the one who's going to live forever!'

'That's not fair,' complained Virginia, who had begun to mimic Renata's tone of voice when things didn't go her way.

'No arguing, it's Easter Sunday. Come on everyone, let's eat,' suggested Romas. 'We don't want your mother's delicious food to get cold, do we?'

There was silence as Kristina served up her mouth-watering roast pork and boiled potatoes sprinkled with dill. Elena had brought over a *bapka* cake she'd made the day before. There were also fat dill cucumbers, marinated mushrooms, hot cabbage with caraway seeds, homemade cheese, rye bread and butter.

'That was an exceptionally delicious Easter lunch my darling. I am so full that I can't eat another bite,' announced Romas, as he leaned back on his chair and unbuttoned the top of his trousers.

'Nor me,' said Elena, as an unladylike belch escaped from her mouth.

'But Mama's made *paska* for dessert,' argued Renata, who panicked that they might not get any dessert at all. As the eldest, she felt that she had to speak up for her sisters, in case they ever missed out on any treats.

'Stop whining and being such a greedy girl!' Elena told her quite firmly. 'You, of all people don't need too many desserts. Go and help your mother! For a start, you and your sisters can pick up some the cracked Easter egg shells off the floor and feed them to the hens, so that they will continue to be good layers.'

As soon as they were outside, Renata poked her tongue out at her grandmother. She knew she was stocky, but she was not fat.

It wasn't her fault that she looked like her father, with her auburn unruly hair. Now for example, her friend Ruth was fat, very fat. The other children would tease her that she looked like a balloon.

'Balloon, balloon, baboon, baboon!' the village lads would yell at her, as they'd run past.

Renata was just a growing girl. It wasn't fair that Mama hadn't made her a new dress for Easter, like she had for Julia. She got very jealous when people said that Julia took after her mother Asta, with her silky blonde hair and big green eyes.

'She'll grow up to be a real heartbreaker, that one,' the villagers would remark when they saw her all dressed up for church.

Virginia on the other hand, was a mixture of Kristina and Romas. Her delicate bones and long neck came from her mother and her dark hair and eyes she inherited from her father.

After lunch, Kristina and Elena cleared the table and Kristina picked over the left over pork bone and popped it into a pot to make soup the next day. After that, she'd give it to Sarga to gnaw on. A few more eggshells were burned in the stove. Later, Romas dug the remaining eggshells into their vegetable garden. Earlier that day it had also been his job to sprinkle the holy water around their cottage, garden and barn.

After all their chores were finished, it was time for the long awaited dessert, a fragrant *paska* with fresh cream. The girls looked forward to the egg-rolling contest most of all. Romas fetched the wooden trays he'd made a few years ago and set them up in the kitchen. He propped the ends up on a block of wood, so that they were on a slant and everyone got their trays ready. Since everyone had a different coloured egg, it would be easy to see who the winner would be.

'Now what colour would you like Elena?' asked Kristina.

'Red! I want a red egg!' shouted Renata.

'Don't be such a rude girl! Wait your turn! Grandma Elena is our guest, she gets to choose her colour first,' admonished her weary mother.

'I would like a green one please,' said Elena.

'Yes, it would be nice if we used all our manners,' Romas reminded his daughters.

'Blue for me, please papa,' said Virginia.

'Yellow for me please,' whispered Julia.

'I get the red one, I get the red one! I'm going to beat all of you!' yelled Renata.

Romas went over to Renata and took away the egg. 'You, young lady can go and sit in the corner since you have forgotten your manners.'

'It's not fair! Not fair!' whined Renata, who was starting to shed crocodile tears at being reprimanded.

'If she were my daughter, I'd give her a good smack on the bottom. That way she'd remember her manners in no time,' said Elena, who thought that Kristina and Romas should be much firmer with Renata.

Romas and Kristina ignored Renata's tantrum and started the tournament by rolling their eggs down the wooden slide. Once everyone had rolled their eggs, Julia emerged the winner since her egg touched Virginia's. Renata looked at her scornfully and poked her tongue out when she thought no one was paying any attention.

February the fifth would always be etched in Kristina's mind. It was St. Agatha's Day and she was getting ready to bake the traditional loaves of rye bread and have them blessed at church. She raised her arms to the sky and called upon the ancient gods.

'Oh hear me Ancient Ones! I call upon you to protect this home from fire, lightning, disease, and other troubles!'

Just as Kristina was putting the loaves into the oven, Sarga pawed at the door to go outside. Kristina looked out towards her pine forest and felt a strange, eerie stillness enveloping the countryside. Sarga took up her usual post on the porch and let out a long, mournful howl. Virginia and her sisters rushed over to the window. Dozens of timber wolves were gathering on the riverbank. One by one, the wolves formed a circle and started to howl until the village echoed. Kristina gasped in fright, clutching her amber pendant around her neck, as she heard Sarga answer their sad calls until the noise was deafening. Kristina clasped her daughters to her side.

'Mama, why are the wolves making that scary noise?' asked Renata.

'They're just talking to their friends in Latvia, nothing to be scared of.'

'I don't like them howling like that Mama,' added Virginia, as she buried her face in her mother's apron.

Even though Kristina grew more and more uneasy as the howling continued, she tried to act light-heartedly and cajoled her daughters to go and play at housekeeping with their dolls, just to keep them occupied.

'I'll be the father going to work and you can be the mother,' Virginia told her sister, as she sat their two wooden dolls facing each other on the kitchen table.

'No! I want be the rich lady of the manor house, because I'm older than you,' retorted Renata. As Kristina smiled ruefully at Virginia's answer, she noticed Birba, the village simpleton, trying to scramble up the slippery path to her cottage. No one knew his real name or how old he really was. Dressed in tattered hand me down clothes, that the villagers gave him, he earned a few kopeks delivering messages. Orphaned at a tender age, he and his sister Magdalena, lived in a tiny wooden hut on the edge of the forest. In his haste, Birba fell over a few times, but he hauled himself upright and pounded frantically on Kristina's door.

'Mm madam! Mm Mrs. Kirvis! Www, watch out! The w..wolves! Mmm Romas, Mmm Mr. Kirvis, he's, he, he's … .'

'Slow down! What are you trying to say?' she cried out. 'What's happened to my husband?' Kristina whimpered, as she remembered the disturbing image she'd seen in her water well.

'He- he's in-in the f-forest, in the f-forest,' Birba stammered out the last bit of his message and ran off to spread his news to the rest of Ventuva.

A terrible lethargy stole over Kristina as she slumped into the chair. Was it a figment of her imagination or did Birba really say that her Romas was lying injured somewhere in the forest? Taking deep breaths, she winced in pain and willed her brain to process what she'd just been told. Surely the wolves hadn't torn Romas to pieces? Yet she had seen the image of Romas' contorted face in the water well on a few days ago. Could her well predict the future again, as it had with Asta? Dare she trust in its predictions? If only she warned her husband to be extra careful this morning, before he'd set out to pick up his workmen's pay.

Her two daughters looked up at her, bewildered to see their mother crying.

'Mama, I don't like Birba! He's scary! I want my papa!' cried Virginia as she clung to her mother's skirt.

'Where's papa? When's he coming home?' whispered Renata, clutching her doll tightly to her chest.

Kristina's fears were soon realized when she saw three men trudging up the narrow, muddy path, pushing her husband's covered body on a handcart. Looking from one man to the other, she gasped, 'Is it true then? Was he torn to pieces by the wolves?'

Their spokesman Jonas Malkas, took off his cap. 'No Mrs. Kirvis, he wasn't, but there seems to be a nasty bruise on his neck.'

Several of the village women came with offers to help Kristina wash her dead husband and prepare him for the vigil. She insisted on washing him herself and in doing so, she noticed a huge bruise that went right around his neck. She'd seen many types of bruising in her healing work and this was no ordinary bruise. Romas' knuckles were red raw, so he'd obviously fought his attackers. There had to be more than one, Kristina thought as she noticed the other bruises on his back. Quickly she searched Romas' leather pouch where he kept his money in his inside coat pocket. Empty! Now, her deepest suspicions were aroused. Who in Ventuva would want to rob her husband? She knew that the authorities wouldn't bother to investigate what happened. They had more important things to do, like line their pockets with bribes from rich people who wanted a favour here and there. Her husband was an ordinary worker like most of the people in Ventuva. From now on her family would have no father, no protector. How would she and her three daughters survive? The family relied on Romas' building skills for an income. As the village's midwife, Kristina was usually paid in potatoes, firewood, vegetables, or anything people could spare.

Kristina knew that she would have to steel herself to keep awake, in order to keep vigil by her husband's side for three days and three nights. Sarga didn't leave her side, as she desolately followed her mistress, everywhere she went. Looking sadly into her mistress' eyes, Sarga would let out a mournful whine at regular intervals. Soon the professional mourners would arrive to begin their age old Samogitian laments for Romas' soul. These women would have to be fed and paid. Long ago, her people had been the last pagans to be converted to Christianity. Some of their traditions still held sway, even though their village had its own little wooden church since the seventeenth century.

'Why? Why was he taken from me now?' Kristina kept sobbing to her mother. She still couldn't believe that Romas was actually dead. Surely he'd wake up any minute, telling her it was all a joke. Surely, tomorrow morning he'd kiss her on the cheek and ask her to make his favourite potato pancakes for breakfast.

Elena tried her best to comfort her daughter and handed her a small glass of *krupnikas*.

'Come on my dear, drink this liqueur, it will calm your nerves. I really know how you feel Kristina. I've been through this. Remember that whenever you see a cuckoo, it will be Romas watching over you.'

Kristina nodded through her tears. She still had the task of washing her husband's body. No one was allowed to come near him. Afterwards she dressed him in his best shirt and trousers.

'No mother, I don't want to wrap him in a linen shroud like you did when papa died,' she snapped at Elena who was fussing about. The village women helped her lift him onto a board covered with a white linen sheet that she'd woven herself as part of her dowry. Romas was placed in her tiny parlour, near the back wall with his feet facing the door. As was their custom, his body would be laid out in this position for three or more days. Soon all her neighbours would come to pay their respects and reminisce about the times he'd helped them to build their barns and cottages.

'Come on Kristina, you've still got to open the windows and the door, so that your husband's soul can fly out freely,' urged her mother, as she placed a warm shawl gently around her daughter's shoulders. Being a widow herself, Elena knew only too well what hardships were in store for her daughter. She bustled about, tending to her granddaughters, helping anyway she could.

The priest preached a long sermon in their church, praising Romas' hard work ethic and asked forgiveness for all his sins. Forgiveness indeed, thought Kristina. I won't be forgiving anyone for killing my husband. That bruise hadn't appeared from nowhere. An eye for an eye was her train of thought as she choked back her tears. After she and her daughters had thrown the last handfuls of earth into Romas' grave, they slowly walked backed home. Despite a lot of coaxing, Sarga refused to leave her master's graveside and Renata and Virginia were sniffling and crying on either side, as they trudged home with Elena. Julia was being minded by her friend Maria.

'It's going to be too noisy at your house with the wake tonight,' Maria had reassured her. 'I'll look after the little one for you, then I'll bring her over afterwards. You've got enough on your plate.' She hugged her friend and urged her to be strong.

Stepping inside her cottage, Kristina took off her coat, shook off the snow and went to lay out the food for the mourners.

'*Nu va*, well then. Aren't we lucky that your Romas kept a supply of *kvasas* in your cellar?' grinned one of the toothless villagers at the wake that followed.

Lucky? Kristina could not believe her ears. The old man licked his lips as he finished the glass of Romas' beer in two gulps.

Oh yes, it was indeed fortunate that she would not have to spend her precious coins for the funeral drinks. She had asked the butcher to slaughter their only pig for the wake, which would last for several days. Later she would make a *skilandis* and ask her neighbour to help her smoke it. Romas would always smoke their sausages and any eels he caught. If there was not enough food and drink, the villagers would certainly gossip about her and how paltry Romas' send off to eternity had been. Her mother Elena and her best friend Laima had been an enormous help and kept passing around the platters of food and filled up endless cups of chamomile tea for the women and beer for the men. Kristina smiled at them gratefully, for the countless bacon buns and cabbage rolls they'd made for the wake. Kristina accepted the condolences from her neighbours gracefully, even though she'd previously overheard them saying that it was a pity she didn't have two strong sons to look after her, now that Romas was gone. What insensitive gossips, she thought to herself.

'*Oi, oi*. You poor dears. You poor, poor little orphans!' Well-meaning villagers came to pay their respects to Renata and Virginia who sat shell-shocked in a corner of the kitchen.

'Pft! Who knows what's around the corner? One day you're a chicken and the next day you're a feather duster!'

After that callous remark, Virginia let out a loud cry. 'Go away! I want my papa!' This outburst was followed by Renata sobbing that she too missed her father. Whenever it was possible, either Elena or Kristina would cuddle the girls, or Laima came and sat with them, telling them that their father was in heaven with the angels.

When everyone had finally gone home after the wake, Kristina was emotionally and physically exhausted. Maria brought back Julia all bundled up in her old fur coat. Unfortunately Renata was still wide awake, as she padded into the kitchen holding her favourite blanket, followed by Virginia sucking her thumb and clutching an old rag doll.

'Come on girls, isn't it time you were asleep? Mama is so tired.'

'But Mama, if you tell us the story of Eglė Queen of the Grass snakes, we'll go to sleep, I promise,' pleaded her eldest.

Even though Kristina felt bone weary, she tucked her daughters back into the bed they shared and began their favourite bedtime story.

'Once upon a time there was a young girl called Eglė. One day whilst after swimming in the sea with her two sisters, Eglė discovered a sea serpent curled up in in her clothes. Speaking to her in a man's voice, the serpent agreed to go away only after Eglė promised to be his wife and only then would he let her have her clothes back.'

Soon all three girls were fast asleep, but later on, as Kristina was stepping out to the toilet hut, she heard Sarga growling. Noticing Vlad on her doorstep, she wondered whether he'd left something behind.

She opened the door slightly. 'Oh, hello. Did you forget your pipe?' she enquired politely.

Vlad pushed open her door and staggered in with a bottle of his moonshine. He made himself comfortable on her best chair, the one that her Romas had made for her as a wedding gift. Carved for her, with a love heart in the back of it.

'Just wanted to be neighbourly and make sure the little widow's orright,' he slurred. 'You'll be wanting a bit of looking after now that you're all alone. How about a drop of my *samagonas*?' he mumbled slyly.

'No, thanks. I'm fine, really I am.' Now why don't you go, Kristina thought to herself.

'Old Vlad here knows how to give a woman a good time,' he winked suggestively, as he leered at her full breasts visible through her night shift. He made a clumsy move towards her.

Kristina's polite smile slipped from her face.

'No!' she shouted in disgust, putting her arms protectively in front of her shift. 'Get away from me you filthy drunk!'

'Don't go all shy with me you Prussian slut! You should be nicer to me, after the gift I've brought you,' hissed Vlad, as he towered over her tiny frame and tore open the front of her nightgown.

'C'mon bitch, let's have a look the rare treasures you've got hidden under there.' Vlad unbuckled his belt, moving towards her.

Kristina's heart gave a wild thump. There was nowhere for her to hide.

'Attack!' she shouted to Sarga, and with a ferocious snarl, the wolf dog sprang at the intruder to protect her mistress. Vlad fell against the table with Sarga crouching over him, her fangs bared, ready to tear out his throat. A puddle of urine trickled down his trousers and onto the floor.

'Get out of my house!' yelled Kristina. 'If Romas were alive, he'd kill you for this!'

Vlad staggered out the door, totally humiliated. 'I won't forget this! You'll pay for this you Prussian bitch! Curse you to hell! I'll get you back, I will make sure that I do!' he shouted as he crawled away. Kristina blacked out. She awoke to find her daughters in front of her.

'Mama! Mama! What happened? Why was Sarga barking?' asked Renata, as she gaped at her mother's torn night shift. Kristina hastily covered herself with her shawl.

'Don't worry, it's nothing. I fell over. You must have had a bad dream,' soothed Kristina. 'Why don't I make you some warm milk and honey and tell you a story.'

'Tell us about Grandma Elena and how she walked thousands of miles to get here,' pleaded Renata. Virginia clutched her wooden doll and sucked her thumb. Thankfully, Julia slept on.

'Well it was a long time ago and no, it wasn't your grandma Elena, it was her grandmother Renata, and grandfather Ignas. When Napoleon was marching through our lands, it was the beginning of a hot summer,' began Kristina, as she tucked them back safely into bed. 'Renata's family didn't want a bar of him, unlike some people who saw him as a liberating hero.'

'What's a hero?' interrupted Renata, who had been named after her great-grandmother.

'Someone who is brave and treats others kindly,' explained Kristina as simply as she could.

'Then the Ancient Ones sent huge thunderstorms and rain which went on for five days and five nights. Our roads became so muddy that the horses couldn't cope and broke down. There wasn't enough food for them or the soldiers. The Frenchmen were supposed to help us be free of the Tsar, but instead, they mistreated our soldiers who had joined them. There wasn't any food or fresh water. Then thousands of soldiers got very sick.'

'Did they spew everywhere?' interrupted Renata again.

'Yes, they were very sick, darling,' continued Kristina.

Virginia giggled. 'Mama, Renata said a bad word and now you will have to go and wash her mouth out with soap.'

Kristina ignored her comment and went on with the story.

'So that's why Grandma Elena's grandparents didn't want to stay in Prussia. They sold their big farm, hitched their wagon and began their long trek to Samogitia. Once they arrived in Ventuva, Renata and Ignas bought a farm from a local noble, near the river with a large parcel of forest around it.'

'People called them "Those Prussians" didn't they?' added Renata.

Oh Lord, will that child ever shut up? Kristina thought, as she yawned loudly and continued with the story.

'Yes, because they were very hard workers. They built an enormous wooden farmhouse, a big barn and established a vegetable garden and a huge orchard. Later, when your grandma Elena was sixteen, she married a tall handsome man.'

'That was Grandpa Pranas, wasn't it?' interrupted Renata for the umpteenth time, since she knew the story by heart.

'Yes, it was,' sighed Kristina. If only her daughters would go to sleep.

'Planas,' piped up Virginia, who was still unable to pronounce the letter "r".

'Yes, your Grandpa Pranas was a very kind man and he always gave us fresh cucumbers to dip into honey whenever we went for a visit,' continued Kristina patiently.

'I don't like going to grandma's toilet hut,' remarked Renata. 'It stinks in summer and it's freezing in winter.'

'You can't do anything about that, that's the way it is for everyone,' replied her mother patiently.

'But, I'm scared that when I squat down, I'm going to fall down into the hole,' complained Renata, who lately had become obsessed with people's toilets.

'Well, aren't we lucky that papa made us a box to go over our toilet? We are one of the few people in Ventuva who have got a toilet with a seat, so that we can sit down in comfort.'

Thankfully, Virginia had fallen asleep and Kristina was praying that soon Renata would as well. Privately, Kristina thought that her father was too fond of his drink, and as a result, her mother's land holdings had diminished at a rapid rate. Elena was forced to sell off more and more land to pay for Pranas' alcohol addiction that eventually was the death of him. If only he'd stayed sober, they could have given her a piece of land as part of her dowry, and she wouldn't be so badly off as she was now.

'What did grandma Elena do after grandpa died?' asked Renata who should have been fast asleep by now.

'You know what grandma did,' Kristina replied. 'She became a midwife and in bad times, always managed to survive by selling her fruit and vegetables at our Friday market.'

'I love grandma's cold beetroot soup best of all,' remarked Virginia.

'Me too, replied Renata sleepily. 'It's so much nicer than that sour sorrel soup.' Kristina smiled at her daughters, knowing that their tastes would change once they got older. She felt a bit sad that she couldn't remember her grandparents who'd died of tuberculosis soon after she'd been born. But she remembered her two aunts well enough who liked to sing her favourite children's songs with her and her uncle, who liked to play jokes on everyone.

By two in the morning, both daughters were finally asleep, but Kristina tossed and turned for the rest of the night, racking her brains as to how she would survive with three growing girls to feed and clothe. She was lucky that her foster-daughter Julia was such a good sleeper. Sometimes when she was teething and grizzly, she'd make up some warm poppy seed milk, which would calm her down, and Julia would revert back to her usual happy self. She'd accepted the fact that by now, that Julia's father Tadas was probably dead and could be of no help to her. His cottage had been willed to his eldest brother in the capital. That was a long way away and since Tadas' body had never been found, the Russian authorities had seized his house and installed their own police official in it. Her mother would probably be able spare her some flour, and she still had her cows.

'If only I'd been nicer to my mother-in-law when she was alive,' said Kristina to herself as she walked about in a daze. Mrs. Kirvis had always been advising her about how to bring up her daughters or coming over to tell her what favourite foods she should be cooking for Romas.

'Your mother will be the death of me,' Kristina would often complain to Romas when he was alive. 'She's always interfering. Nothing that I ever do is good enough. My bread's not as good as hers or my cottage cheese dumplings aren't as fluffy.'

'Calm down sweetheart,' Romas would say and put his arms around her. 'Mama means well and it's not as if we have to live with her, she always bringing us extra vegetables and fruit from her garden.'

'She says that I spoil our daughters too much and that I should give them a whack now and then. Plus she's always criticising me for not giving you a son.'

'How about we just say that God hasn't given us one yet? That should keep her quiet,' Romas would soothe his wife and he'd stroke her hand.

Now she missed her mother-in-law and her husband and would give the world to have them back in her cottage advising her or joking around with her.

'Oh my darling, tell me what to do,' Kristina whispered aloud.

Whenever she felt anxious or frustrated, she had a tried and true method for taking her mind off what was bothering her. She'd roll up her sleeves and bake bread. As soon as she sank her fingers into the soft dough, she felt the calming effect immediately.

Over the next three months, an idea took shape in Kristina's mind. Each day, her friend Laima visited her and as their children played, they talked about the future.

'Apart from your midwifery, what else could you do to earn some money?' asked Laima.

'Do you think that maybe I could make and sell various herbal remedies?'

'Well, you certainly have learnt a lot from your mother about plants that harm and those that can heal people.'

'Yes, but there are only thirty families in Ventuva and some of them are nearly as poor as I am,' remarked Kristina sadly, as she wiped away her tears with her apron and made more cups of strong, black tea for her old bridesmaid and herself. 'I'll think about it.'

One morning, while she was still contemplating her options, she glanced out the window and saw Vlad on her doorstep with a few of Romas' workmen. He wouldn't look directly at her, still smarting from the memory of losing control of his bladder when Sarga had bared her sharp fangs at his throat. He'd learnt from his experiences, so unbeknownst to Kristina, he'd instructed one of his men to throw a huge bone over to Sarga, knowing that food was scarce at Kristina's house. That would shut up that beast and keep her out of their way for a while.

'A very good morning to you, Mrs. Kirvis! I trust you and your daughters are well? We're here to collect our wages,' he announced cockily.

'What? My husband sacked you a month ago,' replied Kristina anxiously, as she drew her daughters behind her. The men murmured uneasily amongst themselves.

'My poor husband, God rest his soul, has only been in his grave a week, have you no shame?'

'Sorry to bother you madam,' said Jonas, who was one of Romas' best workers. He took off his cap respectfully and twisted it in his hands. 'But we have families to feed.'

'You all know very well that Romas was murdered while coming home with your wages,' Kristina pointed out as she stood with her hands on her tiny hips, trying to make herself look bigger.

'Says who? Anyway, what proof have you got that he was murdered?' challenged Vlad. 'It was probably those bloody gypsies who are always roaming about stealing our chickens.'

'I saw the strangle mark on his neck, with my own eyes, as I washed his body for burial.'

'Begging your pardon missus,' interrupted Jonas, cap in hand, 'We are sorry for the loss of your husband, truly we are, but unless we've got some money, our families will starve.'

'What do you want me to do?' replied Kristina. 'I can't conjure up money out of thin air.'

'You're a witch aren't you? That's what everyone says around here. So why don't you just wave your magic wand and I'm sure the coins will rain down on us in a thrice,' Vlad sniggered.

'Look men, I am sorry, but I haven't got any money here,' countered Kristina.

'Well then, we'll just have to find a few of your good husband's tools, won't we? They will go towards settling your debts,' replied Vlad with an air of superiority.

'Come on men, let's go!' They followed Vlad into the barn and began carrying away everything they could lay their hands on. Emboldened by his success, Vlad helped himself to the scythe, a big axe, a saw, and as much as he could take away in his handcart. Only Jonas looked back at Kristina sadly, mouthing, 'Sorry, sorry,' as he left.

Kristina stood frozen on the doorstep, her twig broom still in her hands. Then she ran into the barn. Her husband's tools were gone. Hay was strewn about, barrels were overturned, and her butter churn was lying on its side. Thank God they hadn't discovered the axe he kept under their bed in case of intruders. At least she would be able to chop firewood. What if they came back for more? What if they took away her horse or her cow or her hens?

At nightfall, she buried her grandmother's gold cross and her two silver serving spoons in the pig-pen. Well, she didn't need them anymore, and the pig had been slaughtered for the funeral feast. Thank God that she still had her scrubbing board and tub and her enamel bucket for the cow's milk. In autumn she used it to collect mushrooms, in summer to pick wild berries.

'Curse that blasted man to the four corners of this earth,' Kristina muttered. She recalled how Vlad and his cronies had got drunk at the wake on her poor husband's beer and still kept calling out for more. And all that time, they'd been plotting and planning to come by and take away everything of value that he owned. Vlad was the sort of man who would continue to be a thorn in her side because she'd refused his advances. She wondered why Sarga hadn't warned her of his approach this time. Then she spied her tied up at the back of the barn, gnawing on a huge bone.

'So that's the way he bribed you,' Kristina whispered to her dog. Sarga whined softly and looked up at her guiltily, as if to say that she shouldn't blame her, since she was hungry and there was never enough food to spare. She patted the soft grey head as the dog trotted beside her back to the cottage.

A few months later and Kristina was reduced to boiling up pea pods and potato peelings for meals. The hens weren't laying and the cow's milk had dried up. She had to sell her horse and she no longer had any grain or flour. Her mother wasn't much better off, but she didn't have four mouths to feed. Sometimes, she'd send Renata to beg whatever Elena could spare. Although Kristina still had her cow, it would cost her money to mate her with a neighbour's bull and she still needed money to buy flour to make bread and buy material for her daughters' clothes and shoes from the cobbler. Luckily her daughters' clothes could be handed down.

Even then, their dresses, which she had turned inside out and re-sewn with Maria's help, were patched to the limit.

One market day, as she trudged into the village square up to her mother's vegetable stall, she noticed Ivars, the Latvian farmer whose barn Romas had rebuilt.

'Good day to you Madam Kirvis,' Ivars greeted Kristina polite-ly and doffed his hat. 'I haven't seen your Romas on our side of the Venta for a while,' he continued, making conversation. They were able to understand one another reasonably well, since the Latvian language and the Samogitian dialect shared similar words.

Overwhelmed, Kristina burst into tears. Her mother explained the sad situation. After Ivars politely offered his condolences, he enquired as to how she was coping without her husband. Kristina choked back her tears. 'Frankly speaking, we're not. I don't know how we will survive.'

'I happen to need someone to watch over my herd of cows,' he said. 'Maybe your eldest daughter could become my cowherd and watch over them during the week, then the fishermen could row her back across the river on the weekend? Look, I can't pay her very much but at least your daughter would be fed and housed during the week. My wife Baiba makes three solid meals a day, and there's always some left over,' he said proudly.

Kristina thought of Renata who was five. It would be another two years before she could start at the village school. Then, there would be even more expenses. Maybe, it could work out, and per-haps later, Virginia and Julia could also mind Ivars' cows.

She thanked Ivars for his kindness and agreed to his proposi-tion. She'd made up her mind and saw her mother Elena nodding in approval. For once she didn't argue, usually she had a lot to say about everything and without much tact.

'Everyone's got to do their bit when times are hard. Renata already feeds the hens, and Virginia helps you with the butter churning,' she said. 'I am sure Renata can watch over a few cows during the day. Here, take this smoked fish that I bought. You can have it for dinner.'

Kristina called over her three girls who were playing with the puppies and ducklings at a nearby stall.

'I have some good news,' she said, taking Renata's hand.

'Are we going to get a puppy?' asked Virginia hopefully.

'Well, no, not today. Maybe next year, when you can look after it properly,' smiled Kristina. 'Besides, we don't want Sarga getting jealous, do we?'

After having the smoked fish and a piece of bread each for their dinner, Kristina took aside Renata and told her about Farmer Ivars' offer. Renata promptly burst into tears.

'No! No! You can't! You can't send me away! Papa would have never done that. You don't love me anymore. You love Virginia and Julia more than me! I won't go, I won't!' Renata stamped her foot and continued sobbing.

'Sweetheart, you know that's not true,' replied Kristina, upset herself. 'But there's no way around it. Besides, you'll have nice food to eat every day and come home on the weekend to play with Julia and Virginia.'

'But I'll miss you mama. Please, please don't send me away! What will I do by myself all day? Where will I sleep at night? What will I eat? Do they eat the same food as us across the river?' More and more questions were fired at Kristina.

'I am sure I remember your papa telling me that the Latvians eat the same sort of food like us. They eat rye bread like I make, cold beetroot soup even those bacon buns that you love so much.'

'But Mama, what if they don't? I'll starve to death over there and you won't even know!'

'There, there, you're a big girl now. You have to pitch in and help your mama, now that papa's no longer with us,' reiterated Kristina.

'But I won't understand a word they're saying!' This was Renata's final trump card.

'Be that as it may, but Farmer Ivars and his wife speak a similar language to ours, he'll make sure you understand what he wants done with the cows.'

At about 10 p.m., Virginia came in and woke her mother complaining of feeling sick.

'I think I'm going to spew,' she said, and then promptly vomited all over the floor.

For the rest of the night Virginia retched and then was wracked by stomach spasms.

Kristina rushed to get the toilet bucket as her daughter cried out that her tummy was going crazy.

'Am I going to die mama?' she whispered, as she kept vomiting.

Kristina felt her forehead. Virginia was running a temperature, but her hands and feet were icy cold. Dipping a cloth into a bowl of water, she sponged her daughter's forehead and chest. When Virginia began to vomit up green bile, she became very frightened.

'Is God punishing me for being a bad girl?'

'Shh, shh, no, that's not true. You'll be alright. Take a little sip of water. That's my girl.'

'It must have been the smoked fish that grandma gave us. Your little tummy obviously doesn't like smoked fish. Promise me that you won't ever eat it again, just to be on the safe side.'

The next morning Virginia was pale and listless, but at least she wasn't vomiting anymore. She spent the day sleeping and was given some dry crusts of bread and water. Later on, Kristina made her some chamomile tea. Renata and Julia sat on the bed next to her and offered all their dolls for her to play with. For once, there was peace and quiet.

The following Saturday, Renata was farewelled by her family and taken to the edge of the Venta River where she was rowed across by a fisherman to Latvia and Farmer Ivars' farm. He and his wife Baiba met her, took her home and gave her a good lunch of thick vegetable soup and rye bread. She was introduced to their surly son Maris who ignored her, and later Ivars showed her where she was going to sleep in the barn. Renata felt totally alone and cried that night for her mother and sisters. She had never slept alone before and wondered if she was being punished for being naughty. 'I wish you were still alive papa,' she whispered. As Renata wriggled about on her pallet, trying to get comfortable, out of the corner of her eye, she spied a little marmalade cat sitting on a bale of hay. 'Puss, puss, puss,' she whispered. 'Hello, little pussycat. Do you want to be my friend?' The cat seemed to understand Samogitian, because he jumped down gracefully and came over to sniff her outstretched hand. Renata patted his head, fondled him under his chin and was delighted that he allowed her to pick him up. Satisfied that this small intruder was not going to harm him, Marmalade Cat, curled up beside her and purred. Soon Renata was fast asleep.

The very first question that Kristina asked Renata when she came back on the weekend from cow herding in Latvia was, 'What did they give you to eat?'

'Um, the farmer's wife calls it *Pelēkie zirņi.*'

'That word *zirni* sounds like our word for peas,' exclaimed her mother. 'See, I told you Latvian was similar to Samogitian!'

'What's in it?' asked Julia.

'Um, I think it's a kind of stew Mrs Baiba made from dried peas.'

'That sounds disgusting,' remarked Virginia, wrinkling up her nose. 'Just dried up old peas?'

'It looked as there was some onion and bacon in it as well.'

'That doesn't sound too bad,' said Kristina. 'Maybe I should give it a try one day?'

'Please don't, mama,' begged Renata, as she gave her mother a handful of kopecks. 'I've had it for lunch and dinner every day this week!'

That set the weekend pattern. As soon as Kristina arrived at the river to pick up Renata from the fisherman's boat, she would ask her what she ate that week. Sometimes, Renata told her quite happily that she had cold beetroot soup like her mother made or potato pancakes and sour cream. Kristina was relieved that the Latvians on the other side of the Venta made similar dishes to the Lithuanians.

The seasons came and went as Renata watched over Ivars' cows and each weekend she'd bring back a handful of kopecks for her mother. Sometimes there'd be a small piece of bacon or a loaf of rye bread. The little family was grateful for every morsel of food and Kristina congratulated herself for taking up Ivars' offer. However, a time came that whenever she'd ask Renata her usual questions about her week and the food she ate, her daughter would look daggers at her, change the subject and go and play with her sisters, telling them about her friend Marmalade Cat.

In the meantime, Jonas, one of Romas' workers found excuses to pass by Kristina's cottage offering to split logs for the winter in exchange for mending a shirt or patching a pair of trousers. Jonas was tall, blond, straight-backed man, with a fetching ginger beard. Even though he was a widower he was admired by many women in the village. Sometimes he'd bring Kristina a wooden spoon that he'd carved and etched with flowers. Other days he'd have some chestnuts or raspberries for the girls. His wife had died giving birth to a stillborn baby girl. For reasons known only to himself, Jonas had left Vlad and the rest of the men who used to work for Romas. He made use of his building skills to carve wooden wayside statues of saints and worriers and based them on common peasants he saw, especially those who'd known hardship and sorrow. Being a skilled craftsman, and known for his easy-going nature, Jonas' statues were in demand even in the neighbouring villages. Kristina knew that if she gave him the slightest encouragement, the villagers would gossip about her being a loose woman. As it was, she was sure that they whispered amongst themselves about his visits to her place.

'Well, well, well! The Prussian slut has found herself a new man pretty quickly hasn't she?' Tamara Ivanovitch the village gossip would hiss at her, every time she'd meet Kristina walking towards the main square. She was Vlad's long-suffering wife. People said that he beat her up from time to time, or that he hurled his dinner against the wall if it displeased him. Since she always wore her scarf pulled down low over her forehead, it was hard to see whether he did or not. Anyway, Kristina didn't care, because nowadays she rarely ventured into the village except for Friday's market. She was too busy trying to keep daughters fed and clothed as well as doing all the chores Romas used to do, in addition to her own domestic tasks. Her fingers were encrusted with dirt from working in the garden and swollen from the harsh soap she used to scrub their clothes on the scrubbing board. All their knitted socks were basically a series of patches. Out of necessity, she had taught her daughters to darn and patch clothes and they were also a big help keeping the weeds down in the vegetable garden. Luckily Romas had bought them all new wooden clogs from the cobbler just before he died, so at least they didn't have to go barefooted.

Kristina found herself spending her spare moments at the cemetery behind Ventuva, tending to his grave and telling him about things that worried her.

Many times, over a cup of lemon tea, Jonas would tell Kristina that she only had to say the word and he'd marry her and look after her three daughters as well. Now and then, Kristina thought about his proposal but the memory of Romas was still too strong in her heart. How could another man ever take his place? Besides, she was at least five years younger than him. So, she continued to deliver babies and make up her herbal remedies.

One weekend, a few days before her seventh birthday, Renata returned from across the river and flung a few kopecks down noisily on the kitchen table.

'There's no way I am going back to herding those damned cows for bloody Farmer Ivars!'

'Renata! Where did you learn to swear like this?' reprimanded her mother sharply. 'If you don't tell me, I'll be washing your mouth out with soap this very minute.'

Kristina wondered where her eldest daughter had picked up her bad habits from and vowed that she wouldn't let Renata speak to her that way again.

'Farmer Ivars' son Maris says it and he doesn't get into trouble,' Renata yelled back at her mother.

'Just because he says it, doesn't mean I'm going to allow you to say it,' Kristina scolded. 'Grandma Elena was right all along. You do need a good smack on the backside.'

Renata hung her head and started to sob. 'Come on, tell your mama, what's really upset you?' asked Kristina sympathetically as she put her arm around her eldest.

'I, I don't like the way that one of the workers looks at me when he comes by the stable to take my plate away after my evening meal.'

'I'm sure that he's just being friendly,' said Kristina. 'Maybe, he wishes that he had a lovely daughter like you. Or perhaps he misses his own daughter.'

'He's old and he's got bad breath!' Renata yelled. 'He stinks of tobacco and onions all the time. Last night he slobbered all over me and told me that I was his prettiest little girl in the whole wide world and that it's got to be our secret! If you make me go back there, I'll run away from there, forever and ever!'

Kristina was dumbfounded. She had never seen Renata is such a state. Was her daughter lying to her? But, her sixth sense warned her that all was not right. Over time, she'd learnt to always trust her gut instinct.

'What if I went across the river with you tomorrow and had a talk with Farmer Ivars? Perhaps you misunderstood what the worker was saying?'

'No! I won't! I won't go back there ever again! I'll kill myself!' sobbed Renata, flinging her arms around her mother's neck.

After a few days of mulling over what Renata had told her, Kristina made up her mind to accept Jonas' marriage proposal. Putting on her best shawl, she walked briskly to his house and rapped on his door.

'I'm coming, I'm coming,' Jonas shouted as he struggled with the suspenders over his trousers.

'Oh, hello Kristina! This is a surprise. Come in, come in. What brings you here?' asked Jonas, welcoming her into his tiny cottage. He'd just come in from milking his cow and felt ashamed of his muddy clothes, since he always tried to look presentable whenever he'd call on Kristina. He silently prayed that another tragedy had not befallen her.

'Is there something wrong? Please, sit down by the fire, and I'll make you a nice cup of hot lemon tea.'

Jonas sat down opposite Kristina and looked into her worried face. Something terrible must have happened for her to be so bold, as to walk into his cottage in full view of her neighbours.

'I have thought long and hard about your proposal,' she began. 'I'd like to accept it, but only on one condition. That is, if you solemnly promise me, that you will never ever hurt me or my daughters in any way.'

'Of course I wouldn't, not for all the money in the world,' Jonas reassured her. 'We could have a good marriage, you and me. You know that I'm a hard worker and you are too. We'll make a go of it, you'll see. There won't be any problems, I swear on my mother's grave.'

'I'm five years older than you Jonas. People will talk. Won't it bother you?'

'Not at all, a few years make no difference, I can assure you my dear.'

Back at the cottage, Renata was still crying and cuddling Murk. 'You know, she solemnly told her black cat, 'I think that I am going to marry the first boy who asks me and then we'll live happily ever after.'

In contrast to other couples, their wedding was very modest. Kristina and Jonas had quietly asked Father Casimir to marry them and that was it. Elena presented her daughter with a new set of linen sheets. For their wedding breakfast, Jonas brought along one of his smoked hams and Kristina's three daughters joined in their celebration, cramming big slices of the succulent meat into their mouths together with Kristina's potato and beetroot salad. Elena tried to keep order as they fought each other for more and more food.

'Steady on girls,' Jonas laughed. 'There's more where that came from. No one's going to take it away from you!' He looked at their pinched faces and wondered when they last had a good meal.

'Jonas is right,' Kristina added, remembering Virginia's previous gastric attack. 'You don't want to overeat, then get upset tummies.'

As Kristina ate, she thought about how different this occasion was compared to her wedding to Romas. The Christmas Eve before her marriage, Elena had insisted that she drop two needles onto a plate filled with water. The two needles had floated towards each other and had stayed together. Her mother and her two aunts had jumped up with great excitement, hugging Kristina telling her that she would be married very soon. She was reluctant to believe them, but the following year, the prophecy had come true.

Kristina remembered the first time she'd seen Romas, who'd impressed her even though he was of stocky build, but she noticed that he had a strong, wide chest and she liked his reddish hair and beard. He'd ridden past her parents' farmhouse and had waved to her, calling out, 'Nice flower garden you've got there, young lady!' She'd blushed and stammered, 'Thank you mister,' and hurried inside. It was the first real compliment she'd ever received from a man and wondered why he had spoken to her.

A week later, Romas arrived at her house with the matchmaker, a bad tempered old crone called Vida. She'd driven a hard bargain with Elena and Pranas, after seeing that there was no big parcel of land to go with the dowry. Unfortunately, her father had drunk away most of their land, all that Elena had left was three goats a cow and a few hens. In her great grandmother's day, the farm had about ten buildings including the farmhouse. It had boasted its own granary, pigsty, barn, stable, orchard, cellar, sheds, hen house and a stockyard. All gone down the toilet.

Vida had poked about Kristina's wooden hope chest, examining the sheets, towels and drapes she'd woven, and made comments about her embroidered blouses and shifts.

'You ladies have been very busy I see.'

'Mama's hands are never still,' replied Kristina.

'Not much to do in the evenings,' added Pranas.

'No, you certainly don't do much apart from drinking then snoring in your chair! Not like Kristina and me. We're always knitting, crocheting or doing embroidery, aren't we?'

'Mama's made sure that she passed on her skills to me,' Kristina smiled shyly.

'Not bad, not bad Miss Liepa,' the old crone had muttered. 'A girl can never have too much in her glory box. If you marry Romas Kirvis, there'll be little time for these hobbies, that I can personally guarantee. You two will be busy doing other things, mark my words, girlie!'

Kristina blushed furiously, having been caught out looking at Romas. He had not said a word whilst the women were discussing her dowry. His body was trim and muscular from days working outside as a builder with his father. His hair was thick, glossy, and his brown eyes twinkled when he spoke.

'I am very impressed ladies,' he said, as he kissed Kristina and Elena's hands.

The next time Kristina saw Romas was when he and the matchmaker came on an official visit to ask her parents for her hand in marriage.

So long ago....

Later as she prepared for bed that first night, she examined her body. Would Romas find her attractive, she wondered. If only she was taller and her skin finer.

Matchmaker Vida had praised Romas to the skies, saying that he came from a hardworking and decent family and then she made a big display of touching and squeezing his biceps. The last straw was when Vida swatted his bottom with a tea towel, pointing out to Kristina that she'd have no problem with his lovemaking skills. Kristina remembered blushing violently and the matchmaker cackling. She'd pinched Kristina on both cheeks, till they there were sore.

'Now, here's a pure blushing bride who'll do her husband proud. There'll be quite a few babies coming along soon, I'll guarantee you that, if my name isn't Vida!'

After everyone had finally agreed on the dowry, a date was set for the engagement. What a flurry of activity there'd been at her house! Chickens had to be killed and plucked, cakes baked, the house cleaned from top to bottom. Gifts had to be selected for Romas' family. Kristina agonized over the selection of towels that she was going to present to Dalia, her future mother-in-law. Romas had made her a beautiful wooden jewellery box with tulips carved on both sides for her keepsakes. She still had it in her bedroom on her little bedside table with her grandmother's circular amber pendant with a hole in the middle. Kristina had presented him with two woven neckties and two sashes. She hoped that he would wear them for the wedding. And to her delight, he did, telling everyone proudly that they were his beloved's handiwork.

The time came for the matchmaker to slip Romas' beautiful amber and silver engagement ring onto Kristina's finger and finally they were officially engaged! He later told her that he had it crafted especially for her across the river in Latvia, using a piece of amber he'd found. Afterwards, there were lots of eating and drinking and countless toasts. Romas' father Vytas had drunk far too much and his mother Dalia was very embarrassed as Vytas slurred his words and swayed about towards the end of the night. On the other hand, Elena and Pranas were very pleased with Kristina and their new son-in-law.

'Didn't I always tell you that a neat flower garden would make a good impression on your future husband?' Elena asked Kristina, as she hugged her proudly.

Still deep in her reminiscences, Kristina glanced up at Jonas and felt let down by the lack of romantic courtship, but she knew that nothing could bring back the heady excitement of her wedding to her first husband. They'd both been young and eager for married life.

Laima, her maid of honour had organised Kristina's hens' night. The bridesmaids brought along delicious poppy seed and walnut cakes they had made to the bachelorette party. Laima had baked the *Karvojus*, a traditional braided wedding cake, which she presented to Kristina later on at the wedding reception. Of course, Vida the matchmaker had to explain to all the guests that the cake was symbolic of Kristina letting go of her two childish plaits she'd worn up till then and that Romas would make sure of that. At Kristina's party, her friends had sung a few traditional Samogitian songs about love and courting, then reassured her that they would not abandon her once she was married. After that, all her friends began make wreaths of rue and Kristina was asked to choose the best one as her bridal wreath. She found it hard to choose, since she didn't want to offend anyone. So she asked them to put their wreaths in a circle, stepped into the middle and Laima wrapped a scarf around her eyes. Dana then spun her around three times and Kristina found herself stopping at her own wreath. Her friends clapped in delight and then it was placed on her head, and each girl stepped up to kiss her and whisper a wish into her ear.

'I wish that Romas will never be unfaithful to you,' said Dana.

'My wish is that you will have a son as your first born,' whispered Laima.

And so it went on, wishes for everlasting love, happiness and that Kristina's mother-in-law Dalia would not turn out to be a bossy one. Of course, there was a long debate about the sort of bridal dress that Kristina would wear. Her mother had already bought a length of beautiful white, material from Moshe, one of the Jewish pedlars. The rumour was that it came all the way from Vilnius.

'Maria is going to help me make my dress, since she is the best dressmaker in Ventuva,' Kristina informed everyone. They nodded in agreement and made a mental note to ask for her assistance to make their wedding dresses when they would become brides.

'What gifts are we going to give the groomsmen?' asked Laima.

'How about woollen gloves?' suggested Donna, who was the most sensible one in their group.

'Excellent idea. Very suitable and practical as well,' agreed Jurga.

At the end of the evening, Kristina presented each of her four bridesmaids with a colourful sash to wear around their waists.

'They are beautiful. Thank you so much,' exclaimed Laima.

'I could never dream up such intricate patterns that you design. Where do you get your ideas from?' added Dana, whose weaving skills left a lot to be desired.

Soon it was time to go out to bid farewell to Kristina's garden, because once she left her parents' house, she would have to establish her own outside the cottage that Romas had built for their life together. He and his men made it in true Samogitian fashion using horizontal logs, with the roof constructed of rafters with a four-sloped form, with a broad loft. The two windows were made low and wide and Romas put in six small panels of glass in each one, with wooden shutters either side. He decorated the rafters, beams, the gables and the hip knobs with his own modest carvings. There was even a small cellar under the house and wooden floors. Her husband was not the type of person to show off, but he was very pleased when Kristina threw her arms around him in delight the first time she saw her new home. Kristina glanced at Jonas and then around her cottage. Yes, it was neat, but she certainly didn't have time to clean it from top to bottom like her mother's house before her wedding to Romas.

Her uncle Richard had chosen two of his best horses to take them to church. He had had attached little jingling bells to the harness and, brushed the horses' manes and tails till they shone. It was a pity that his two brothers had been killed during an argument with the village official and his henchmen. Elena had told Kristina that her other two uncles had died in the Uprising of January 1863 against Tsar Alexander II. Bad luck seemed to run in her family. She knew that her mother missed her brothers every day and was convinced that they could have stopped Pranas from drinking away his land.

'Oh yes, a good flick with the horsewhip would have set Pranas on the straight and narrow,' she often would say when she got upset about having to make do.

At the wedding, the matchmaker had worn a strangely decorated hat. Valdas, the Master Of Ceremonies, carried a huge bag stuffed with gifts. Since Ventuva only had one bridge across the Venta River, Romas had to carry Kristina across it seven times for good luck. Elena and Pranas had met their daughter at the door with the traditional offering of bread and salt. Kristina grimaced as she recalled her embarrassment in front of the wedding guests when the cackling Vida demonstrated how they should sleep together by pushing them onto a narrow bench in the middle of the room.

'Come on my lovebirds. Get closer together,' Vida had shrieked to all and sundry. 'Come on Romas my lad, you'll never give Kristina any babies if you don't get closer!' cried the old crone as she pushed Kristina off the bench and demonstrated herself, pressing her shrunken body lasciviously against Romas. Then long pieces of cheese that Kristina had made beforehand were handed out to the guests, who made all sorts of jokes about how hard they were.

Kristina kept a false smile pasted on her face, willing herself to breathe, while the knots of anger built up inside her. She was so nervous, she couldn't eat a single thing on the bridal table which groaned with everyone's beautifully prepared dishes. All the women had wanted their dishes praised and voted the best ones. After the embarrassing demonstration with Vida, Romas came back to sit beside his wife at the wedding table. He squeezed her fingers.

'I'll wager that the old crone enjoyed that part,' Kristina said indignantly to her new husband.

'Come on, it's only a joke. Don't be jealous sweetheart,' Romas teased her, as he stroked her arm.

The singing and dancing started after that and Romas whirled Kristina about the room energetically in a fast polka. Then her bridesmaids performed a stately traditional flower dance especially for her. More people got up to dance, as the musicians continued to play their fiddles and accordion till well past midnight.

Later, as Kristina lay nervously in her new bed, dressed in an exquisitely embroidered linen nightgown, she wondered what Romas would expect from her. Elena had only given her a few words of advice before the wedding.

'Be guided by your husband on your honeymoon night. He will show you what to do.' And that was that. Now as Kristina trembled under the feather quilt, she hoped that whatever Romas was going to do to her, that he would be kind and gentle.

Her husband could see that his new bride was jittery and he knew that tonight, he must not force himself upon her like a wild stallion on a reluctant mare.

'Aš tavi dėdlė mīlo - I love you,' he whispered to Kristina in Samogitian. 'Do what you want to me. I am yours.'

Kristina's eyes widened in surprise. She had not expected this. From what she had observed around her, Samogitian men were usually quite reserved. Yet, she had heard some of the village women complain in the communal bathhouse, about how they had to put up with their husbands' demands in the marital bed. Some had to endure a beating if they didn't submit.

'Can I touch your chest?' she whispered. Romas encouraged her by taking her hand in his and guiding it over his chest. Slowly the couple learned the lines of each other's body and when the moment came, Kristina was ready for Romas to make her his own. Before they fell asleep, Romas whispered again that he loved her and given time, things would get better. Waves of tenderness washed over Kristina, as she looked at Romas, grateful that she had such a loving and gentle husband.

The next day, Elena looked at her daughter, scrutinising her face for signs of disappointment and pain. There were none and she breathed a sigh of relief that the matchmaker had indeed chosen a good husband for her daughter. More wedding festivities had begun.

A group of guests, some more sober than others, began the traditional custom of trying to hang the matchmaker in jest. Quick as a flash, Vida read out her so-called Last Will and Testament to the assembled guests to avoid her fate.

'I hereby leave my billy goat to Elena, whose lady goats haven't had a good going over for years. Then my rooster to Kristina and Romas, since he can teach these two youngsters a thing or two about lovemaking.' Vida continued in this bawdy vein, the guests laughing good naturedly until tears rolled down their cheeks.

Then it was time for Kristina to save Vida from being hung. So she reluctantly stepped forth to tie a sash around the old crone's waist, all the time wishing, that she could hang her quite cheerfully herself, after all the embarrassment she'd caused. Later, Valdas, the Master of Ceremonies, was seized and was threatened with a drowning in the horse trough. Again, Kristina rescued him by tying one of her sashes around his waist.

While Kristina and Romas were occupied helping Vida and Valdas, their table was taken over by a pair of imposters. Antanas, their best man, had dressed up as a bride, and Laima the maid of honour was dressed as a bridegroom. They insisted that this was really their wedding reception. Kristina and Romas had to prove that this was in fact their wedding, by paying a ransom to get their own seats back. The wedding guests roared their approval.

'Quick! Where's Valdas and his bag of ransom gifts?' shouted Romas. Valdas made a big show of trying to find his bag of presents, looking carefully under all the chairs, asking each guest whether they'd seen such a bag. This went on for ages, until Elena agreed that indeed the bag might be under her chair.

Looking back, Kristina thought that all those customs had been good fun, even though she had been very embarrassed at the time. She and Romas had waited long time before Renata had come along. Every month, she'd hope that she was pregnant. Seven years! After that Virginia came along and then there were no more pregnancies. Kristina often felt dejected that she could not give Romas the son she knew he'd hoped for. Her mother-in-law would click her tongue and mutter some Samogitian proverb and end up by saying, 'Well it's obvious that God hasn't been kind to you, but it wouldn't hurt you to go to church more often and pray for a son!'

'I've got my two beauties,' Romas would assure his wife whenever she was feeling sorry for herself. It was usually after some gossip had thrown a sarcastic remark at her about not having a son to look after her in her old age.

However, the hour would soon arrive for her to go to bed with her second husband.

After the wedding breakfast, Jonas kissed her hands. Turning to Virginia, Renata and Julia, he told them, 'You are now my daughters. Even though I am not your real father, I expect to be obeyed and in turn I will love you and treat you with respect.'

Kristina's three girls just stared at him. They hadn't known what to expect, since none of their friends had stepfathers.

Renata began to speak on behalf of her sisters. 'Mr. Malkas,' she began timidly, 'I am the eldest, so I will make sure that we listen to what you and mama tell us, but please don't send me or my sisters across the Venta to be cowherds.' Then she broke down, her chest heaving with sobs.

Kristina stared at her daughter with her mouth open. She prayed that Renata would not keep talking and give away the reason why she had knocked so hastily on Jonas' door.

'Jonas, I'm so sorry. I really must apologise for Renata's rudeness,' she said in weary tone, as she glared at her daughter.

Jonas smiled and went up to Renata and shook her little weather-beaten hand, then those of her sisters. He knew that he had to take their concerns seriously, if they were going to accept him.

'Today, I give you my solemn promise, that none of you will ever be sent away. We will work together as a family and I will protect you as long as I live. I might even take you fishing for pike,' he added with a big wink.

Renata clapped her hands and hugged her sisters, relieved at last that neither she nor her sisters would ever be forced to bear the burden of sleeping in dirty stables and herding some farmer's cows. Kristina looked at Jonas gratefully. She had chosen wisely and she'd known instinctively that he would turn out to be a good husband and father to her three daughters.

That night when the three girls had been tucked up in the bed they shared and their favourite fairytale had been told, Kristina and Jonas prepared for bed. He noticed the dark shadows under Kristina's eyes and saw the strain on her face.

'We're not young honeymooners, my dear,' he said. 'Why don't we have a good sleep tonight, then take each day as it comes?'

Kristina was taken aback. She had steeled herself for Jonas demanding his marital rights on their wedding night and was relieved that he hadn't chosen to do so. It had been three long years since she'd been with a man and she still wasn't sure whether anyone could ever take the place of her first husband.

Kristina was still a bundle of nerves, so Jonas put his arm gently around her, kissed her gently on her cheek and whispered to her what a lucky man he was to have such a pretty wife and a lovely ready-made family. As a widower, Jonas knew the signs a wife would make to let her husband know when she was ready to be his lover. His own wife, God rest her soul, would tie a pretty new ribbon in her hair or make his favourite dish of *cepelinai*, those delicious zeppelin-shaped dumplings to show him that she was in the mood. Jonas knew that he wasn't a romantic man, but at least he was patient one. He could remain patient a bit longer, he thought as he fell asleep with his arm still around Kristina.

As they were getting used to each other, an unexpected event occurred. During the middle of harvest, as the full moon shone, Sarga's frantic barking woke everyone up.

'Holy Mary, Mother of God! What's going on out there?' yelled Jonas as he grabbed his trousers off the wooden chest and ran out the door. As he looked across the road, he could see that half of the Ventuva was ablaze.

'I've got to go and help the men!' he shouted to Kristina, as he ran towards the burning cottages. Kristina silently prayed to the Ancient Ones to protect Jonas. What if he was killed by a burning log while he helped fight the fire, which could be seen from kilometres away? She touched the amber pendant at her neck and began the magic chant, *'Turn circle turn, turn to the East. Turn circle turn. Turn to the West. Turn circle turn, turn to the North. Turn circle turn. Turn to the South.'*

But this time the Ancient Ones didn't answer her. Perhaps they were too busy with more important things, Kristina thought to herself.

The three girls huddled against their mother as Kristina drew her shawl around their shivering bodies.

'We'll be safe here, won't we Mama?' asked Julia.

'The fire won't come up to our house will it? whispered Virginia.

'No, Jonas will make sure that the fire won't reach us,' Kristina reassured her girls. Through the windows, they watched the fires burn until sunrise.

At midday Jonas limped through the door. He was covered with soot and one leg was bandaged. Kristina rushed over to him.

'Are you all right Jonas? What happened to your leg?'

'Just a fence post that crashed over it. I'm fine, just need a drink and a rest, that's all,' he reassured her.

Kristina ran to get him some milk and put bread and cheese on the table.

'Let me look at your leg.'

'Just let me eat in peace, I'm starving.'

After Jonas had eaten his fill of cold beetroot soup and warm boiled potatoes, she waited for hear him to speak.

'Half of Ventuva has burnt down. I'm sorry Kristina, but there was nothing anyone of us could do to help Elena.'

'What? What do you mean?' stuttered Kristina.

'The sparks from the neighbours' houses, set your mother's house alight,' explained Jonas.

'We had all the buckets and hoses going. The wind was just too fierce. The flames must have engulfed her as she was trying to get out to the barn to save her chickens.'

'No!' Kristina fell into his arms. 'Tell me it's not true.' I can't bear it.'

Jonas held Kristina whilst she sobbed until there were no more tears left. The three girls looked at him in disbelief.

'Do you really mean that our grandma died in the fire?' asked Renata.

Jonas looked at her hopeful face. He couldn't lie to her.

'Yes, she did. I am so sorry.' He went to put his arms around her and comfort her.

'Why didn't you save her? I hate you! I hate you! I wish you'd never married my mama.'

Jonas tried to put his arm around Renata again, but she twisted away from him and went running to the barn and picked up Murk.

'What am I going to do?' she asked the cat, who just looked at her. Virginia and Julia peered around the corner. The three girls hugged each other, not knowing what would happen to them now that they'd lost their father and grandmother all within a space of a few years.

Later, after Kristina had calmed down with the help of a glass of honey mead, she and Jonas began to discuss the cause of the fire and how it could have reached her mother's house.

'Do you think someone lit the fire deliberately?' asked Kristina.

'We're not sure yet, but most of the men think that it started in the bathhouse,' replied Jonas, twisting his beard nervously. 'Then once it started, it spread to the church and over to the other houses, including Elena's.'

'But that's near Tadas' old smithy,' Kristina gasped. 'And he hasn't been seen for years!'

'Surely you don't think that he could still be alive?' muttered Jonas.

'No, I feel in my heart that he's definitely not here,' replied Kristina. 'But, my sixth sense tells me that Vlad had something to do with it. Everyone knows that he became a spiteful drunk after my Romas sacked him for stealing.'

Kristina found herself telling Jonas, how Romas told her about Vlad's thievery one spring day, when he'd come home for lunch. Of course, Vlad had denied he had been stealing any building materials, and swore on his mother's grave, that he'd just taken a few palings to fix his barn. He'd shouted at Romas that a man was obliged to look after his family and make sure the barn didn't leak. He'd always complained to anyone who'd listen, that Romas paid him a pittance. Mind you, most of Ventuva knew that he spent at least half of his wages making and drinking moonshine.

'You could be right my dear,' agreed Jonas.

'I'll never forget that night he came back here after the funeral,' Kristina shuddered at the memory she'd buried away. Vlad's evil black eyes had burned fiercely as he vowed revenge that night. She found herself blurting out the events, bit by bit to Jonas.

'By the devil! That damned cur! I swear that I'll kill him, if he ever tries to harm you ever again!' vowed Jonas indignantly. He thumped the table so loud with his fist, that their three girls came running in from their bedroom to see what was going on.

'Anyway, Igor told me that the authorities will be here tomorrow, to conduct a very thorough investigation,' intoned Jonas. 'Half of Ventuva has gone up in flames. Someone's got to get to the bottom of this tragedy.'

After a week of questioning people, eating and drinking, the Russian authorities concluded in their report to Igor, that the fire had started accidentally and that the villagers would just have to rebuild everything themselves.

Kristina was heartbroken. After organizing her mother's funeral, she seemed to age overnight and walked about in a daze, dressed in her black mourning clothes. Donna and Dana, two of her friends had also perished in the fire, trying to save their cottages from burning down. Homeless villagers wandered from door to door, begging for food and shelter from those who still had their houses standing. Most days Jonas would have to pull Kristina up and out of bed, dress her and hope that she would be alright until he got home. Sometimes, she'd still be sitting in the same chair that she'd sat on that morning. Sometimes he'd find her at the cemetery babbling to Romas or her mother. Just as well the girls are at school, he thought as he watched Renata take over the mothering of Virginia and Julia. One afternoon when he came home from work, Jonas saw the table set and his three daughters bustling about in the kitchen.

'Where's your mother?'

'She's at Laima's house,' answered Virginia.

'We've made you some *cepelinai* for dinner,' announced Renata proudly.

'My goodness! That's a treat, but aren't they a bit difficult at your age?'

'I think that we got them nearly right. Sit down papa.'

Jonas tried not to look too astounded when Renata served him two huge potato dumplings and two big boiled meatballs smothered in sour cream.

'Mmm, these are delicious!' he exclaimed. 'How did you girls come up with this novel idea?'

'Ah, we weren't too sure how mama gets the meat to stay inside the potato dumplings, so we just thought we'd have the meat next to the dumplings. You can mash them up, it tastes just the same, doesn't it?' asked Renata nervously.

'I thought that we could wrap the meat around the dumpling, but that didn't work,' added Virginia.

'We tried to put some meat inside the dumpling, but it wouldn't stay there, would it Renata?' Julia explained.

'I think that you girls have made an outstanding effort! From now on I will call this dish the *Cepelinas Duet*!' When Kristina came home she saw the remains of their meal and felt ashamed. She vowed to make an effort to shake off her listlessness and fatigue.

Kristina realized that it wasn't for Renata and her sisters, her family would not have been able to cope. Mind you, half of the village was in the same boat, everyone had lost either a family member or a friend. Ventuva had to be rebuilt and Jonas' skills were called upon once more. Their beloved church was gone, and also the synagogue.

While he was out helping the men to rebuild houses and barns, Jonas heard some of the men were complaining that Ventuva was lost without its post office. A brilliant idea formed in his mind. Jonas was convinced that he could build on a little room at the side of his cottage to serve as a temporary post office, since the original one would take ages to rebuild. Letters had to be written, important telegrams had to be sent. He told Kristina about his idea as soon as he came home. That seemed to cheer her up and she felt as if she was going to participate in something useful once again. Her girls could lend her a hand when they came home from school or prepare the evening meal. Once he told her more about his idea, Kristina began to plan what shelves were to be put where, what stationery she'd need and how she could also sell other things besides stamps. Soon their village had a new post office and Kristina had a new lease of life.

Finally Ventuva had been rebuilt. Everyone breathed a sigh of relief. Life was back to normal. That peace was shattered when one summer morning, Kristina was alarmed to see a strange telegram arrive at the Post Office. All it said was, 'GERMANY AND RUSSIA AT WAR!'

'Oh God, what if they call up Jonas?' was her first thought. Her next thought was that the Tsar was a madman. She raced down the street with the telegram to spread the news.

'Not so fast Madam Kristina!' Igor Gregorovitch the Russian official warned her. 'I believe that the telegram you are holding was meant for me!'

He knew everyone by name and very little escaped his notice. As long as people obeyed the law and did their work, he was happy to leave everyone in peace. Sometimes he even joined some of the men for a drink and a game of cards. However, once the war started, he was promoted and strutted about in his new uniform like a peacock. News about the war spread like wildfire in Ventuva and all the eligible men were drafted to fight for the Tsar.

'Count your lucky stars that you're too old to fight the Huns,' Jonas was informed when Igor paid them a visit.

'Just as well, we have daughters and not sons,' remarked Kristina, after he'd left.

One afternoon after her daughters had arrived home from school, Virginia remarked casually to her mother that all Jews were dirty and traitors.

'Why are saying stupid things like that?' Kristina demanded. 'Your two friends Helena and Ruth are Jewish. You know very well that Maria our neighbour is Jewish too. She came here with her husband, because her parents were murdered in a pogrom when they were living in Russia.'

'But, our teacher told us that they killed Jesus and that they have poisoned the wells all over our country,' replied Virginia.

'Did you know that for centuries the Jews and Lithuanians have lived peacefully side by side Kristina asked 'There are hundreds in our village.

Virginia hung her head and wouldn't look up at her parents.

'But, but Mr. Šorkov said that's why the Tsar ordered pogroms against them before! Papa has always told us that the teacher is right.'

'Well, your papa may have said that, but even Igor, our Russian village official, has always been very friendly with the Jewish people who live here,' added Jonas carefully. 'He knows all their names and how many children they have.'

Later on, most people in Ventuva were truly shocked when they heard that orders had come from the Tsar to expel 200 Jews. Kristina and Jonas knew quite a few of them and had helped rebuild their synagogue after the Great Fire. Back then, they had seen a true camaradie and determination amongst the villagers to help one another. For years, their girls had always played with other children irrespective of who they were. Suddenly their friends were being classified as enemies.

It was early in May, whilst Kristina was looking out the window, that she saw her neighbour Maria being bundled into a wagon with some other women. She recognized one of them who was the oldest Jewess in Ventuva.

'Oh my Lord! They're taking away a ninety year old woman! We've got to stop them,' she shouted to Jonas, as she rushed outside carrying two of her thickest shawls. Men, women, children and the elderly were being pushed onto wagons, then onto trains and exiled forever to the vast artic wastelands of Siberia.

'Kristina! Stop! Don't do anything rash,' Jonas warned her.

'Please sir, let them go in the name of justice and fairness,' she sobbed, on her knees in front of Igor. 'My neighbour Maria's just a poor dressmaker. I've known her all my life!'

'She's a spy and traitor,' Igor coldly informed her. 'You can't trust a single one of them. They've been been plotting with the Germans against us. The men have been sending secret messages in those long beards to the enemy!' He pushed Kristina out of his way and she fell heavily onto the ground. Sarga sprang at him to protect his mistress, but with one shot from Igor's revolver, Sarga lay on the ground.

'No!' cried out Kristina, as she fell across her beloved dog.

'Get back to your cottage or I'll shove you into the wagon with your Jewish friends!' he snapped.

Jonas put his arm around his wife, who was sobbing hysterically over the body of her faithful protector. 'Go, go back inside and wait for me. Go!'

'Please Mr. Igor, sir. Please permit me to give Maria these two shawls.' he asked politely.

'Hurry up!' snapped Igor and motioned the wagon to depart.

Once they were back in their cottage, Kristina broke down completely.

'How could he? How could he just shoot Sarga like that, in cold blood? And who can possibly believe that silly rumour that our Jews have been throwing cats down the wells to poison the water? Those poor, poor people. What's going to become of them?'

'Looks like the Tsar and his army chiefs have found a scapegoat for their lack of success on the battlefield,' replied Jonas who had been secretly reading an underground newspaper, "The Dawn," that was being smuggled in regularly by traders from Prussia.

'Look, I am going out to bury Sarga behind the barn. Don't say anything to the girls, we'll pretend that she's run off after some fox who was trying to get in the hen house.'

Kristina nodded dumbly and held Murk close to her. His heart was thumping wildly. He had seen what Igor had done to his best friend. He jumped off Kristina's lap and followed Jonas out the door. When the girls came home from school, they noticed immediately that Sarga wasn't in her usual spot on the porch to greet them. After Jonas explained the story about the wily fox, they seemed to accept it, but when the next morning they couldn't find their dog, they became agitated and wanted to search for her.

'She'll be back as soon as she's hungry,' Kristina said softly. A few days later, Virginia found Murk lying behind the barn as stiff as a board.

'Mama, mama! Come here! Murk's dead!'

'Surely you're mistaken my darling.'

'No, I'm not. Look!'

Kristina looked up to see Virginia carrying Murk in her arms.

'Sweetheart, Murk was old, he's at least ten. Maybe it was something he ate?'

Renata was not convinced. She found it very strange that within a few days, two of her pets were no longer with them. But there was nothing she could find out, because all that she heard was the villagers talking about the war and nothing else.

Some people speculated that the ancient gods had unleashed the Great War, because women were following all sorts of frivolous fashions. One Sunday morning, the priest told his congregation that Almighty God had sent the war as punishment for not following the Church's teachings.

'Those who don't believe in God,' he thundered, 'are to blame for this calamity!'

As people shuffled out of church, Jonas could hear others saying that reading newspapers was to blame for the German war.

'How could these crazy rumours help the men like my two brothers who've been drafted to fight for the Russians?' Jonas muttered angrily to Kristina on their way home. 'They had no choice. You can bet they're being used as cannon fodder!'

She had never seen her husband so bitter. 'Sweetheart, have you heard from your brothers recently?'

'No, the last letter I had from Leonas came three months ago.'

Kristina gathered the girls around her. 'How about we make some *spurgos*? My jam donuts always cheer up everyone, don't they?'

As Kristina and her daughters started on the dough for the donuts, she was determined to do anything to make her husband feel happier. But in her heart she knew the chances of his brothers making it home were very slim. She'd seen their bloodied faces in the well only a few days ago. She shuddered as she remembered seeing a similar omen before Romas had been murdered.

'Have you heard from Leonas or Algis?' Kristina asked her husband again, noticing that he was lost in his thoughts and not really listening to the girls.

'Nothing.'

As if by magic, the very next morning, a letter addressed to Jonas appeared at the Post Office. It was postmarked Yaroslav. Where in the world was Yaroslav? Kristina pondered whether she should open it or wait for Jonas to come home for lunch. She bit her lip. Maybe she should steam it open carefully and he wouldn't notice. She waited with baited breath until he came in at midday, rubbing his hands from the cold. Over his shoulder he carried two rabbits.

'Something for your pot,' he smiled, knowing it would please his wife, for meat was scarce. The Germans had been plundering the countryside, talking all the agricultural and dairy produce for their war effort. It was also about this time that people started calling the big potato dumplings *cepelinai*, after the German zeppelins that were being used in the war.

'How dare they nickname our potato dumplings *cepelinai*?' Kristina raged. 'We've always called them *kleckai*. I'm certainly not going to start calling them *cepelinai*!'

'No, we don't have to call them that, sweetheart. Let's have some of your lovely sorrel soup.' Jonas was eager to change the topic because once Kristina got a bee in her bonnet, he would have to listen to her for the next fortnight.

Once they'd had lunch, Kristina took the letter out of her apron pocket and placed it silently in front of him, then kept pestering him to open it.

'It's a letter form Leonas, I'd know that writing anywhere.'

'Go on! Read it! What does it say? Is he alright?'

Jonas ran his fingers through his bushy beard and let out a deep sigh.

'Oh my Lord, it's very graphic,' he exclaimed. 'Are you sure you want to hear this?'

She nodded silently, and so he started reading.

Yaroslav, Russia.

Dear brother,

I hope that this letter finds you and Kristina well and that Ventuva has not suffered too much from the invaders. We have been stuck in the trenches for months but last week we were finally able to repulse an attack by the Huns. They didn't get closer than five hundred steps! We forced them to turn back and retreat with their tails between their legs. They tried to get into our trenches four times and we could even see their horrible faces. We fired at them with everything we had, and lucky for us, they could not withstand our gunfire and eventually we forced them to turn back.

Algis and me lay next to each other in the trench, and Sergeant Mozorov told us to shoot at the Hun's officers and pick off the big soldiers first. Well, we got quite a few of those bastards! They were just walking towards our trenches really quiet without firing a shot. Stupid! So, we let them come closer, so they were in full range and then we let them have it. Blasted them to eternity! You should have seen them fall like flies!

The ones who were in the front dropped like a sack of potatoes, and the ones behind, ran back like rabbits. I think that Sergeant Mozorov was happy with Algis and me, because we sent a lot of those Huns back to hell where they came from. But, dear brother, just between you and me, I have to admit it was absolutely terrifying. Just as well, you're too old be drafted. A few times Algis and me nearly crapped ourselves. At least there are a few Samogitians in our trenches. None from our village though. One man even brought his harmonica with him, can you believe it? He's been warned not to play it, as it will give away our position to the Huns. I hope that this war doesn't last for too much longer, winter's coming

and it won't be much fun in these bloody cold trenches.
Give my love to Kristina and my three little nieces.

Until next time, your brother,

Leonas.

There never would be a next time, because the next letter that arrived, informed Jonas that his brothers had been killed in action in Yaroslav. He was cut to the core and buried himself in his work. Over the next few years, his eyes would mist over whenever anyone mentioned his brothers' names. He carved two beautiful crosses, inscribed them with their names and erected them in the village cemetery. Apart from the deaths of Algis and Leonas, Kristina's family was spared from any other misfortunes during the Great War, so she lit a candle on the night of February 16th 1918, when her country declared its independence from their Russian overlords and gave thanks to the Ancient Ones. After almost two hundred years of slavery, her people were free once more.

RENATA

Life improved once all the Russian officials left the towns and villages. All sorts of advertisements began to appear for tools, skincare and medicines in the newspapers. Jonas would read out the most interesting ones to Kristina after dinner. As much as they laughed about some of the most ridiculous claims made by various remedies, both knew that they couldn't afford any of them.

At that time Renata had her eye on a boy she'd known all her life. Petras Baras, the village's organist, would often invite her to go strolling with him after church, along banks of the Venta River. He was a short, solid type, built like a boxer with fair, curly hair and a chubby moon face. He admired people with business acumen and had built up a good relationship with all the local traders. Petras would give anything to step out of poverty and the never ending Sundays of playing the church organ with a pious look plastered on his face. During his walks with the village girls, he'd slyly promise to take them away from all the dreariness in their lives. Sometimes he'd even take them out in his row boat if it was a fine day.

He'd taken a fancy to Renata, because he felt superior when he was with her and as he'd hold her hand, he'd tell her witty stories about how he was descended from a rich noble family, but that his grandfather had drunk away the estate. Other times he'd mention his brothers who had been killed in the Great War and was rewarded with a lot of sympathy and tenderness.

'Did you know that my ancestors were called the bare-bottom nobles?' Petras laughed cheekily after one of his tales. 'And so, now you know where I got this long, noble nose,' he added.

He also began to hint at an inheritance from an uncle who lived in Memel. Flattered for the first time in her life, Renata smiled and replied that his background was so much more fascinating than hers. She walked on air, dreaming of living in a castle surrounded by servants. He was so courteous and polite unlike the other village ruffians.

'What's got into our Renata?' her sisters would complain to their mother. 'She never has time for us anymore. She's always mooning about singing silly love songs.'

'You are so gorgeous Renata. You and I will have beautiful children,' Petras would whisper in her ear, until she finally succumbed to him on St John's Night.

When it was over, she cried at the excruciating stab of pain she'd felt and tried to wipe away her shame with her petticoat. Is that all there was to it? She had dreamed of romance, champagne and grand gestures. What would her mother say when she got home? Maybe she could wash the petticoat before Kristina noticed the bloodstains.

'Shh, don't cry my love. We're engaged now,' Petras reassured her.

Emboldened by her lover's promise, Renata hurried home.

'Where have you been?' whispered Julia. 'We lost sight of you after they lit the bonfire. Jonas was upset you weren't there to wish him a happy name's day. Have you been looking for the St. John's fern that blooms only at midnight?' She prided herself on being the romantic one.

'I know where you've been. You've been strolling about with Petras, haven't you?' Virginia was older and smarter than her youngest sister. 'And now you're in big, big trouble!'

'Renata! There you are! Finally! Explain yourself! Where have you been all this time?' scolded Kristina when Renata walked in after midnight. 'Jonas and I were going to send out a search party for you, when we couldn't find you when they were making the toasts!'

'Um, Petras and I were just talking and time got away with us,' said Renata coyly.

'Talking? Just talking, were you? I wasn't born yesterday! Where did you disappear to? Look at yourself in the mirror!' Kristina kept on scolding.

'What do you mean Mama?'

Kristina hauled her eldest in front of the mirror. Renata blanched when she saw the top buttons missing from her blouse and her hair full of leaves.

Jonas could only look glumly at her. He wasn't her father, but he knew that this called for some drastic action.

'As a matter of fact, Petras and I got engaged this evening!' Renata announced to her family.

'Says who?' Jonas spoke up.

'Petras said so. He told me tonight.'

'Really? Then why didn't he come to see us tonight like any well-mannered young man? We have brought you up as a decent, virtuous girl.' Kristina was quietly furious at her daughter.

After everyone had finally retired the night, Kristina couldn't sleep. She tiptoed into her daughters' room and saw the stained petticoat lying crumpled on the floor.

'Oh no!' she cried to herself as she clutched her amber pendant, walking outside and leaning for support against her oak tree. She stroked the tree and called upon the god of the woods, 'God of the forest, god of the rain, grant me the strength to ease my daughter's shame.'

This is where Jonas found her, still sitting against the tree just before dawn. He'd reached for his wife and had found her side of the bed cold and empty.

'Couldn't you sleep sweetheart?'

'How can I? That damned devil Petras Baras has seduced our daughter! Why did it have to be our village's church organist! What if he abandons her? What if she's pregnant already? Oh, the shame of it all!' Kristina wept as Jonas held her in his arms.

'I think that I might be paying his parents a visit tomorrow,' Jonas promised as he stroked her hair. 'Come to bed now sweetheart. I am sure that Gedas and I can make Petras see sense.'

Jonas was true to his word and called upon Petras's parents just as they were all sitting down for their midday meal.

'Come in Jonas, come in and have some lunch with us,' invited Gedas. His wife Janina bustled about and brought in more hot potatoes to have with their *kefyr*.

'Looks like your roof's still in good shape,' remarked Jonas.

'Indeed it is, thanks to your good workmanship,' replied Janina, as she brought in her plum cake with fresh cream.

When they'd finished their lunch, Petras kept glancing at Jonas, still trying to work out why he had paid them a visit.

Gedas invited him outside to sit on the porch. 'I've made some good *gira* this summer. Fancy a glass?'

'Don't mind if I do, thanks.'

'I'm sure that your son would like to join us for a beer, wouldn't he?' bantered Jonas.

Petras stepped outside, still wondering what Jonas was doing at their house.

'Our Renata told us last night that you asked her to marry you.'

Petras' face reddened. 'Umm, really? Is that what she said?'

Furiously, Gedas turned on his son. 'Well, did you or didn't you? Answer me! Now!'

'Well, not exactly, we just talked a bit, that's all,' Petras replied airily, squirming on the bench. Sometimes, he felt a slight frisson of guilt, after taking advantage of the village girls, but they were willing, weren't they? Yes, he'd found all his previous dalliances very pleasurable and without any problems, until now.

'So how did Renata's petticoat come to be stained and the front buttons of her blouse ripped off?' Jonas asked angrily.

'By God! Don't tell me you assaulted Renata!' Gedas got up and loomed over Petras, ready to knock him down.

'No, father! I didn't. You know me better than that! I would never hit a woman!'

'So, Mr. Petras, pious church organist, why don't you tell us what really happened last night after you disappeared from the bonfire?' Jonas looked up coolly at Petras.

'Ah, all right. W, w, we're engaged!' Petras finally managed to stutter. 'But I'm off tomorrow to join the partisan unit at Joniškėlis to fight the Bolsheviks!'

'What? With those lily-white pianist's hands and flat feet?' laughed Jonas.

'They wouldn't let you join the army when you ran away from home when you were 15!' echoed Gedas.

'Well, that's settled then. I guess that Lithuania will obtain its independence without your supreme efforts Petras. I expect you to organize the banns to be read out in church as soon as possible. I am sure that since you are on such good terms with our Father

Casimir, he'll be delighted to marry you and our Renata. Good day to you!'

When Jonas finally returned three hours later, Kristina pulled him inside their bedroom.

'Quick! Don't keep me in suspense! Tell me exactly what happened. Tell me everything, don't leave anything out!'

'Well, my dear, all I can say, is that Petras is definitely going to marry our Renata, though just between you and me, he's a shifty character. At first, he wouldn't admit that he'd seduced Renata. Not in so many words. Then he tried to weasel out of it by telling us that he was off to be a partisan and fight the Bolsheviks!'

'What?' Kristina felt as if a huge stone was pressing down on her chest, as she went to talk to her eldest, after Jonas had told her what had transpired at the Baras household.

'Renata, now tell me the truth. Are you absolutely sure that you wish to marry Petras? You know he's the first man who's ever paid any attention to you. And remember what people say. Baras by name, baras by nature.'

'What has Petras's surname got to do with what sort of man he is?' retorted Renata. 'That's just one of your silly pagan superstitions. Yes mama, I am well aware that his surname means a tavern, but he's not a drinker. Look at me mama. I'm a short, dumpy girl with a big ugly mole on the side of my nose. Who's going to ask me again?'

'Oh, I'm sure there'll be other fellows who'll come along to court you. You're only seventeen. There'll be plenty of other opportunities.'

'But mama, Petras always looks so sad and he says that only I can cheer him up. His two brothers were killed on the Eastern Front like my uncles, Leonas and Algis. He says that I make him happy. Besides, what if there's a baby in my belly already?'

This was her final trump card and Renata was not going to let her chance slip away. Petras had promised her that they would live in a big, fancy house in the seaside town of Palanga and she'd have all the new clothes and shoes that she could ever want. She would be the envy of all of Ventuva. Renata would never have to wear clogs again or hand me downs from her mother. She'd have two boys and two girls and they'd live happily ever after.

'Just think! You'll be my bridesmaids and wear gorgeous dresses and after my honeymoon, you can come and visit me,' she told her excited sisters.

'And then, we'll be real ladies and eat lots of eat dainty little cakes and sip real coffee from your gold-rimmed coffee cups.'

'Alright then. The only thing I ask, is that when Jonas and I come to stay with you in Palanga is that you take me to Birutė Hill,' acquiesced her mother.

Renata's wedding took place a month later and everyone agreed that she made a beautiful bride, even sour-faced, terrible Tamara Ivanovitch, the village gossip, who never had a kind word about anyone. Still she couldn't help but let a few snide remarks slip once everyone had gone out of the church.

'You can bet that she used some of her mother's witchcraft to snag our organist,' Tamara remarked cattily to anyone in the church who would listen.

'Ha, ha, Tamara, I'm sure that there'll be quite a bit of organ playing at their honeymoon, that's for sure!' cackled another gossip.

Compared to Kristina's first wedding, Renata's was very modest, since it wasn't long after the end of the Great War and the Lithuanians were still fighting the Bolsheviks. Virginia baked her sister a wedding cake in the shape of a figure eight and inserted two wine bottles decorated with rue and ribbons into the holes.

There was no matchmaker, but Petras's father played the part of the Master of Ceremonies and welcomed Renata into their family, adding that Petras's brothers would have certainly been there if they had survived the war. A few of Renata's school friends were also invited, bringing with them dishes of roast chicken, pork, ham and salads. Jonas provided the beer he had brewed from left over bread.

'Where are you two going for your honeymoon?' asked Virginia, after all the guests had gone home.

'I've booked us a room at the Kurhaus resort for the weekend!' Petras replied imperiously.

Renata gasped, 'Oh my goodness, Petras! That's the oldest and most luxurious hotel in Palanga! How can you afford it?'

Petras tapped the inside of his nose. 'I've got contacts, you know.' He was extremely satisfied when he saw that Renata's family was very impressed.

'Are you going to have dinner in the big restaurant?' asked Julia timidly.

'Well, we are staying there. Of course we'll eat dinner in the restaurant.'

'It's very famous all over Lithuania for its cuisine, isn't it Petras?' asked Renata proudly.

'Definitely, my dear, and I just happen to know the head waiter. He promised me that he'd give us a table with a view of the sea. It's a done deal!'

'Petras, do you think that we could dance the night away afterwards in the ballroom?'

'I've heard that you can even go to a concert, since they've got their own entertainment centre,' added Virginia.

'I would love to see a musical production in the theatre, when it's on,' remarked Julia.

Renata was in raptures. Her hotel was perfect. She, an ordinary village girl was actually spending her honeymoon at the Kurhaus resort!

Afterwards, she couldn't wait to tell her sister about the smoked fish kiosk, and the café overlooking the beach, where they drank icy cold fruit cordial and kefyr.

Once the honeymoon was over, Renata and Petras moved into a rented one-bedroom apartment in the main street of Palanga. To all appearances, Petras was a model husband, but as she had discovered during her honeymoon, he could be rough and demanding. Renata had no choice but to give in to his wishes. She suffered in silence, overcome with disappointment and prayed each time that he would finish quickly and she could go to sleep in peace.

After Renata was two months pregnant, she pleaded with Petras to stop insisting on his marital rights so as not to hurt their unborn baby.

'I'm sure that I'm having a boy,' she'd say. 'You don't want to injure our baby son do you?'

'Of course it will be a boy, boys run in our family,' replied her husband, strutting about like a rooster.

So for seven months, Renata was free of Petras's unwanted attentions, and he spoilt her with little gifts and flowers. Once he had received his inheritance from his uncle in Memel, Petras turned out to be quite the entrepreneur and became the owner of two food shops that had become vacant in the main street of Palanga. He bought a two-storey house just as he'd promised and once their son Simas was born, Petras was so pleased with his wife, that he suggested hiring a wet-nurse and a maid. They had the baby's christening at the beautiful Church of the Assumption of the Virgin Mary in the centre of town.

However, Renata wanted to look after her own child, take him for strolls in his pram with the other young mothers in Palanga or knit cute little sailor outfits. When her sisters came from Ventuva, Renata would proudly show off the jewellery Petras had bought her on his numerous business trips. She made no mention of her disappointment in married life, pretending that everything was wonderful. They'd all walk along Palanga pier in the evenings, taking turns to wheel little Simas in his pram or go and listen to the military bands play in the park in the evenings.

'Why don't we listen to some records on your phonogram?' Kristina asked her daughter one night when she had come to stay. 'Can you put on my favourite, *The Last Sunday*?'

But Renata couldn't admit to her mother that she had stopped listening to music at home. She found it too sad and evocative and in her mind, it was easier to forgo such emotional stimulation. Instead she tried another tactic.

'Come on mama, you deserve a treat whilst you're staying with us. Let's go to the band pavilion where they play such lively marching tunes. I find them very stirring.'

Renata and her sisters loved seeing all the handsome officers and their families in the ice cream parlours or strolling about in the Botanical Gardens.

'Oh what I would give to stay here longer with you,' said Virginia to Renata wistfully one evening. 'Ventuva is such a dull and boring place compared to Palanga.'

'I know! Why don't you ask mama if you can do the sewing course that's been advertised?'

Virginia begged and pleaded saying that being a seamstress would give the family extra income, so Kristina and Jonas finally relented.

94

'Yes, why not? I'm not getting any younger my dear,' said Jonas one night.

So Virginia enrolled and began to learn the art of dressmaking and soon made herself a pretty light blue floral summer dress. Next, she was making clothes for all her family.

'Tell me your secret Renata. Why does your Napoleon cake taste so much better than the one I try to make?' asked Julia one day as the sisters were devouring big slices of the rich cake for afternoon tea and sipping coffee from dainty china cups made in Germany.

'Well, first you have to rest the pastry, then roll out the layers very thinly,' explained Renata who was very proud of her cooking ability. 'Of course, the filling has to be rich and creamy.'

'Do you think there's some sort of Home Management course I could do in Palanga?'

'Leave it to me, I shall make enquiries at the Town Hall tomorrow.'

Renata was so delighted to have both of her sisters stay with her whilst completing their courses, because that meant she didn't have to spend so much time in Petras's company by herself. Petras didn't mind, saying that it was good for his wife to have some help with little Simas whilst he was away on his frequent business trips. It meant that he didn't have to deal with any domestic issues and could go and visit his mistresses whenever he pleased. On very hot days, the women would pack their lunch and go to the women's section of the beach, where they didn't have to worry about wearing their cumbersome swimsuits or being gawked at by lanky, spotty youths. From time to time, a light plane would fly low over the beach and all the women would promptly turn over onto their stomachs.

'For heaven's sake! Why do they do that?' asked Julia.

'Because they can!' replied Virginia.

'Because all men are filthy pigs!' retorted Renata with such force that her sisters looked at each other and raised their eyebrows, as if to say, 'What's got into her?'

One afternoon, dressed in the new outfits made by Virginia of Paris, as she liked to call herself, the three sisters were taking another stroll around the Botanical Gardens.

'I wouldn't mind taking a turn around the park with that one,' whispered Virginia conspiratorially to her sisters, as she spied a handsome officer walking past with two others. Little did she know that Sergeant Marius had noticed her as well, in her pretty, blue summer dress, and decided on the spot that she was the only one for him. He was on leave from his unit in the eastern part of Lithuania and had often heard other men talking about the earthy sensuality of Samogitian women. Smiling cheekily at Virginia, he doffed his officer's cap, saluted smartly, said hello and gave her a broad wink.

'Oh my goodness! 'Did you see that?' giggled Virginia excitedly to Julia. 'That officer gave me a wink, didn't he?'

'You be careful,' warned Renata who considered herself an experienced woman of the world now that she was a married lady. 'Some of these soldiers can't be trusted, especially him! You can tell by the way he speaks that he's not from Samogitia.'

Virginia ignored her, saying that if she wanted him, nothing was going to stop her, including her bossy older sister. Whenever she'd see him, she'd give him an encouraging smile, and he'd wave to her and doff his cap. The next morning as she went out to buy some pastries from the bakery for breakfast, Virginia spied her officer in the queue. He smiled at her and she self-consciously ran her fingers through her hair. As they left the bakery together, he spoke to her for the first time.

'Good morning, young lady. Please don't think me rude, but I have often seen you and your sisters strolling about Palanga. Can you at least tell me your name? Please! I can't get you out of my mind. Do you live around here?'

'Good morning. My name's Virginia Kirvis, I live in Ventuva, not far from here.'

'Ventava? Isn't that across the river in Latvia?'

'No, it's Ven-tu-va! With a *u* not an *a*'.

'I see. Sergeant Marius Plonas at your service. Now that we're properly introduced, may I see you again, sweet Virginia of Ventuva?'

'I, I'm going home tomorrow. I have to help my parents with the harvest.'

A week later, whilst Virginia was helping her mother to pickle endless jars of dill cucumbers, she noticed a man in uniform riding up their path on a motorbike with a sidecar.

'Oh no,' she thought to herself. 'That's Sergeant Marius and I look a right mess.' She rushed back into the cottage and hid behind the bedroom door.

'Are you lost sir?' asked Jonas politely, when Marius alighted from his motorbike.

'No, I've come to call upon a young lady, whom I have been told lives here.'

'I have three daughters. Just what sort of game are you playing at? It's quite obvious from your speech, that you're not from around this area!' scolded Kristina.

'Begging your pardon, madam, it's just that I have come to ask for her hand in marriage.'

'Whose hand? Which girl are you talking about?'

'The one who has the pretty blue summer dress!'

'*What*?' shouted Jonas. 'When did all this happen? Virginia! Come in here this instant!'

All three girls crept into the kitchen. Marius smiled at Virginia who shyly returned his smile.

'Now, who wants to tell me what's been going on behind my back?' threatened Kristina.

'Nothing untoward, I can assure you madam,' answered Marius all too quickly.

'Spit it out young man!' demanded Jonas.

'I have often seen your daughter, strolling in Palanga's Botanical Gardens with her sisters and I truly feel that she's the only one for me,' explained Marius.

'Oh do you now?' replied Kristina brusquely. 'We know nothing about you or your family, it's obvious from your dialect that you are not from Samogitia. What makes you so sure that we can trust you?'

'Yes, that is correct, madam. I am from a small town near Kaunas, but I can get my commanding officer to vouch for me, and my family,' Marius replied in a dignified manner. 'I have asked for a transfer here, if you will allow me to marry your daughter.'

'Well, which one is it?' Kristina demanded, even though she knew very well who it was.

Virginia peeped out from behind the door where she and Julia been eavesdropping.

'I think he means me,' she said softly.

'Hmm,' grumbled Jonas. 'In that case, you'd better have a glass of my krupnikas to celebrate.'

'Oh thank you papa, thank you mama,' cried Virginia, relieved she had her parents' consent.

'It's just like Cinderella, isn't it?' whispered Julia to herself, hoping that one day she'd meet her knight in shining armour. Life in independent Lithuanian was an exciting period for her, even though she was still at home helping her mother and Jonas. She couldn't wait be a bridesmaid at Virginia's wedding and hopefully, an aunt soon after.

Renata's little family prospered in Palanga. One winter's day she saw an advertisement plastered on a street lantern and on the spur of the moment, she decided to enrol in the French cookery course. She was already a good cook, but she wanted to be famous in Palanga for her culinary skills and hospitality. She wasn't living in the back woods of Ventuva anymore. Renata craved to become Palanga's most popular hostess when she entertained Petras's business colleagues and her friends. She was going to outshine everyone.

It was a freezing, cold morning in January of 1928, when Renata came upon a remarkable article in her newspaper. The government had decreed that the first of May was going to be a celebration called Mother's Day. About time, she thought, as she sipped her creamy coffee and bit into her rye bread and cheese. No one appreciated what she did each day. She excitedly showed the newspaper article to Petras who was slurping his macaroni and milk soup.

'Just imagine! Our government wants to honour all mothers with their own special day!'

'Hmm. And what about all the fathers who work every day to support their families?' he demanded angrily.

'I work just as hard as you do! Everyday there's washing, ironing, mending, cooking, cleaning, polishing and gardening to do,' exclaimed Renata. 'The meals that take me ages to prepare are gulped down by you in five minutes!'

'How many times have I told you that you can have two maids to help you with all that? But no, you want to be a martyr and do it all yourself! So don't play the poor, overworked peasant woman with me. It is your choice!'

'Well it would be nice, wouldn't it, if on Mother's Day, you could take our family out for lunch to a restaurant in Palanga, instead of me slaving over a hot stove!'

'Don't you think it would be better if we went back to Ventuva to see our mothers, since you're so keen on this Mother's Day business?'

'Yes Petras, you're right as usual. That would be better! Whatever you say. I will have a think about what gifts to take to our mothers. Leave it to me.'

That first Mother's Day in Ventuva was the one that Renata remembered for the rest of her life. The look of surprise on her mother's face when she opened the door and saw her daughter standing there with an enormous bunch of tulips and the biggest box of chocolates that she'd ever seen.

'What a surprise! What's this all about Renata? Why have you spent so much money on me? Mothers don't need presents! Just a simple thank you after each meal is enough!'

'No mama, you deserve this and more. You've had a hard life bringing me up. I know that I wasn't the easiest child to love when I was little.'

Tears formed in Kristina's eyes. Poor Renata, she looks so tired and unhappy, she thought to herself as she glanced at her eldest.

'Well, I'll just leave Renata and Simas here, whilst I go and see my mother now,' Petras said gruffly, and off he strode down to his parents' house.

'So what did Petras give you for Mother's Day?' asked Julia, who had made Kristina a new skirt with Virginia's help. Well, if the truth be known, Virginia had sewed most of it.

'Um, Petras said that he would probably take me out for dinner,' mumbled Renata. 'But our Simas is only two, so we'll have to find a baby sitter.'

'You could leave him overnight with us if you like, then we could bring him home to you the next day, couldn't we papa?' Julia was longing to get married herself and the prospect of playing with her cute little nephew delighted her no end.

'I suppose I could hitch up the wagon and we all could take a drive to Palanga,' said Jonas. 'The little fellow would probably like that, wouldn't you?'

'Horsey, horsey!' gurgled Simas delightedly, as Jonas hoisted him onto his leg and jiggled him up and down.

'That would be wonderful papa. Simas is at the stage of waking up several times each night, wanting to get into bed with me. I just don't know what's wrong with him. He grizzles from morning till night.'

Kristina noted that her daughter did not say 'our bed,' but she held her tongue. Renata looked frazzled and she noticed the dark circles under her eyes. She couldn't remember any of her daughters wanting to climb into her and Romas' bed at that stage. Perhaps it was because the three girls all slept in the same bed.

'Maybe he's teething? His two year old molars should be coming through soon. Give him some hard rusks to chew on or make him some poppy seed milk. That should quieten him down for the night.'

Renata recalled how placid Simas was during his christening at Palanga's beautiful Church of the Assumption of the Blessed Virgin Mary. Somehow, she thought that he would remain the same placid baby forever. She hadn't even thought about the different stages of her son's development, so she just nodded at Kristina, thankful that there was a logical explanation for his grizzling and that her mother had a solution.

When Petras got back from his mother's house a few hours later, Renata told him about Jonas' offer to look after Simas overnight. He readily agreed, since he had his own plans for Renata when they got home from dinner at the restaurant that night.

Since Petras was often away on business, Renata felt that she needed to fill in some time once Simas was older. She was determined to learn to use other herbs besides dill and parsley. Once she had enrolled in the French cooking course, she became Pierre's star pupil and he would often use her dishes as an example of the way the meal should look. Encouraged by his praise, Renata bloomed and found her sensual experiences in the food she learnt to create. For Simas' birthdays, she would create a multi-coloured jelly tower or various farm animals fashioned from marzipan. One evening, she decided on a roast goose stuffed with prunes and apples, accompanied by roast potatoes for Petras's business colleagues. Pierre had taught her to parboil the potatoes first, cool them, then sprinkle them with mustard powder before she put them in the hot fat to roast. That way, they come out a golden crunchy brown. As her guests tapped the toffee on the top of Renata's *crème brulée* for dessert, they gasped in wonder as they tasted the delicate custard beneath.

'Mrs. Baras! If you weren't married already, I'd be on my knees proposing to you, right this very minute!' exclaimed Mr. Vacel, who owned a big department store in Tallinn.

Renata flushed a deep red and stammered her thanks, knowing that Petras hated to be upstaged and would certainly punish her later that night, by roughly demanding his marital rights. That night, as she stared up at the ceiling, Renata began to form a plan in her mind. Pierre had told her at the end of the course that he'd be only too happy to employ her in his restaurant Le Grand Lapin, if ever she wanted a job. If she was careful with the housekeeping money, perhaps she could save her fare to France, that way she would be free of Petras and the unhappy life she was leading.

However, nine months later, Renata found herself pregnant with her second child. She prayed daily for a daughter, and after she had spun her wedding ring on a cotton thread over her belly, the ring had indicated that she would have girl. Simas's birth had been an easy one and she'd always planned to have four children.

When Petras came in to visit her in hospital, he took one look at his daughter and snarled, 'By the devil! What an ugly kid! She looks nothing like you or me! You've been playing around behind my back, haven't you?'

Renata fell back against her pillow stunned. Where had that accusation come from?

'That is not true,' she whispered. 'How can you say such a thing to me? You know that all I do is tend to the house, our son and my flower garden.'

'You gave yourself to me easily enough before our wedding night! How do I know that you haven't been playing up with that fancy Pierre who runs your cooking course or any man who asks?'

'Petras, you tricked me into giving myself to you. Surely you haven't forgotten what happened on that St John's night?'

'Well, you tell me why this kid's got high cheekbones and black hair like a bloody Tatar!'

'How do I know that you haven't got a Tatar somewhere along your side of the family?'

'There are certainly no Tatars on my side. I, for one, don't believe that she's my daughter! I don't want to have anything to do with her! So keep her away from me!'

Renata turned her face to the wall and sobbed. The nurse ushered out Petras, scolding him for upsetting his wife.

'Mr. Baras, please keep your voice down. You're upsetting all the mothers in my hospital. If your wife's milk doesn't come in, then we know who's to blame! Shame on you!'

'The Devil take you and all the other stupid cows in this blasted hospital!' Petras muttered as stalked down the hospital steps and headed straight for his favourite tavern where he knew that he'd be king after buying a round of vodka shots for his business cronies.

From that day on, a silent war raged between them. Renata refused to let Petras back into their bed, forcing him to move into the guest room. He ignored her most of the time and instead talked to his wife and daughter through his son, asking him to tell his mother to pass the salt or get his slippers. Other times, he'd just point to an object and Renata or Ella would have to run and fetch it for him. He made it quite clear that he was the provider and his wife and daughter should be grateful for what he gave them. After a bout of drinking in the main tavern, he'd stumble back home and call Renata, 'a cold, heartless bitch,' or his daughter, 'that bloody Tatar.' Petras's affection was lavished solely on his son whom he boasted to everyone, would inherit his shops and business acumen.

'He'll be a rich man, mark my words. Simas will be known all over Lithuania.'

As soon as he was old enough, Simas accompanied his father on business trips all over Lithuania, Latvia and sometimes to Estonia. Over the years, Petras had amassed a collection of anecdotes and stories that he trotted out for all his customers, after they'd shared a few drinks. When Renata tried to protest that Simas was too young to be accompanying him, Petras would retort, 'I'm making a man out of him, you stupid woman! What's he learning at school, that I can't teach him? Do you want him to grow up to be a sissy?'

In the end, Renata gave in, although she insisted that her son keep up his music lessons reminding Petras that playing the accordion at some business function, might seal a deal or two. She knew by then that was the only way to appease her husband.

Ella grew up to be a timid and fearful child who hid behind her mother's skirts. Her brother Simas would tease her on a daily basis, pull her plaits or throw her favourite dolls against the wall. Her high cheek bones and black hair earned her the nickname of 'Gypsy girl' from the children in their street. Renata did her best to protect her daughter from the taunts, but then even Petras and Simas adopted the nickname and started to call Ella 'Gypsy girl' as well.

When Simas got older, Petras spoilt him by buying him a bicycle, and he'd peddle like the wind down the main street of Palanga. When he got older his father bought him a motorcycle to visit his aunt Virginia, or go fishing with his cousin Darius. To his credit, the fact that Darius had been born with dwarfism didn't faze Simas. That Darius could catch any size fish never ceased to amaze him. His aunt Virginia didn't treat her son differently from anyone, else apart from calling him 'my little man.' Often people remarked how strange it was that his twin sister Milda had been born normal.

'The Devil's put his mark on that family,' Tamara the gossip would say to all and sundry. 'Mark my words! No good will come of him!'

'Should have been strangled at birth!' others would chime in.

'It's God's will,' Virginia would say, and vowed to herself that she would let no harm to come to her little man. Like her mother, Virginia strongly believed in destiny. She would often argue with Marius that one couldn't change fate. He in reply, would point out Petras as an example of a person who'd changed his destiny.

'If your brother-in-law can rise above his station, then there has to be hope for our son.'

After his business trips, Petras would return back to Palanga elated and brimming with ambition and new plans for expanding his delicatessen business. One day, he threw a red fox fur collar onto Renata's bed.

'Here! Put this on! No one can accuse me of not buying you anything!' Renata's hair was a reddish brown, and once she'd put on the fox fur she thought that she looked like a fox herself and told her husband that it didn't suit her.

'So that's the thanks I get! You are a fussy bitch, aren't you? Here, give it to me and I'll take it back,' he snapped.

A few days later, while Renata was shopping in Palanga, she overheard Agata, one of the town's notorious hussies gossiping to the serving girl behind the counter of the shoe shop.

'So I said to him, darling, that red fox fur collar is the very best present you have ever bought me. You know, his wife's such an ugly, dumpy thing! So I wore it to bed, you know, with nothing else! That got him going!' she added with a sly wink.

The shop assistant laughed. 'You certainly know how to reel them in! Don't forget that we're meeting up this Saturday night at the band pavilion. I'm sure that some of the army officers on leave will show us a good time!'

Renata felt her face flush as she rushed out of the shop. So that's where Petras spent his time. Certainly not at all those business meetings! From that day on, her heart hardened towards Petras even more. Whom could she tell? She could almost hear her mother say, 'You've made your bed Renata, now you have to lie in it,' or 'It's a bit late now, it's spoons after dinner.'

Afraid to confront her husband about what she discovered, Renata withdrew into her garden. In a silent fury, she decapitated all the rose blooms and pulled out all her flowers. Gathering up the rose petals, she made rosewater, just like her mother had taught her. The next week, dressed in her oldest clothes, Renata began to plant potatoes, tomatoes and cucumbers. She began to polish her furniture religiously, the smell of beeswax calming her. She scrubbed the floors on her hands and knees. Stopped wearing the fine dresses she had. Her pretty manicured fingernails became encrusted with dirt.

'Looks what the cat's dragged in!' Petras would sneer. 'Can't you fix yourself up woman? Look in the mirror! Wouldn't hurt you to go and get your hair done once in a while or wear a bit of lipstick, would it? People in Palanga are starting to say I married a mad woman.'

Renata was coping the only way she knew how. Looking back, she had really been happy in Ventuva. Her family had lived a simple life, her parents loved each other and her stepfather Jonas was a good decent man.

One summer morning, Renata closed her front door and walked along the main street towards Palanga beach. Simas and Ella were safe at school and she felt the balmy breeze caress her skin. Pine trees swayed and rustled. She saw lovers sitting on benches whispering to each other. The seagulls seemed to nod in agreement. In a daze, she came to the water's edge. The silky, white sands sighed beneath her bare feet. Slowly, Renata started to walk towards the edge of the sea, giving herself up to the ocean, until she felt the waves tumble her in their sandy currents.

Suddenly, strong arms were dragging her back to shore.

'Madam, madam! Are you alright?' A young man was pounding her on her back.

Renata stared back glassily at him.

'You're Mr Baras' wife, aren't you?'

'Who, who are you?' she tried to speak, as she coughed up more seawater.

'I'm Lukas, one of his delivery boys,' he replied. 'Don't you recognize me?'

'Of course, of course! Thank you for helping me out Lukas.'

'You were going to drown yourself, weren't you?' Lukas asked gently.

'Was it that obvious?' asked Renata, fearful that he was going to tell Petras the whole sorry tale. Then she'd have to put up with more of his shouting and swearing.

'Perhaps, you were just wading in the shallows and a wave knocked you off your feet?'

'Yes Lukas, that's exactly what happened!'

'Can I help you walk back to your house Mrs Baras?'

'I'm alright now, thank you for helping me. I will never forget your kindness young man.' Renata knew if any of her neighbours saw her walking along the street with a young man, there would be hell to pay once Petras got wind of it. There was no way she was going to play into his hands.

'I'll just sit on the sand and wait till my dress dries out, thank you all the same.'

Feeling ashamed, Renata smoothed down her dress and thought that she'd pay a visit to the grotto at Birutė Hill, since it was on her way home, through the Botanical Gardens. She remembered her history lessons and her old teacher intoning in his boring voice to the class how back in the tenth century there used to be a village there and how later on in the thirteenth century, the villagers built a high wall with a look-out tower. Now there was a pier and row boats. She and her classmates had yawned with boredom at the time, but Renata thought that she could recall quite a few of the facts, so something must have sunk into that dull brain of hers.

'Birutė was a vestal virgin, a pagan goddess, a keeper of the eternal fire.' Her teacher's words came back to her. She remembered how overjoyed her mother had been when she had taken her to the grotto and the chapel built on top of the hill. Kristina had raised her hands to the statue of Birutė and prayed, 'Dear Birutė, keep my family safe and bestow health and happiness upon them.'

Renata had been so embarrassed, when she saw a group of tourists from another part of Lithuania turning round to stare at her mother and shake their heads at the Samogitian dialect they couldn't understand. Now here she was, at Birutė's grotto, praying as well, asking for help with her marriage and her philandering husband.

When Renata finally got home she was exhausted physically and emotionally. Ella and Simas were already back from school.

'Where have you been mother?' exploded Simas. 'Where's my apple strudel and the glass of milk that I usually have?' He went into the kitchen flinging open all the cupboard doors.

'Mama, when do you think we can go and stay with Grandma Kristina?' asked Ella timidly.

Renata ignored her son's rudeness and tiredly looked at her daughter.

'Soon. You can go soon.'

Simas looked away furtively. 'I'm not going! Grandma Kristina's a witch! It's the truth! Papa told me! I'm definitely going to stay here and help Papa in the shop!' he announced imperiously. He had promised a girl he'd met on the Palanga pier that he was going to get to know her better that summer. Besides, he and his friends were going to spend a night at 'Villa Sophie.' When they were little children, they had been warned constantly by their parents never to go anywhere near the huge mansion belonging to Count Tiškevičius. Rumours swirled around that it was haunted by his daughter. Others said that his wife had a roomful of mirrors where she conducted séances, getting in touch with spirits who had not passed over to the other side. Simas didn't care about any of the rumours. He was going to win the bet and he insisted again that he wasn't going to go to Ventuva that summer.

Renata ignored her son's outburst and thought that staying with Kristina might give Ella a break from her obnoxious brother, who tormented her at every opportunity. She could also play with her cousin Milda, whom she regarded as a good influence because of her outgoing nature.

'As long as you promise to help grandma, it's all right with me,' said Renata.

'But what if papa doesn't let me go?' asked Ella.

'You leave your father to me,' replied Renata with a smile. 'I'll deal with him.'

Summer was always a magical time for Ella in Ventuva. Her grandmother took her into the forest to show her where to find all the types of berries that grew there. They picked bucket loads of bilberries, cranberries, raspberries and strawberries.

'In autumn, I will show you where all the mushrooms are, and then we'll fry them in butter for our supper.' For their lunch, Kristina made a fruit soup by gently simmering the berries. While it was cooling in front of the kitchen window, she taught Ella how to make strawberry jam.

'Watch and follow me. See? Use equal amounts of strawberry and sugar and the juice of one lemon. Put it in a big pot and stir it for an hour until it thickens.'

'All right grandma, but how will I know if the jam's ready?'

'Take a bit on a spoon and put it on a saucer. If the jam's not runny, it's ready.'

Next they boiled up the cranberries with some sugar and water and poured it into jugs. 'Nothing like a few glasses of cranberry juice to help you with any women's troubles.'

Ella wasn't quite sure what she meant, but she nodded and waited for her cousin Milda to come over.

'Do you want some of the cranberry juice I made?' Ella asked her proudly.

'Thanks, but I'm not really fond of cranberries,' Milda admitted, 'But I'd love to have some of those fat juicy strawberries with cream.'

'Is it true that our grandma's a witch?' asked Milda curiously after she'd made short work of at least a dozen strawberries.

'I don't think so,' replied Ella feeling scared. 'I'll ask her and tell you tomorrow when I come over to your house.'

While they were sitting on the outside bench, Ella told Milda that she wished that she could live in Ventuva forever with her grandmother. 'I could go to school with you, it would be such fun.'

'Who's coming to live with me?' Renata said jokingly as she strolled by with the washing.

'Grandma, do you think I could I live with you here?' asked Ella.

'But you live in Palanga with your mother and father, and your brother Simas.'

'I hate them! I hate all of them!' Ella shouted. 'I wish that I'd never been born!'

Milda was frightened at Ella's outburst and scampered home as quickly as she could.

Kristina was taken aback, to see her granddaughter sobbing so bitterly.

'Come on sweetheart, tell your grandma what's wrong,' she said softly putting her arms around Ella.

'They all hate me. Papa says that I'm not his daughter. He never speaks to me.'

'That can't be true. Are you sure?'

'Papa calls me a Tatar and he never gives Mama any money for my clothes. Last year I had to borrow my friend Monika's folk dancing costume for our end of school concert.'

Kristina pondered about all the dresses that Virginia had made for her niece. She wondered how Renata had managed to wrangle the money from Petras for the materials. When the time was right, she was going to get the truth out of Renata.

'And, and, Simas and Milda say you're a witch! You're not a witch, are you grandma?'

Kristina was horrified. 'No, I am not a witch. I just know what herbs can be used to help people. You know when I put vinegar on your mosquito bites, the itch goes away, doesn't it?'

'Yes, but.'

'And when you have an upset tummy, my chamomile tea helps, doesn't it?

'Yes, but.'

'And when you get sunburn, I put slices of tomato on your burns and your skin cools down.'

'But, but?'

'And what about the time you burnt your hand, picking up the hot saucepan handle without a cloth?'

'Um, you made me stick my hand in some grated potato.'

'And were there any burn marks on your hand the next day?'

'No, but ... '

Ella didn't seem fully convinced. 'But Papa says that you drink blood and ride your broomstick at midnight.'

'What?' Kristina laughed till tears rolled down her cheeks.

'The only blood I handle is when I make blood sausage with your aunts!'

'I could never eat blood sausage,' declared Ella.

'But you have my dear. You've had it with eggs for breakfast here many times.'

'Oh that's really horrible grandma,' replied Ella, pretending to gag.

'How about I speak to your mother and see what we can work out about you staying here? Now, have I ever told you the story about the thieves? Stories had always calmed her own children, she was sure that she could do the same with her granddaughter.

'Once upon a time, my grandmother was working for a very rich Samogitian nobleman.'

'Is this a true story?' asked Ella.

'You'll just have to wait and see,' replied Kristina. 'Now my grandmother wasn't alone there in the big manor house, there were two housemaids working there as well. One was old and one was young. The nobleman had a stable full of beautiful horses and two big dogs.'

'What were their names?' asked Ella, who was disappointed that her father hadn't allowed her to have any pets, saying that they were a waste of time and money.

'One dog was called "What are you sitting there for?", and the other one was called "I can see you".'

'What silly names!' laughed Ella as she relaxed and fell under her grandmother's spell.

'One afternoon, the noble left to go visiting, but of course the maids had to stay behind to do their work around the manor. That night, the maids heard somebody trying to break into the stables. Thieves had come to steal the noble's horses. What were the maids going to do?'

'Hide?' asked Ella. 'I'd be scared stiff of thieves.'

'No, the older maid, who was smarter, ran outside yelling, "What are you sitting there for?" "What are you sitting there for?" and "I can see you! I can see you!"'

'She was calling the dogs wasn't she?' remarked Ella.

'Clever girl! Yes she was,' answered Kristina. 'She kept yelling in this fashion and the thieves thought that they'd been spotted. So they ran off and in this way, the noble's horses were saved.'

'What did your grandmother do then?' asked Ella.

'That can be a story for another day,' smiled Kristina. 'But now it's time for us to bake a honey cake for your Aunt Julia's birthday. I'll check the beehive and you go and check to see how many eggs the hens have laid.'

Soon both of them were working at the kitchen table mixing up a cake to surprise Julia.

The next year, Renata, instead of travelling back to Ventuva to spend Easter with her mother and sisters, decided to invite everyone to Palanga for Easter Sunday lunch. This was going to be her secret farewell, before she went off to Paris. She'd saved enough from her housekeeping for the trip and had written to Pierre to say that she was coming. She knew that she could stay in the little attic in the apartment above his restaurant, where he lived with his wife

Yvette. Later, she would write to her family and explain why she had to leave and when she'd saved enough money, she would send for Ella. She knew that Petras would never let her have Simas.

Petras was quite pleased to have Renata's family at his house for Easter but insisted that his parents should come as well. After attending Mass in Palanga they all came back for a sumptuous feast. Renata had relented and had hired a young girl to help her with the preparations for the lunch. Both of them had worked for days and had this time Renata had outdone herself. Petras flitted about playing the genial host. Virginia and Julia hadn't seen so much food in all their lives! However everyone had to admire the new ice chest that Petras had bought to keep food cool in summer.

'It's the latest thing! I can have the ice delivered whenever I need it,' he exclaimed proudly.

As an entrée, Renata had prepared herrings with sour cream, with diced hard boiled eggs on the top, finished off with a sprinkle of shallots. There was smoked plaice and a dish of cold fish fillets with tomatoes and onions. Later, Renata brought in her famous roast goose and a leg of roast lamb. Potato sausages and baked ham with horse radish sauce were placed on the other side. Quick as a flash, Milda and Darius grabbed a soft white bread roll and a potato sausage before anyone had started.

'Stop that, you two! People will think that I never feed you,' admonished Virginia.

'But mama, breakfast was six hours ago, we're really, really starving!' whined Milda.

'That may be true, but you know very well, that grace is always said first,' Marius added with a smile.

'Um yes, yes of course,' Petras mumbled. 'Bless this house and bless this food. Amen.' He went around filling glasses with the German wine he'd bought on his last business trip to Berlin. He liked to show off for his parents and in-laws as he carved the goose and lamb at the head of the table. Smiling benevolently, he offered pieces of lamb or goose to his relatives.

'No wine or *kvasas* for you,' he told all the children. 'You can have some homemade lemonade or milk'

'Ella and Milda remained silent as their glasses were filled up. 'Bottoms up! Cheers! Happy Easter!' were heard as the adults toasted each other.

'I should be allowed to have some gira,' protested Simas. 'I am old enough! Papa has let me have some plenty of times, when we've travelled to Riga and Tallinn!'

'No Simas, you're definitely not old enough to drink beer!' replied Renata in a firm voice.

'Oh, let him have a little glass of *kvasas*,' relented Petras. 'He's a lad after my own heart, after all.'

Renata saw her mother's raised eyebrows and quickly began to pass around dishes of her marinated mushrooms, potato salad, dill cucumbers, vinegretas, and her mother's favourite beetroot and bean salad.

After everyone had eaten their fill, they all went outside for the Easter egg rolling contest.

'Remember the fun we used to have with Papa at Easter time?' Renata asked her sisters.

'You always got into trouble for being naughty,' laughed Virginia. 'I remember you having to sit in the corner more than once.'

'You certainly were a high spirited little girl,' Kristina reminded her eldest. She saw that the spark had left her daughter who seemed more determined than ever, to show everyone what a wonderful housewife and cook she was. 'Have you started to teach Ella to cook?'

'Yes I can make *kotletai*,' replied Ella. 'But my meat patties turn out very hard and father complains about me being useless.'

'What if I told you about a secret ingredient to make your meat patties really outstanding?'

Kristina whispered in her grand-daughter's ear, 'After you've added the egg and the piece of bread soaked in water or milk and squeezed it out, finely grate a quarter of an apple into the meat mixture. Then mix it all really thoroughly by hand so the mixture feels soft.'

'Really, is that all?'

'Yes, it's very simple isn't it, when you know a few tricks!'

Whilst Kristina was explaining a few more of her cooking secrets to Ella, the men were discussing politics. Petras favoured the current president Antanas Smetona, whereas his father-in-law was for his deputy, Augustinas Voldemaras.

'Disgusting the way Smetona got rid of Voldemaras,' Gedas said to Petras.

'Well he deserved it, it's well known that he was plotting to overthrow Smetona!' shot back Petras.

'Your Smetona's always been in bed with the Germans!' shouted back Marius. 'I bet that the Estonians and Latvians don't treat their politicians in this way.'

'Now that you mention it, I actually met President Päts when I was in Tallin last month and President Ulmanis when I was in Riga last year,' boasted Petras.

'Of course, and I'm sure they told you all about the economic plans they have for their countries,' joked Marius.

'It was when I was at a big business conference,' retorted Petras.

'Ah yes, of course! Your very important conference about cheeses and sausages!' laughed Gedas.

'Well, when are you going to serve dessert?' Petras snapped to Renata. He was very miffed that he wasn't given the respect he craved from Marius and his father. To top it off, his nephew Darius had beaten his son Simas in the egg rolling contest, although he was very careful not to let his anger show in front of Virginia's family. Pete was about to say something, but stopped himself. Kristina had heard him utter 'stupid dwarf' under his breath and wondered if all was well in her daughter's marriage. Even so, she felt she should not interfere. She wondered if her daughter's in-laws had noticed anything.

Helped by her sisters, Renata brought in a creamy *paska*, a plate of mushroom cookies topped with chocolate, a poppy seed cake and a *bapka*.

Jonas groaned. 'Oh my Lord, I don't think I can eat another bite!'

'There's plenty of time,' answered Kristina giving his hand a friendly squeeze under the table. 'It's only three o'clock!'

Nevertheless, the family made short work of the desserts, even though they'd all protested like Jonas, that they couldn't eat another thing.

'I wonder why Aunty Renata didn't make her Gypsy cake this year? Milda remarked to her cousin Ella, who still had a mouth full of *paska*.

'When I'm married, I'm going to cook this sort of delicious food, just like mama, and then I'll make a Gypsy cake just for just you and me,' replied Ella.

That summer, whilst Renata was in the final stages of planning her escape to Paris, she awoke to an unfamiliar sound of boots marching along Palanga's streets. Rushing to the window, Renata saw people waving strange looking flags in front of the Viktorija holi-day resort and raising their arms shouting, 'Heil Hitler!.' German soldiers were flooding their streets and soon Hitler's name was on everyone's lips. Petras had just heard on the radio that Lithuania's government had been given an ultimatum by Hitler, but dismissed it, telling Renata that his business contacts in Germany had reas-sured him that he had nothing to worry about. Hitler just wanted to get rid of some undesirable elements in their society, and that was a good thing. However, Renata clearly remembered the day she'd been told how her mother had bravely rushed out of their cottage, trying to save their Jewish neighbour Maria from being carted off to Siberia.

'But war's a terrible thing,' she told Petras. 'You lost your two brothers last time.'

'I'm too old to be called up, and fortunately Simas is too young. But it will be good for business, you'll see! We can trust the Germans, they helped us get our independence back in 1918. You should know that soldiers need food and provisions. I'll make a fortune!'

Renata glanced out the window again. Some of her neighbours were running out to hand posies of flowers to the marching sol-diers. From that moment she resolved to keep her opinions to her-self, because she could never be sure, whose side people were on. Once the Nazis established themselves, they took over all the buildings and shops in Palanga and commandeered Petras's two delivery vans. His dreams of making a fortune were shattered and he found out very quickly, that he wasn't a big shot anymore. Ella and Simas continued to go to school, but their teachers began to talk about the Jewish problem and Ella would come home and tell her mother what the teacher had said. Renata remembered their teacher in Ventuva saying the same thing during the Great War.

119

One afternoon when Ella came back from school, she saw a German officer talking to her father.

'Meet my dear daughter Ella,' her father was saying in an unusually affectionate tone. 'She's going to start high school in a year or two.'

Ella looked up in fright at the officer and then back at her father. Why was he being so nice to her all of a sudden?

'Major Friedrich has been billeted to stay with us Ella. Another officer might be joining us next week. You must make sure that you make them feel welcome in our home.'

Once the two officers installed themselves in the guest room, there were no more visits from her aunts in Ventuva. It was deemed too risky. Major Friedrich and Major Dieter often brought back chocolate and real coffee in exchange for Renata's home cooking. Renata hid her feelings and only spoke when she was spoken to, as her German was limited, unlike Petras's, who had travelled on business to Berlin and Dresden before the war. He had learnt German at high school, whereas she'd only grasped the basics of French. Often they'd have a bottle of Schnapps and invite Petras to play cards with them or ask Simas to play some lively marching tunes on his accordion. They told Renata what a pretty woman she was and that they missed their families and generally were very polite.

As Renata and Ella were queuing up to get their weekly rations one morning, they noticed big yellow stars painted on the Jewish stores. Groups of people with a yellow star were being loaded into trucks and those who were reluctant to climb in were being beaten with rifle butts.

'Mama! Look! There's Mrs Weinstein, the lady who ran Aunty Virginia's sewing course!'

'Don't look Ella,' cautioned Renata. Quickly she turned the next corner and took the short cut home. Agitated beyond belief, she felt an overwhelming urge to pack up her belongings and go back to Ventuva. As she started to fling open her wardrobe doors, Petras came in from the kitchen. They were forced to share a bedroom once more, now they had two German officers under their roof.

'What do you think you are doing, you silly bitch?' he hissed.

'It's happening again! They're taking away those poor Jewish people somewhere.'

'Don't be stupid. Major Dieter told me that they're re-settling all the Jews on farms in Poland. Everyone knows that they've kept our people from prospering here.'

'But what about poor Mrs Weinstein and her family. Her parents must be the same age as our parents. How could they possibly do any hard farm work?'

'Leave it! It's none of our business. The two majors are in the know, they tell me everything.'

Privately, Renata doubted that any of that was true, but then what did she know about war or politics? She thought that she would try another tack.

'You're right of course, what would a silly woman like me know about these things. But I must confess that I am a bit worried about the way Major Friedrich looks at Ella.'

'What are you talking about woman? Are you mad? She's only eleven!'

For once however, Petras listened to his wife. He shuddered to think what could happen, and knew he would not be able to do anything. He had to agree with his wife that although Ella still looked awkward and gawky, she was starting to blossom into a young woman. Unlike Renata, she was growing tall and her high cheekbones gave her an exotic look.

'Alright, alright! I'll invent some excuse that her grandmother needs her back in the village, that she's sick or something. Maybe I can take you next weekend. I am sure the majors will let me have one of our wagons back to take you there.'

Renata fell on her knees. 'Thank, you, thank you,' she cried as she kissed his hand.

'Well now, that's more like it. Now I think you owe me something, don't you?'

Ella stared glassily at the ceiling as her body was invaded again and again.

When Renata arrived back in Ventuva, she observed that there were no animals anywhere. As she stepped in the door, she immediately noticed that Kristina had lost a lot of weight and that her clothes hung off her tiny frame.

'Mama! How good to see you!'

'You too, Renata. And is that my Ella that I see? Look how you've grown into a beautiful young lady? And there's my boy Simas! Where's that motorbike of yours?'

'The Huns took it.'

Why can't we see any animals around here grandma?' asked Ella.

'The Nazis requisitioned them,' answered Kristina, 'And gave us a receipt to cash in after the war.' She spat on the floor in disgust.

'Where's Grandpa Jonas? He promised to take me fishing!' Simas suddenly realised he was not in the room.

'It's a long story,' replied Kristina. 'Sit down and I'll get you some bread and jam and then I'll tell you about it.'

'No, you sit down Mama, you look tired, let me do it.'

'One day, the Nazis came and pounded on the door. They took away our cow and told Jonas to pack his things, he was going to be taken somewhere in Germany to work on a farm. He and your uncle Marius are still there.'

'But why?' asked Ella.

'There are no men left to work their farms, since all the able bodied ones have been called up to fight for Hitler.'

'But Jonas isn't as young as Marius, what can he possibly do?' asked Simas, who was grateful he hadn't been taken as well. Little did he know that his father had done a deal with the billeted German officers. He'd given them Renata's silver tea service and a painting they took a fancy to in their living room.

'I am sure that he'll tell us all about it when he gets back,' replied Kristina hesitantly. During the last full moon, as she had sat outside, the Ancient Ones had whispered that Jonas wasn't coming home. Her amber pendant had spun about in her hand and stopped in the direction of the east.

After hearing more news from his village friends, Petras finally decided that they wouldn't go back to Palanga. He hid his horse and wagon in the disused tunnel he'd discovered after The Great War. There he found a group of men who had banded together to form a resistance group, calling themselves The Forest Brothers. They invited Petras to join them. Each day he disappeared to feed the horse with whatever he could find and walked him up and down the tunnel. Renata became the lookout at the Post Office for any news of the invading troops and then would jump onto her rickety blue bicycle and peddle as fast as she could to warn the Forest Brothers.

'You know, your father Romas would have joined the partisans as well, if he was still alive, God rest his soul,' Kristina would often tell her daughters.

Virginia's husband Marius, being the village policeman, joined the partisans as well after he returned from labouring on the German farm. He was well regarded for his organisational skills. Petras was pleased to have his brother-in-law with him. Maybe after the war, he could recoup his losses, when Lithuania became independent once more. Since Petras was in his early forties, he was given the job of being the look out.

At night, along with her sister and the other village women, Renata would take food to the Forest Brothers. Sometimes Kristina would go with them. Julia had a close call with the Russian patrols a few times during the day, but was always able to invent some female complaint and holding her stomach, would limp away.

One night Marius tried to talk him and five others to pay their families a visit.

'Come on brothers,' Marius cajoled. 'I know that you've missed your wives and sweethearts. We've been hiding in these forests for three months now. How about we slip away and see them for an hour or so?'

Petras declined, since he knew that there was no warm bed waiting for him in Kristina's house. Instead, he offered to stay behind and keep watch.

As soon as Marius slipped in quietly into his cottage, he crept up behind Virginia and put his hands over her eyes.

'Guess who sweetheart?'

'Marius! You gave me a fright! I thought that I was a goner. You are taking a big risk to come back here!'

'I couldn't keep away from my family, you know me.'

'But what if they catch you? The patrols have been here every week.'

'We know. My Forest Brothers have got good eyes, they'll hoot like an owl three times if they see a patrol coming this way.'

As his children slept, Marius knew that this could be one of the last times he would see his wife. He handed her a package and told her to bury in the barn under the haystack.

No sooner had Marius renewed his acquaintance with Virginia when he thought he heard an owl hoot.

'Did you hear that?' Virginia jumped out of bed.

'Shhh, come back to bed darling, that was only one hoot, not three.'

An hour later, Marius dressed quickly and with a hunk of cheese and bread wrapped inside his shirt, crept out of his cottage towards the covered tunnel in the forest where the rest of the partisans would also be heading. As he skirted around the bend, he felt a cold sharp object at the back of his head. Then his world went black. When we he awoke, he was on a cattle truck with dozens of other bruised and battered men.

What did Marius think about after he was deprived of everything that mattered to him in a remote Vorkuta gulag? The back-breaking work deep in a Siberian coalmine, where no one knew where he would be for twenty five years, or whether he was dead or alive. As Marius gnawed on the hard black bread, he dreamt about the food Virginia used to make, steaming bowls of plump dumplings filled with pork and veal, pastries stuffed with poppy seeds, honey and nuts. The smells of his childhood. A bucket of earthy autumn mushrooms, freshly picked radishes and beans eaten straight from the rich earth. Peas straight from the pod, some went into the bowl, but his mother never reprimanded him, she smiled as her son gorged himself on their home grown vegetables from their little plot of land surrounded by pine forests. Twenty five years! How could he survive working in these bloody coalmines for twenty five years?

Marius was surrounded by pine forests now, but they were filled with hungry wolves who wouldn't hesitate to tear out his skinny throat to feed their litters of pups. He shivered as he drew the threadbare blanket around him and warmed himself around the fire along with the other starving men. He wondered where the rest of his Forest Brothers, were at this moment. Had they escaped or had they died a terrible death? Were their mutilated bodies strung up in the village square? He fished out a wrinkled fish-head from his watery soup and sucked out whatever nourishment he could find.

Not at all like the freshly caught carp and pike his Virginia would bake whole in the oven with potatoes, carrots and mushrooms. For Christmas she would mince up the fish and sew it back into the skin and decorate it with cucumber slices, radishes and fresh sprigs of dill. There'd been a time when he'd never thought very much about his next meal. Sometimes there'd be fish in aspic for their Christmas Eve meal, along with mushrooms and beetroot salad, pickled dill cucumbers, cabbage, freshly baked rye bread, and a berry pudding. On Christmas Day, after church, they'd share a roast goose with apples, ham that he'd smoked himself, and his mother-in-law's delicious poppy seed cake. Marius remembered how his wife would complain that her arms were aching after kneading the dough. His mother-in-law would look wearily at her and say, 'My Virginia doesn't really know what real pain is, does she?' Smiling at her son-in-law, she'd offer him another *kibinas* pastry or a dish of her home-made cottage cheese and strawberry jam. If he ever got out of Vorkuta alive, he'd never take his freedom or food for granted ever again.

Marius understood what real pain meant now. The beatings, the roll calls at any hour of the night, were his life and he surrendered his body to this regime. Plotting every night, planning for revenge and escape kept him alive. He noticed Alex hiding in the shadows, and signalled with his eyes to meet him outside the barracks in the artic snow.

'What do you want?' Alex sighed wearily. 'You know very well that we could get caught at any moment.'

Marius slipped a piece of mouldy black bread into Alex's callused hand.

'Happy Birthday, Forest Brother.'

'Prisoner 4521 is accused of crimes against the Party. Communicating with spies and disobeying camp rules!'

The rest of the prisoners, the old and the weary, were forced to line up in the freezing snow to be given a taste of what their destiny would be. They all knew the outcome before the sham trial, yet they still hoped that a miracle might happen, and deliver one of their own from his fate. They craned their necks to see this terrible spy, whom, the camp commander assured everyone had committed a multitude of heinous crimes.

'The prisoner is to be executed. No need for any further evidence. No need for that,' proclaimed the camp official. His apparatchiks nodded in agreement.

'Let him speak!' a few prisoners mumbled bravely.

Marius struggled awkwardly to his feet, his body leaning against the post. Crippled by the beatings, he tried to express himself, but the outcome had already been decided for him. The last things he saw as the bullets ripped into his chest were the faces of his beloved wife and children.

That evening Virginia's rocking chair began to rock by itself. 'Someone's going and someone's coming,' she whispered to herself, remembering her mother's sayings. Perhaps Marius would be coming back to her and she would run out to the gate to welcome him back home.

Three months later, Virginia received an official letter from Vorkuta stating that her husband had died from liver failure. Both she and her mother were now widows and there were only a few old men left in their village. When the Russian army arrived, they had forcibly conscripted any young men, before that it was the Nazis.

After Marius' arrest, Petras knew that it was a matter of time before the rest of the Forest Brothers would be ambushed, betrayed or killed. He would give anything to know who'd betrayed his brother-in-law, but he understood that it was high time for his family to go elsewhere, or otherwise they could very well be forced onto the cattle trains to Siberia where the sun only shone for a month at the most.

One moonless night, Pete crept out to retrieve his horse and wagon from his secret hiding place and told Renata to pack them a small suitcase each.

'Of course you must go, my darlings, I'll be all right here. I'm too old to go anywhere.'

Kristina sobbed as if her heart would break into a million pieces as she watched sadly while her daughters and their children loaded their belongings onto Petras's wagon. Her beloved Jonas hadn't returned from the German farm where he and Marius had been forced to labour. Upon his return, Marius had told her about that fateful day, when they were both hitched to a plough like horses and forced to plough the fields. In the heat of the midday sun, Jonas had collapsed and couldn't be revived. The farmer's wife ranted and cursed them about how her wheat and rye wouldn't be planted if they didn't hurry up and bury that old peasant who'd caused the delay. Of course, Marius couldn't tell his mother-in-law that part.

Kristina went outside to the pigsty where many years ago she had buried her silver spoons and cross. Opening the rusty tin, she gave them to Renata and held her close.

'They're of no use to me Renata,' she said sadly. 'Perhaps, they may be useful to you one day. It's all that I have to give you, my darling girl.'

Renata's throat tightened and tears ran down her face as she hugged her mother for the last time, breathing in her familiar scent of dill and parsley. For most of her life, Kristina had been her source of comfort. She'd taught her where to find edible mushrooms, how to pickle a cucumber in brine and leave it on the windowsill for two days, how to add some lemon juice to the potato mixture for making *cepelinai*, so that they would not turn grey. At the simple wooden table, Renata had learnt to make potato sausages and a cabbage rolls, how to tell whether the poppies were ripe to harvest, then bake into a poppy seed cake, how poppy seeds, crushed in milk, would soothe a crying baby. Would she ever smell the newly baked rye bread coming out of Kristina's oven and smothered with her freshly churned butter? Renata looked up at her mother, trying to hold back her tears. Only then did she realise that not only was she leaving Ventuva, but that she was also leaving her soul behind in her mother's simple wooden cottage.

Kristina's blue eyes were misty with tears, as she felt a vast hole burning into her very soul. 'Renata, Virginia you will always be in my heart. And you, my precious Ella, I will watch over you forever and your daughter as well.'

'But how do you know that I will have a daughter?' asked Ella.

'The Ancient Ones have spoken. Think of me whenever you need me and you will see me in your mind's eye. Here Ella, take my journal, you'll find it full of all sorts of remedies. Heaven knows where you all will end up.'

Come on!' shouted Petras. 'That's enough blubbering! If we don't go now, you'll be blubbering at the end of some Ruskie's rifle!'

'As soon as we get settled, we'll send for you and Julia, I promise that we will.'

Renata was crying as she and her family together with Virginia and her two children climbed into the wagon. After only a few kilometres out of Ventuva, Virginia panicked and changed her mind, making the decision to stay in Lithuania.

If we're caught by the enemy, that will be the end for Darius and Milda. Anyway, I've realized, that I just can't leave mama and Julia behind,' she told Renata sadly. 'She's eighty-three and now that she hasn't got Jonas, what will become of her?'

The sisters parted at the cross road, and Virginia began her slow trek back to Ventuva with her two children. Along the way, they saw many of their villagers going the opposite way, carry or wheeling their belongings in simple farm carts or wagons. They didn't realise that the wooden carving of the old man at the cross-road had been made by their very own Jonas.

After her two daughters had gone, Kristina continued to watch sadly until they were only specks in the distance. She then went into the forest and saw that her trees were all twisted and broken. She stroked their trunks gently and whispered to them that the war would be over soon and then they could heal themselves. Her maiden name was not Liepa by chance, of that she was positive. The trees swayed and cried piteously to their linden tree sister, that their own people had betrayed each other. Kristina was angry at the terrible destruction around her, but she was getting old. Where could she run? She half expected her old friend Laima to be there.

Both had taken many walks in the forest when they were young. Both had loved their birch and pine forests. Their husbands had joked that they were off on another pilgrimage when they would say they were going for a walk. But Laima was feeling her age as well, the war had taken an unbearable toll on her family. She'd lost her husband and brother when the Russians had rounded them up for deportation to Siberia in 1941. And now she could barely shuffle, as her legs had become terribly swollen. Laima's mother, whom had been friends with Elena, had died just before the Nazis had invaded.

Overcome by sadness, Kristina took out her amber pendant and once again called upon the Ancient Ones to guide her children to safety.

'Turn circle turn, turn to the East. Turn circle turn, turn to the West. Turn circle turn, turn to the North. Turn circle turn, turn to the South.'

A stillness descended around her. Not one tree swayed, no birds sang. She heard Vėjas, the Wind God whisper to her from beyond the pine trees, 'Linden tree, never fear, for I will speed your daughter, far, far from here!'

Kristina gave thanks to Vėjas and started her trek back to her cottage. How could it be possible that only one of her daughters was going to be saved? Perhaps she'd misheard?

When she awoke the next morning, and as she was cutting herself a piece of rye bread for breakfast, Kristina thought she heard the voices of Milda and Darius. Surely she was dreaming? But Virginia burst through the door and hugged her mother.

'We just couldn't leave you and Julia here all by yourselves mama. We just couldn't!'

She went into her old bedroom only to see Julia retching into a bucket.

Julia looked up at her sister gratefully. 'Thank God you're here,' she said. 'I don't know how I would have coped without you.'

'What's the matter? Oh no Julia, you're not pregnant, are you?'

'Um, yes, I am, but don't tell mama.'

'Oh Julia! Mama's no fool. I think she would have guessed by now. Where's your baby's father?'

'It was Eagle Eye.'

Virginia turned pale. 'You don't mean Eagle Eye the freedom fighter, do you?'

'Who else do you know who goes by that name?'

'Oh my God, Julia! The Russians tortured him and strung him up in the market place with the other Forest Brothers they caught last week.'

'Yes, and those Russian invaders forced us to file past and we had to pretend we didn't know them. I remember how the soldiers were watching us for any signs of emotion.'

Virginia put her arm around her. Like her sister, she possessed the uncanny ability to sense danger, much like creatures in the wild.

'That must have been horrible for you,' she said at last. 'But now I'm back, I can help you through this. Are you sure you don't want me to make you some rue tea?'

'Rue tea? Are you mad? No, I don't want any horrible rue tea! I can't murder an innocent baby! You know very well that it would probably induce a miscarriage. I want to keep it. How can you even suggest such a thing to your own sister?'

'How will you explain a baby all of a sudden in our village? You're not married. What if someone informs on you and says that you slept with the enemy? They'll shave off all your hair and parade you in the market place. The Russians will then send us all off to Siberia, that is, once they torture the father's name out of you. Have you forgotten about my Marius? Or what happened to our classmate Rita? How the Russians took her down to some basement and raped her for weeks on end, until she gave them the names they wanted. Then they shot her and threw her naked body into a ditch!'

Julia shuddered. 'Have you quite finished with your lecture Virginia? Keep your voice down. Of course I haven't forgotten! No one, and I mean no one, must know about this baby. You mustn't breathe a word to anyone.'

Virginia knew how Ventuva's villagers liked to gossip and during war time, vicious rumours spread with the speed of lightning. It was hard to know whom to trust.

'All right Julia, then we'll have to invent an excuse why you can't be seen in the village once you start to show. Milda and Darius can't be told the truth either, they could accidentally blurt something out, without even thinking.'

Virginia didn't have the heart to tell her sister that she'd found out earlier that Eagle Eye's family had all been exiled to Siberia, even his elderly parents. If they didn't perish on the long train journey, then they'd die of hunger or drop dead from exhaustion. Making sure Julia was comfortable, Virginia trudged back to her own cottage to look through her old trunks to check if she had any baby clothes left. She'd bartered most of them for food, but she didn't do that dressmaking course in Palanga for nothing. Soon, she was making baby clothes out of old sheets and pillowcases. Kristina just nodded thankfully at her daughter whenever she brought them over. She wrapped them in an old shawl and hid them in Elena's ancient leather suitcase under her own bed.

In her sixth month, even though she was thin, Julia could no longer hide her pregnancy. After talking to Kristina, it was decided that her mother would develop a bad back and she took to

shuffling slowly about the village, bent double over one of Jonas'
walking sticks.

'*Ai, ai, ai*,' she would moan, as she walked about. 'I don't know
how longer, I'll be able to walk this far,' she'd announce to anyone
who'd listen. 'I'm an old woman, who knows how much longer
I'll be on this earth! *Ai, ai, ai*! May the good Lord put me out of
my misery!'

The ruse worked and soon people accepted that Virginia was
going in and out of the village in her mother's place. She told
everyone, who asked, that Julia was at home helping their old
mother. Kristina sat behind the counter of the Post Office, with
Julia nearby.

When Julia's labour pains came, Kristina felt her belly and knew
that her baby was in the wrong position. She desperately hoped
that it would turn itself around before the birth. For three days, Julia was in labour. Virginia did everything she could to distract her.
One day, she even pulled her up to do a simple folk dance. In the
early hours of the morning, after Kristina finally turned the baby,
it was stillborn. Blue with the cord wrapped around his neck. The
three women wept as they washed him and looked at his perfect
tiny fingers and toes.

'Oi, oi, oi! It's all my fault! I should have been able to turn the
baby much earlier,' Kristina lamented, rocking back and forth on
her chair.

'Mama, we know that you did all that you could. Maybe it's
for the best?' Julia looked sadly at the little boy whom she'd never
feed, rock to sleep or see grow up to be a brave young man like his
father. She cuddled little Darius, whom they named after Virginia's son and wrapped him in the tiny clothes Virginia had sewn for
her nephew. The three women kissed him for the last time and at
midnight, Kristina took her grandson in her arms and gently bur-

ied him under her oak tree. She then cried out to the Ancient Ones, beseeching them not to send her any more sorrow.

'Turn circle turn, turn to the East. Turn circle turn, turn to the West. Turn circle turn, turn to the North. Turn circle turn, turn to the South.'

The Ancient Ones answered her with such a heavy a gust of wind that she fell over backwards.

'A singing revolution with three nations linking hands, will drive the tyrants from our lands!'

'A singing revolution? What sort of revolution could that be? You Ancient Ones have got something mixed up this time!' Incredulous, Kristina sat on the ground and laughed to herself, shaking her head at such a preposterous prediction.

In the following days, the villagers commented upon Kristina's miraculous recovery from her bad back and kept asking her for the secret remedy. Kristina smiled and said that they could get it from her for a certain price.

'Well, what is your remedy mama? What can I tell people who ask me' asked Virginia curiously.

'White willow bark tea,' replied her mother with a twinkle in her eye and pointed to the big tin on the shelf in her kitchen.

In the meantime, Petras and his family were travelling at night, hiding during the day, slowly making their way to Germany. When they arrived in Dresden, it was close to midnight. He expertly manoeuvred their horse and wagon into a small cobblestoned laneway.

'Wait here!' he cautioned his family, wagging his finger at them. 'Don't any of you dare make one single sound. Understand?'

He crept up to the back door and tapped three times. An old bedraggled woman he barely recognized answered the door. 'Good evening Frau Mueller,' he whispered, 'Is Gunter home?'

Frau Mueller crossed herself. 'Nein,' she answered, 'He's been drafted to fight for der Führer. They have even drafted boys as young as ten!'

Petras hesitated, but pressed on. 'Gunter always said that we would be welcome here, if the need arose. Can you shelter us for a night or two?'

'Ja, ja, but of course. I vill never forget your kindness to our family when our daughter Irmela was injured in that terrible wagon accident in our main street. You saved her life. Wilkommen. I am sorry but I vill have to put you down in the cellar.'

Petras tethered his horse to a tree and motioned for his family to creep carefully into the house. Frau Mueller bustled them inside, looking fearfully over her shoulder to make sure the neighbours weren't spying on her. As she led them down to the cellar, the air raid sirens sounded and she clattered down the stairs to huddle with them.

'Schrecklich, schrechlich,' she kept moaning.

They stayed there till daybreak and then crept upstairs and looked out the window. All around them were scenes of devastation, houses that they had seen the night before, were no longer there and their horse lay dead. Their wagon was smashed into tiny pieces. They observed their kind hostess' neighbours who had begun to gather around the horse, wondering where it had come from. Some of the old men started to drag the horse away, commenting that it had come just at the right time, since they were all starving. Fights broke up as to who was to get what portion. A huge knife appeared from nowhere and their beloved horse was butchered on the spot.

Ella burst into tears, 'No! No, they can't eat our Simon,' she cried, as she tried to run for the door.

'Shut up, you stupid girl!' Petras grabbed her by the arm and slapped sharply her across her face.

'Pull yourself together! There is nothing and I repeat nothing,that any of us can do about this situation. Not one of us can be seen here! We must remain invisible. Do you understand?'

His children looked glumly down at their feet, knowing that their father was right.

'I haf some bread and surely you must haf brought somezing mit you,' Frau Mueller said. 'We can drink some ersatz coffee with it, ja?'

'I still have a bit of cheese left in my bag,' said Renata, who had been given it by a farmer in Bavaria in exchange for Kristina's two silver spoons.

Not long after, Frau Mueller's footsteps were heard clattering down the steps to the cellar.

'Och mein Gott im Himmel!' she gasped. 'The Russians are here! They are fighting mit our troops. We must disguise ourselves as very old women,' she cried looking pointedly at Ella. 'They will not show us any mercy. They are not as disciplined as our men. It is well known that they will rape any woman in sight!'

She got out the flour bin and smeared their faces and their hair. Ella's hair was put into a bun on top of her head and an old moth eaten scarf was added to her disguise.

'It will look suspicious if they find us in the cellar,' rasped Frau Mueller. 'I vill have to pretend that you are my relatives from the provinces. It is best that Simas and Petras disguise themselves as old men as well. Do not say anything except ja or nein. Ella you have to pretend that you are deaf and dumb.'

The very next day, they heard an enormous pounding on the door. Two Russian soldiers kicked open the door and pushing Frau Mueller roughly against the wall, they started to ransack the house. Renata sat in the armchair and rocked and moaned. Ella kept her head down and Petras and his father pretended to be sleeping on the sofa. Taking a cursory glance at the old people, the Russians continued to take whatever took their fancy and then gestured to Ella. Frau Mueller quickly made gestures to indicate a deaf and dumb person to them. The soldiers cursed them all and left to ransack the other nearby houses that had withstood the bombardment.

After they had left, Petras told his family it wasn't safe to stay one minute longer.

'They could change their minds and come back for something that they liked before.'

'Maybe we should keep our disguises and see if we can make our way to one of those UNRRA Displaced Person's camps we've been told about.' added Renata.

As they were leaving, a stray bullet whizzed past, hitting Ella in her left leg. Again they were delayed as Frau Mueller took them inside and hastily removed it, then sent the family on its way again. Ella moaned in the wagon while Renata tried to keep her quiet.

'Shh, Ella, for God's sake keep quiet. It's lucky that Frau Mueller used to be a nurse.'

Finally, they reached a refugee camp in Bremen where they had to wait four years for a ship to take them far away from Lithuania's brutal invaders and plunderers. One day, Petras told Renata excitedly that he'd found out from the camp's official that they could line up in a few days' time for a medical check-up by Australian

Red Cross officials, who were looking for migrants to go to Australia for work.

'You can go over there and now strip down completely Mr. Baras.'

'What did you say? What for?' demanded Petras in a pompous tone. 'I'm in perfect health!'

'You might think so, but we have to check your lungs for tuberculosis,' replied the doctor.

When Renata came back, she was angry with her husband. 'You didn't tell me I'd be force to strip to the waist like a common criminal,' she yelled.

'You think that's bad? The men had to take off all their clothes!'

Later Petras found out that the real reason, was to check if any of the men had their blood group tattooed under their arm, which would have indicated to the officials that they were Nazi soldiers and that their genitals would have revealed if they were circumcised or not.

'Apparently Jews aren't welcome in Australia,' remarked one of Petras's friends.

In 1948, they boarded a Norwegian ship called the Svalbard, and the Baras family crowded like sardines, into their tiny cabin on the ship that was going to take them to Australia. Bedraggled and bewildered, nine hundred people from war-torn Europe attempted to make the best of their situation, as they tried to cope again after their lives in displaced persons' camps. They soon found out that there were architects, doctors, painters, dentists, teachers and other skilled people sailing with them. Seasickness affected half of them as soon as the ship left the port. Petras was the first one to become ill. For once, he wasn't in control and had to rely on his wife to hold the bucket as he retched and vomited up whatever he'd eaten that day. At times, he'd push her away, totally humiliated. Other times, he was grateful for the cup of water she held out to rinse his mouth. Then Simas fell ill, but luckily Renata and Ella didn't suffer. They swayed about the ship, as they made their way to English classes where they learnt to repeat the phrases that would help them adjust to their new country.

'I haf won brudder, ah mudder ant ah father,' repeated Ella with the others her age. She usually sat next to a girl called Dalia and they would giggle at their teacher, who used to be to a high ranking diplomat. Even though they were eighteen, sometimes they behaved like naughty little schoolgirls mimicking their teacher, until tears rolled down their cheeks.

'What a coincidence,' remarked Ella to her new friend. 'One of my friends in Ventuva was called Dalia!'

'We must polish the furniture with furniture polish,' was another sentence that brought forth gales of laughter from Dalia. Even more so, when Mr Bendras explained that if the word 'polish' was written with a capital "P", it would describe the inhabitants of Poland.

'What a crazy language English is!' Ella would constantly complain to her parents who had also decided to attend English classes. Petras was confident he would be able to set up a new business. When Ella was homesick she'd pull out her grandmother's leather bound journal and read. Sometimes she'd read out aloud to Renata.

'To stop potatoes from sprouting, put an apple in amongst them! Is that true, mama?'

'Yes, that's what my mama used to do. She also used to rub half lemon on her hands after chopping onions, to get rid of the smell.'

'Yes, I read that too. What about smearing egg yolk in your hair if it's dry and brittle?'

'Mama did that a few times, she also used to rub mayonnaise onto her face to plump it up.'

'Wrong! Grandma writes that you should whip up some egg white and put it on like a mask.'

One evening after their usual dinner of tasteless mutton and mashed potatoes, a Lithuanian woman began to sing in the plaintive voice of her region.

'I'm sitting behind the table, looking through the window. I see a boat bouncing up and down on the waves. And on that boat a maiden sat, washing and combing her hair.'

Those who knew the song joined in and soon the ship echoed with hundreds of women's homesick voices. Soon, the Latvian and Estonian women learnt the chorus and offered to sing some of their traditional songs. A Latvian woman sang one of her favourite folk songs, then an Estonian woman sang a sad song of longing for her homeland.

Enticed by the singing, the men came to see what their women were doing. Someone produced a harmonica, another a small accordion, whilst the others improvised with spoons. Each country sang its National Anthem. Even Petras became very animated and his fingers itched to play the ancient piano on board the ship, which was in dire need of tuning.

'If I had an accordion, I could play a few tunes,' offered Simas.

The Latvian man who had a small box accordion, gestured for Simas to try it, and soon Simas was playing the polkas and waltzes he'd learnt back in Palanga. At 21 he was at least six foot tall, with sandy wavy hair and a cheeky grin that was attracting a coterie of admirers on the ship. Petras was jealous of his son's gaggle of adoring females who'd always surround him at the end of an evening, begging him to play just one more tune.

'Don't even think about getting lucky with any of them!' he'd snap at his son. 'You don't want to be saddled with a screaming brat soon after you step ashore,' he warned. Fortunately Simas listened to his father. He had already heard some of the men talk lasciviously about the women they fancied and what they would like to do with them, if they got them in a dark corner of the ship. So instead, he began to write song lyrics whenever he felt lonely at night. He was particularly proud of a song he composed and sang at the talent quest organized on the ship to lift everyone's spirits. He stood confidently and began playing the accordion, singing to his parents and those around him.

> *I am the Lithuania in your dreams,*
> *Warming you with the sun's beams,*
> *The snow-capped forests of Ventuva,*
> *The majestic streets of Palanga.*
> *Tired and lined fishermen's faces,*
> *We are the warriors from distant places.*
> *Buried in the Curonian sand dunes,*
> *No plunder left, just a few plumes,*
> *I am the Lithuania in your dreams*
> *Warming you with the sun's beams.*

Even his father's eyes misted over as he saw Simas presented with the first prize, a bottle of wine. 'That's my son Simas!' he shouted to everyone. 'That's my son!'

The day they were going to cross the Equator, the ship's crew organized a Miss Equator contest.

'Why don't you go in it Ella?' cajoled Dalia.

'Who me? No! Why don't you?' bantered Ella. 'Your figure's better than mine!'

'I'm skinnier, but you have got a better bosom than me! That's what the judges will look at!'

'I'll go in it, but only if you do!'

To her utter mazement, Ella was crowned Miss Equator. At eighteen, she finally had shaken off her gawky awkwardness and felt proud of her high cheekbones. After being congratulated, Ella was presented with a bag of oranges and an artificial posy of flowers.

Once they had docked in Australia and had been processed by government officials, Renata and Ella were set to scrub hospital floors and lift heavy dirty laundry baskets whilst Petras and Simas worked as cleaners in the same Sydney hospital. Often, Renata felt guilty that she'd left her old mother behind in Ventuva. Still her sisters were there to look after her. She wrote a letter to the Russian Embassy begging that her sister be allowed to join her in Australia, but the answer that came back a few weeks later was "Permission Denied".

Across the other side of the world, in 1956, letters with strange looking stamps began to arrive in Kristina's little post office. The first one was addressed to her. She was afraid to open it for several days, but the bright, cheerful stamp intrigued her.

Dear Kristina,

I don't know whether you still remember me, but I want to tell you that I am in a big city called Chicago in America. At first I thought that the streets would be paved with gold, but I soon learnt that everyone had to work hard. I got a job in a slaughterhouse killing pigs. I lived in a room with 6 other men. We slept on mattress-

es on the floor. There was one shower and one toilet for 40 men in our tenement building.

For years I saved my money, hoping that I could send for my little Julia, but then came the Depression here in America and I found myself poor again. I joined the American Navy and I found myself wounded on a beach in Normandy. We were just like those pigs in the slaughterhouse. Nowhere to run.

I hope that you and Romas survived the war. I have no one else to write to, and I know that you two have kind hearts and would have looked after my Julia. I am truly sorry that I left her the day after my Asta died, but I just couldn't face bringing up a baby by myself. I am dying of liver failure, and it would be good if Julia could come to Chicago and look after me. I can send her the money for the boat trip. If she's married, I can send money for her husband as well.

I look forward to hearing from you or my daughter.

Best wishes,

Tadas.

Kristina put the letter in her apron and went outside. She walked to the banks of the Venta River and sat down. Should she show Tadas' letter to Julia? From his letter, she thought that he sounded like the same selfish person, he'd always been. She debated with the Ancient Ones, asking for their help.

What good would it do for Julia to travel all the way to America to nurse an old dying man who was her father in name only?

Who knows where he was living, and amongst what sort of people?

What if Julia hated America? She would have no money to get back to Ventuva, to her family who loved her.

Besides, she and her old school friend Kestas were getting along so well, now that he was back from the Siberia. Julia deserved some happiness in her life. There was every chance that they would get married, for on March 25th, Julia had told her that she'd seen the first stork of spring flying across the sky. That day was fixed in her mind. It was a clear sign from the Ancient Ones.

Kristina made her decision. She tore the letter into tiny pieces and threw it into the river.

'Do we know anyone in Austria?' asked Julia one day when another strange letter arrived. Kristina's heart skipped a beat, hoping that there wasn't another letter from Tadas, for then she'd have a lot of explaining to do.

'No, it says Australia, there's a picture of a queen on the stamp,' explained Virginia.

'Give that to me!' said Kristina and immediately began to read the letter aloud.

Bankstown

Sydney, Australia.

July 1956.

Dear Mama, Virginia and Julia,

We hope that all of you have survived the war. I tried writing before, but my letters were returned every time. Now that Stalin is dead, it might be easier for us to write to each other. We have read in our newspapers that Kruschev is very popular. Please, please let us know, we have been worried sick. You may have been wondering where we ended up after leaving you that fateful day, twelve years ago. Our ship took us to a huge island called Australia surrounded by sea with a smaller island about the size of Lithuania, called Tasmania at the bottom of it. We could have gone to America, but we just wanted to get on the first ship that came along.

Ella and I have been promoted to working in a hospital kitchen, whereas Petras and Simas are working as orderlies in the same hospital. The other workers call them Peter and Simon. My nickname is "Rennie". It's been difficult, but we have scraped and saved to qualify for a bank loan, and buy an old run down house that has five bedrooms!

As soon as I hear from you, we will be able to organize to send you a Red Cross parcel. Tell me what you need. As soon as I can find out where to get the proper forms, I will put in an application to have you all come to Australia to live with us. Now that I earn my own money, Petras can't tell me what to do. Please for the love of God, write back to me!

I kiss all of you.

Renata.

At first, Virginia was too scared to write back to Renata at the strange address in a place called Sydney, Australia. She thought that she might be deported to Siberia. Then cautiously, she told Julia to write the first letter, praying that the authorities would not blacken anything out, the way Marius' first and only letter had been from the Vorkuta gulag in Siberia.

Ventuva

October 1956.

Dear Renata,

Thank you for your lovely letter and we are glad, now that we know that you are alive and well. Just think! You are in an exotic country called Australia. Here, having American relatives holds more status. So if you were an Amerikonka, like our neighbour's sister, people would envy us. Thank you for your thoughtful Red Cross parcel. It certainly has made a difference, though under the Soviets, we don't really need anything, since life is so wonderful. However, it's a bit hard to get proper shoes for Darius, with him being a Lilliputian and all. Virginia makes all our clothes, you know that dressmaker's course she did in Palanga, was the best thing she ever did. She also does some sewing for other village women as well, to earn a bit extra. Right now, she's at work, cleaning at the medical centre. Yes, I can hear you gasping in surprise! It's certainly very handy to have such a fine clinic in our village. The Soviets also built us a train track too, now we can go to Palanga on the train and if we wanted to, we could hop

*on another train and go to Kaunas or Vilnius. At one
stage, they wanted to build a dam but that fell through.
Mama is well enough, but her age is finally slowing her
down. She's ninety five now, would you believe? Getting slower and slower, this time her back really does
ache, and so Virginia and I take turns in massaging it
with camphor oil. It would be lovely, if you could send
her a warm woollen coat. Darius still loves fishing and
catches us some sort of fish just about every weekend.
Milda married a farmer across the river in Latvia, so
we don't see her very often. His mother is Latvian,
but his father is Lithuanian. Got drafted into the Russian army during the war and would you believe, got
wounded in the crossfire on his way back in 1945. So
close to coming back home. But there you go, what can
you do? Last year, Milda brought their little girl Dana
here, she wants her to go to school in Samogitia, so that
she doesn't forget her heritage. Virginia and I look after
her. She a pretty little thing, with curly blonde hair and
grey eyes. So, yes a few ribbons would be nice for her
plaits, and maybe a pair of shoes and a warm dress.
Now that Kruschev is in power, a few people like my old
school friend Kestas have been allowed to come back
from exile in Siberia. Their stories are harrowing and
their children are not allowed to go to any of our uni-
versities. People here are scared to be seen with them,
but I don't care. I want to know what happened to them
over there. Don't worry about me or Virginia, we don't
really need anything. We look forward to your next letter and whether you have been able to get permission
for us to visit you in Australia.*

Lots of love to everyone,

Julia.

'Look at this warm woollen material that my sister has sent us,' Virginia said, overjoyed as she opened up yet another parcel from Renata.

'I don't like grey,' complained Dana. 'Why can't we have something more colourful?'

'Beggars can't be choosers, my dear,' reprimanded Virginia. 'We are very lucky that we get a parcel every so often. Renata must be very rich that she can send us this tin of International Roast coffee and a big block of dark chocolate.'

Ventuva, 1957

My darling daughter,

You asked me in one of your letters if there was any-thing new in Ventuva. The big news is that Vlad Ivano-vitch and his wife Tamara have disappeared! No one knows where they have gone or if something has hap-pened to them. No dead bodies have been found. It's as if the earth has swallowed them up. I for one, am glad that those two are gone. I have never told you this be-fore, but Vlad threatened me after your dear Papa was killed by bandits. I suspect that he had a hand in it, but of course I could never prove it. Some people say that he also betrayed Virginia's husband Marius. That Vlad is the incarnation of the devil himself. By the way, thank you for all the things you have sent us, I have been able to barter some things on the black market, so that we can buy some firewood for this winter, which we haven't been able to do for years. Strangers have cut down most of our forest and the Venta River isn't as clean as it used to be, if you know what I mean. Some of our neighbours have disappeared to God knows where. But then, I'm a silly old woman, what would I know. Tell me your news.

Love from your old mama in Ventuva.

Ventuva
June, 1961.

Too soon enough, a new letter appeared in the letterbox. Renata's hands trembled as she opened it.

Dear Renata,

I have some very sad news. I am sorry to have to tell you that our mama died last week. She went to bed as usual, had her warm milk and honey beforehand like she always has, you know, so that she can sleep better. Anyway, in the middle of the night I heard a scream. I rushed in and she was crying that an evil thing was choking her. I tried to comfort her, but she kept staring at the foot of the bed, then she suddenly stretched out her arms and said 'Mama!' and then she was gone. Just like that. Anyway, we had the traditional three day vigil and then we buried her next to our dear papa and Grandma Elena, in our little cemetery. Do you follow our traditions over there in Australia, I wonder? We didn't have a big wake, just our little family, no one can afford those anymore, even though everything's possible here, thanks to the Soviets. Your tin of biscuits and packet of tea came in very handy after our funeral lunch of potato pancakes that Julia made. She hasn't been feeling well lately. Milda came across the Venta River for the funeral, but she had to go back the next day to work at the canning factory. Poor little Dana she was hysterical. Kept clinging to her, wouldn't let her go. Misses her mother. Only natural. I am enclosing a photo of mama in her open coffin.

Lots of love always,
Virginia.

Julia attempted to open her eyes, but was unable to. She didn't want to leave, having been quite happy in her own surroundings, cramped as they were. She was always happy living in Ventuva and the familiar, comforting noises and smells of their mother's cottage. She glanced momentarily at her hands, and was shocked to see that her nails were very long and that her skin felt paper thin. 'Well, at least I've got my own hair,' she thought to herself.

There was a cacophony of noises, and amongst them a voice that Julia recognized.

'She may not make it,' Dr Markozova said in a worried tone. 'If she pulls through this operation it will be a miracle. Why wasn't she brought in before her appendix ruptured?

It made Julia angry hearing the doctor's prognosis. She wanted to say that she was alright, but at that moment she was too weak to do or say anything.

'Her pulse is getting weaker, doctor.'

Doors banged in the wind, as she listened to snatches of conversations around her.

'What a shame, Julia used to be a nice looking girl.'

'And she was such a good dressmaker,' replied the second voice. 'Her sister taught her well. We'll miss her now she's gone.'

'How rude to discuss me whilst I'm lying here helpless,' she thought to herself. She attempted to move her cramped limbs, but a light, delicate hand restrained her. Why are these lights so bright? Her mother Kristina had always preferred candlelight. Everyone knows that a woman looks much more attractive by candlelight. She saw her grandmother Elena beckoning her towards a beautiful garden filled with sweet smelling roses. Her grandfather Pranas came up to her. 'It's not your time yet,' he said. 'Go back.'

'Why do I feel so cold? Where are my clothes?' Someone was washing her, making comments about her body. Startled, Julia found herself trying to push them away, then she folded her arms across her chest in a feeble attempt to preserve some dignity. How humiliating!

Finally Julia opened her eyes and stared at her surroundings.

'Doctor, doctor! Come quickly! The patient is still alive!' The orderly raced from the morgue back the hospital as if he'd seen a ghost.

'It's a miracle!' Kestas whispered, as he held her hand as she was wheeled back into the ward. '*Aš tave myliu* - I love you. It's time we got married. From now my dearest, I'm not going to let you out of my sight ever again.'

ELLA

'Well hello gorgeous! Where have you been all my life?' A young stranger complimented Ella, as she sipped on her orange juice at the annual Baltic folk dancing concert, at the Bankstown Community Centre in Sydney.

Was this tall, dark and handsome man actually speaking to her? Surely there must be some mistake. She glanced around to see if anyone was behind her.

'You're a really good dancer you know. You're so light and graceful!'

'You're just saying that. My friend Dalia is much better than me.'

'Don't be modest, it's obvious to me that you come from a long line of professional dancers!'

'No, I don't! My family comes from Palanga. That's probably why I speak with a touch of the Samogitian dialect. Before we came out to Australia, my father was a businessman there.'

'Oh really? My father was an army officer back in Lithuania. We managed to get out, just in time you know. Otherwise, we would've been shoved onto a train to Siberia, like most of our relatives were. We still don't know whether they survived or not.'

'That must be so sad for you. Before we left, my aunt Virginia got a letter that my uncle Marius died of liver failure in a Vorkuta gulag somewhere in Siberia.'

The stranger lit another cigarette. 'I suppose that we should introduce ourselves. My name's Algimantas Kelmas, but my workmates insist on referring to me as Al Kelm. They say it's much easier. Oh well, we're in Australia now.'

'Nice to meet you Al. I'm Ella Baras. Yes, same here. All our names got shortened at the hospital as well. Not mine. Mama's called Rennie. Um what were you talking about before?'

'We were talking about terrible times. I still dream about our two horses frothing at the mouth. I was petrified with fear, alongside my family in our wagon, as we were travelling towards the German border.'

'I was scared that we'd get stopped by the army and be turned back,' replied Ella. 'How did you know when it was time to leave Lithuania?'

'I'll never forget, Ella. It's etched in my mind forever. It was on the morning of the eighth of June, back in 1944. I was working at the Kaunas Post Office, and thought I'd take a peek at some very official documents that had just arrived, whilst the Russian official had gone outside to use the toilet. Just as well that I'm a curious person. They turned out to be those dreaded deportation lists to Siberia, and our family's name was on one of them!'

'Oh my Lord! What did you do Al?'

'In a flash, I was at the front door and running towards home as fast as I could, and then I blurted it out to my father.'

'That's a coincidence. My Grandma Kristina ran the Post Office in Ventuva. I wonder what I would have done. So what happened then?'

'My father told us to throw as many belongings as we could into a suitcase each. I saved my family from a fate worse than death, can you imagine?'

'You are my hero Al. Not like me. I didn't want to leave my Grandma Kristina and my aunties behind in their village. Which way did your family go?'

Al pauses and takes a deep breathe. He hasn't talked about this to anyone outside of his family before. 'We crossed into Prussia by going through the townships of Kudirka and Širvinta. We stopped to rest our two horses in Insterburg, but father said that we couldn't stop for long because we had to keep travelling.'

'We had to sleep in barns in Bavaria,' added Ella.

'When we got to East Prussia, we were taken in by a kind farmer, a Herr Schmidt. We were allowed to sleep in his barn, but in the morning, we all had lice. Everyone was itching and cursing like mad. Dad, my brother Vygis and I decide to shave off all our hair. Mother just washed hers as much as possible in the stream nearby. There was no soap of course. We had to make do. On Schmidt's farm there were two POWs who worked alongside of us doing farm work. We got paid with food and shelter in their barn.'

Ella listens to Al intently. She is reliving her own experiences in her mind's eye, but she lets him continue.

'From other refugees, we learnt that the Russian army was not far behind us. My father's a retired army colonel, and he knew that we couldn't stay there any longer. People told us that the best thing to do, was to travel through West Prussia, then cross into Pomerania.'

'Yes, as long as we kept one step in front of the approaching Russian army, we hoped that we'd be safe. That's what my papa told us,' said Ella.

'When we get into Jastrow, the officials took away our two horses, telling us they'd pay us after the war ended!' Al was indignant at the memory.

'Now that's a laugh, as if they knew where you'd be or whether any of us would still be alive by then. Our horse was butchered during in the Dresden bombing.' Ella shuddered at the memory.

'And get this! To compensate us, they gave our family official papers to travel on a train, that is, if one would ever came along! Can you believe it?'

'Terrible!' agreed Ella as she glanced at her watch and saw that it was after midnight. She and Al had been talking for two hours. She was going to get into trouble for being late home, but she didn't care. She was talking to a very good looking man with thick, shiny, black, wavy hair and piercing blue eyes.

'Anyway, what could we do? We had no other option but to sit there huddled together on the platform, exhausted and terrified. The Germans wouldn't let anyone on. But my father, being an experienced army man had a few tricks up his sleeve. At nightfall, we sneaked below the platform and hid behind the wheels of the last train carriage. My parents are middle-aged, but I think that the urge to survive at any cost, must have kicked in at the last minute. While there was a change of guards, we took a chance and hauled ourselves into the last carriage. By then, the weather had changed and our feet were absolutely frozen.'

Ella recalls sitting cold and hungry in the Dresden cellar. Al lights up another cigarette and continues his story.

'When we arrived in Stalpmünde, we managed to get on another train to Gartz, then a later one to Berlin. In Gartz, we had relatives, my maternal aunt Cecilia and our cousin Algis lived there. He's about my age. Unfortunately, she was injured during one of the bombing raids on the city and died of her injuries. We had to bury her in the back garden and leave Algis to fend for himself. Poor boy, he was only eighteen. Lucky for him, he wasn't drafted into the Wehrmacht.'

Al looked away, trying to erase the memory of his aunt lying on the street, her body riddled with shrapnel.

'Are you alright, Al? You looked a bit lost there for a few minutes. I'm sorry, that must have been awful for you and your parents.'

'Just thinking Ella, there are some things you can never forget.'

'Yes. We were lucky to stay with someone papa knew in Dresden,' Ella told Al. She raised the hem of her folk dancing skirt just a little, to show Al the small hole in her leg.

'Christ! How did that happen?'

'I got caught in some sniper crossfire as I was crossing the street,' Ella explained. 'The German lady was a nurse, so she removed the bullet, otherwise I would have died.'

'You must have been very brave,' Al said as he slipped his arm around Ella and continued with his story. Ella was entranced. Here she was sitting with a handsome man who not only listened to her, but found her attractive as well.

'Next we arrived in Ingolstadt. There the German officials tried to haul us off to Dachau. We managed to escape, by father telling them in his perfect German, that we'd come to stay with relatives. As soon as it was dark, we hurried out of there and found ourselves in a small village, where an old lady called Brunhilda let us stay on her farm as long as we fixed her windmill.'

'Do you remember the utter chaos everywhere, once we heard that the Germans had lost the war?' said Ella as she settled back in Al's arms.

'Do I ever! No one was in charge, it was a shambles, wasn't it? People running around everywhere, trying to save themselves and their families in any way possible. There was lot of looting and stealing, I certainly remember that. Every man for himself!'

'We fell on our knees and thanked God when the Americans arrived,' recalled Ella. 'But they wanted to repatriate us back to Lithuania. Imagine! But we weren't stupid, were we?'

'Not on your life Ella. Funny how those Yanks fell for all those Russian assurances, that we'd be welcome back in Lithuania without any reprisals. But we Lithuanians know our history, don't we Ella? The Russians have always been well known for their brutality, right throughout the ages. Two hundred years of Russian domination have taught our people a thing or two! Dad knew he'd be executed and the rest of our family would be sent to Siberia. He was forcibly conscripted into the Tsar's army during World War One, so he knew first- hand what the Russian army and their secret police were capable of.'

'We were lucky to get into a DP camp in Bremen,' said Ella.

'We finally found ourselves in Wiesbaden,' replied Al. 'There were about seven thousand of us there. About four thousand of them were Poles. I joined the scout group and was able to finish high school and get accepted into the university to study philosophy or architecture. My German improved too, because I had to speak it to the officials. I really wanted to study architecture, but at that time, men like me were being offered assisted passages to migrate to America and Australia. My parents wanted to get away as far as possible.'

'Same here, it didn't matter what ship we boarded,' rejoined Ella.

'I listened to my father's advice so in 1947 along with some other men, we set sail for Australia on an American ship called the USS Sturgess. I can tell you, it was a sad twenty first birthday on that ship without my family.'

'We came a bit later than that,' remarked Ella, 'On the Svalbard in 1948.'

'Those huge waves and did you get those storms when you sailed across?'

'Don't remind me! The wind was howling and the ship creaked and groaned. We had to hold on to everything in the dining room, dishes were sliding everywhere!'

'I was glad when we finally docked in Melbourne,' said Ella. 'But it was freezing cold. No one told us that the seasons were all upside down here, compared to Lithuania. I traded my fur coat for a bag of bananas in Africa, I can't believe that I was so stupid.'

'Don't blame yourself. We were all naïve back then. When my ship docked, we were taken to the Bathurst Military Barracks,' Al continued. 'They'd been turned into a DP camp. It was freezing in June, and we only had a thin blanket on our bunk beds. Later, I was transferred with other men to the Walter Morris Timber Mills in Adelaide, South Australia. Believe me Ella, that was a back-breaking work.'

'I am sure it was Al. You are so brave. Did you have to work there for long?'

'No, later on I was sent to Queensland to cut sugar cane, hot as hell up there. Then I came back to work on The Snowy Mountain Scheme. Saw lots of kangaroos in the snow there during winter. Can you believe it? Snow in Australia! Afterwards I started work as a shunter at the railway yards in central Sydney. I'm still doing that job now.'

'We were sent to Bonegilla.' Ella was pleased that she was being favoured with Al's attention. She didn't have to say much, just be sympathetic. It never occurred to her that Al wasn't asking very much about her own war experiences.

'What about your parents? I was lucky enough to be able to come out with mine.'

'Now that you mention it Ella, I started to worry about my parents and my younger brother Vygis who'd been left behind in the DP Camp. Luckily, I was able to sponsor them out to Australia, but I had to be the guarantor for their welfare.'

'That must have been a huge responsibility.'

'You're right Ella, it certainly was, but I'm a determined person. Back in 1948, my parents at 52 were considered too old to migrate to Australia. They just wanted young people like us to work on big government projects. At sixteen, my brother Vygis was considered too young.'

'What happened then?'

'Last year, the rest of my family was allowed to join me, but first they were sent to the Bonegilla Migrant Camp in Albury. That's on the Victorian and New South Wales border.'

'What a coincidence! That's where we got sent as well,' remarked Ella. 'My brother Simas got involved in a rebellion against that smelly old mutton they trotted out for breakfast, lunch and dinner. In the end, they let some of us do the cooking. My mother did a lot.'

'Revolting! I will never eat mutton as long as I live, give me a piece of pork any day,' laughed Al.

'Same here!' agreed Ella. 'Mama is an excellent cook, but my grandmother Kristina was the one who taught me how to make traditional Lithuanian dishes like *cepelinai.*'

'Will you make some *cepelinai* for me one day, Ella?' whispered Al, as his lips brushed her cheek.

As Al walked her home, Ella was already picking out her wedding dress, planning her honeymoon and the type of house, that she and Al would live in when they were married.

'Goodnight, Ella. How about going to see a film with me next weekend?'

Six months later Ella knew she was pregnant and that sooner or later she'd have to tell Al. She could no longer hide the awful nausea that she felt every morning.

Al, there's something that you should know,' she said one night after they'd been to the movies to see *It Happened At The Word's Fair*. They were sipping their favourite chocolate milk shakes in the café near the picture theatre.

'Hey there Kitty, why are you looking so sad? It was just a movie.' Al replied, using his pet name for her.

'Well, um, Al, you see, I'm pregnant.'

'What? How can you have been so stupid? I should have known! You've probably been plotting and scheming all along to saddle me with a kid that I don't want!'

Ella reeled back as if she'd been slapped.

'But you told me that you were going to take care of things,' she sobbed. This wasn't the reaction she had hoped for. She had dreamt that Al would take her in his arms and tell her how happy he was and that they'd get married immediately.

'Anyway, how do I know that it's mine? You can always get rid of it! Surely you can borrow some money from your brother? You all work in a hospital, some one will know a doctor who'll do the job for some extra cash.'

Ella was horrified. 'No! There is no way that I'm going to get rid of this baby!'

'Do your parents know yet?'

'I am pretty sure mama suspects. I have been going outside to the toilet to throw up my breakfast every morning.'

Al considered his options carefully. The Lithuanian community was a tightly knit one. Everyone knew that since he'd volunteered to become Ella's folk-dancing partner, they'd become inseparable. Anyhow, he and his family were renting one room in Darlinghurst from a cantankerous old landlady. If he married Ella, all of them could get a room each in her parents' big house in Bankstown. He'd be a hero in his parent's eyes. He was sick of trying to get to sleep on a thin mattress on the wooden floor, next to his snoring brother and father. His mother hated having to go into the landlady's filthy kitchen and putting up with her snide comments about smelly foreign food. Turning towards Ella, who was quietly sobbing into her handkerchief, he said, 'Well then, I guess we'll have to get married. I am a decent man, after all. I feel obliged to do the right thing by you and my kid. But my wage isn't that much, you'll have to go out to work later, so that we can make ends meet.'

Ella smiled in relief. 'I am sure that I can do that, darling,' she said as she kissed Al in gratitude. She was going to be married, none of the gossips in her community would be able to point their fingers at her and call her a loose woman. No, she was going to be a respectable married woman. Mrs. Kelmas. Despite her father's angry protests about the cost, Ella insisted on wearing a white, silk wedding dress, white high-heeled shoes and she carried a bouquet of white roses. Al's brother Vygis was his best man and her friend Dalia was her only bridesmaid.

'That husband of yours is too handsome for his own good! He's a ladies' man, mark my words! One day you'll be very sorry that you didn't accept the money your father offered you not to marry him!' Renata was telling her daughter at the wedding reception, back at their house in Bankstown. Ella picked at her food, thankful that her nausea had eased.

'Oh for heaven's sake mama. Stop it! This is supposed to be a happy occasion. Don't worry mama, my marriage is not going to be like yours. We love each other!'

Petras insisted on making a long speech telling everyone that when he was back in Lithuania fighting the Bolsheviks, he never dreamed that he would have such a lovely daughter like Ella. In the long run, his speech was more about him than his daughter.

Ella swiftly looked up at Simas, who'd just got out his new accordion. He nodded, knowing that it was time for a song to lift the sombre mood. Softly he began to sing an old song, "Beer, beer,

God will give us beer". Everyone joined in, even Rasa, her snobby mother-in-law. For two hours, they sang Lithuanian traditional songs and many others from the pre-war years.

Please sing "The Last Sunday" for me Simas,' begged Renata. 'It used to be my favourite.' She held back her tears as she recalled the carefree days strolling in the Palanga Botanical Gardens with her sisters, singing the old Šabaniauskas songs of the 1930s.

'I wish mama and my sisters were here to share this day with us,' she whispered to Petras.

'Yes, we certainly had some great holidays at the Kurhaus Resort,' Al's father was saying to Renata who was sitting next to him. 'When I'd get leave from my batallion, Rasa and the boys would join me there, or sometimes we'd go to Nida on the ferry from Kaunas.'

'Did you ever come across a Sergeant Marius?' asked Renata.

'Why yes, I knew his family very well,' replied Bronius. 'Why do you ask?'

'You wouldn't believe it, but he married my sister Virginia,' exclaimed Renata.

'Oh, isn't that a coincidence! Do they still live in your village in Samogitia?'

'Um, Marius was deported to a gulag in Vorkuta in Siberia, but my sisters are still there.'

All that Ella and Al could afford for their honeymoon was a night at a hotel opposite Bondi beach. Ella felt uncomfortable in her old swimsuit, as she noticed her husband ogle and comment on the endless parade of bathing beauties.

'Mmm, just look at her! What a luscious figure! What fabulous legs! Al would say, licking his lips, imitating her parents' Samogitian dialect.

Ella looked glumly at the sand. 'Al, I want to paddle in the water. Help me up.'

Perhaps her mother was right after all about Al. Maybe he really was a ladies' man. Her honeymoon was not turning out as she had imagined it in her dreams.

Six months later when Ella gave birth to a little baby girl with a fuzz of white blonde hair, whom she decided to name "Gaila". Renata kept on knitting baby clothes and made no comment that the child's name meant "sorrow". She just remarked that the baby looked just like her when she was born, apart from her hair and skin.

'Run, run for your lives! Get out of the house, get out of the house!' Petras yelled as he swooped three month old Gaila up out of her cot and ran into the street. The walls shook and everyone rushed out into the street in their dressing gowns. When the earthquake had passed, they noticed big cracks in the walls of their sandstone house. It would take ages to patch up the cracks on the weekends. Still, they couldn't afford to hire anyone to fix the damage. They would have to do it themselves, in between their shifts at the hospital. Maybe Al could help out?

As it was, Renata and Rasa would take it in turns to look after Gaila whilst her parents went to work and had to put up with Gaila's crying, 'I want my mama. When's mama coming home?' umpteen times during the day. Gaila would start up as soon as her mother left for work at David Jones, one of Sydney's big department stores. Renata would try to distract her by telling her that if she was good, her mama would bring her back her a treat from the cafeteria where she worked behind the counter. Usually she did, even though it was a left over stale bun that she'd refresh, by heating it in a small frying pan with a bit of water and a lid on top. From time to time, Ella would see some of the ladies from the Lithuanian community, all dressed up, having lunch with their daughters in the cafeteria. They would urge her to join the choir, but Ella always politely refused, since every bit of money was needed to help feed and clothe her family. Besides, on the weekend there were household chores to catch up on, and the garden needed attention. Al would never let her go and she knew better not to ask.

Like Renata, Rasa had also lived through two world wars and prided herself on being frugal woman. She'd come from a small, country town in the south of Lithuania where her father was a schoolteacher. She liked to lecture Renata about being thrifty. She kept every bit of soap, then boiled it up in an ancient pot on the stove and then poured it into a long narrow cake tin that she'd greased with butter beforehand. When it had set, Rasa would get out a knife and cut it into square pieces.

'Oh that's too much work,' Renata would say. 'I just help myself to a cake of soap now and then from the hospital's toilets.'

Undeterred, Rasa would insist on showing her how to make her own hand lotion by mixing lemon juice and glycerine that she kept in a bottle on the sink. She also made her own face cream that she kept in the fridge, even though everyone would complain that it took up too much space. After a roast chicken for tea, the carcass would be put in a pot the next day and made into soup with any leftover vegetables. All the vegetable and potato peelings were washed, cooked and blended into a soup. Inside the kitchen drawer, there was a separate section for bits of string, ribbon and safety pins. In another container were all her buttons, which Gaila was allowed to play with and that's the way she learnt her colours and how to count.

If it were a rainy day, Renata would take out her old photos and as Gaila sat on her knee, she would weave stories about the people in them. Instead of children's stories, she grew up with tales of how the wolves came down to the village one day, to mourn the death of her father Romas or when Gaila's father narrowly escaped from the Russian army when it was hunting down the partisans in the forests around Ventuva.

Renata often told Gaila about her sisters and mother she had to leave behind in her little village. All the times they'd applied to have Virginia come to Australia and the countless rejection slips from the Soviet government said the same thing; "Permission Denied". Sometimes, Gaila helped her grandmother make up a Red Cross parcel for her family.

'What would a little girl your age like?'

'A doll! Definitely a doll that walks and talks!'

It didn't matter what Gaila suggested, because the little girl her age on the other side of the globe, would find very practical things in the parcel, like thick woollen socks knitted by Renata or sturdy lace up shoes.

The long awaited day finally came, when Al and Ella had saved enough money to move out of Renata's house and buy another one with Bronius and Rasa. Although it wasn't the best arrangement, Ella had to accept it. They managed to make ends meet until Al broke his leg one morning on the way to work.

'You came in last night? Broke your arm? That's a bit of bad luck, seeing it's your right arm!' Al waved at the newcomer lying next to his bed.

'My name's Algimantas Kelmas, but just call me Al. Everyone else does. Told me my name was too hard for them to pronounce!'

'Where do you do come from?'

'I'm Lithuanian.'

'So you're Lutheran? I'm an Anglican myself.'

No, I mean I come from Lithuania.'

'Where's that?'

'It's next to Poland.'

'Okay, now I getcha. Pleased to meet you Al.'

'Been here a month myself. Broke my leg on the way to work. Skidded on my motorbike on the wet road. When I woke up, I was in here. I'm a shunter, you know, on the railways.

'Dirty work?'

Yeah, you're right there mate, it *is* dirty work. My wife complains she can never get the grease out of my clothes and that she's got to scrub them separately. Women!'

'By the way, me name's Jim. I'm a builder.'

'So you're a builder, mate. Got any kids?'

'Five.'

'Jim, you're kidding me. Five? We've just got one. Cute little girl. Loves riding on the motorbike with us. Likes going to the beach the most. Your wife work?'

'No.'

'Guess not, with five kids. My wife used to work at the hospital. Since she hurt her back, she works a few days at the David Jones cafeteria. Not much pay, but it helps pay a few bills. Hates our chooks, 'cos they poop everywhere, pecking the tops off her carrots and radishes. Told her not to plant them near the coop. Nothing like a fresh boiled egg for breakfast is there?'

'Porridge for me mate! I love porridge.'

'Nah, I hate the stuff. Invalids' food. Yeah, I know some people swear by it. Well, they are welcome to it. Not me, mate. I can ask the wife to bring you in a few eggs. No worries.'

'Bought your own house yet, Al?'

'No, we live with my parents. Have to. Can't afford our own house yet, but someday, we'll have one. My old man's still a bit shell shocked from the war. Up and down every bloody night, checking every room. Asking if his sentry's come back. Wakes us all up.'

'What can you do?'

'Nothing. That's life, mate.'

'Have a smoke Al?'

'Don't mind if I do, thanks. Look, my mother does her best. Mending, darning all the time. The way she turns a collar, you'd swear I'm wearing a new shirt. She's been teaching my wife to cook some different meals, you see. I reckon the wife never really learnt, said that her mother wouldn't let her into the kitchen, in case she made a mess'.

'Too right Al! How do kids learn, you tell me, if you don't let them make a mess? I'm going to make sure our kids will learn to make stuff in the kitchen with their mother.'

'Anyways, has your wife has learnt to make a real Aussie meal now?'

'I mean to say, no offence Al, but you live in Australia now, so it's stew, chops, snags, some mashed spuds, a few carrots and peas on the side.'

'Ah well, you know what they say, old habits die hard.'

'My wife's pavlova is the best. Can't just stop at one slice. Not like this horrible hospital muck.'

'You're right there Jim, it's bloody disgusting. I'll get Ella bring in some nice Lithuanian meat dumplings when she makes them. I'll give you a taste next time she comes to visit. I save the hospital's red jelly for my little girl. It's a little treat she looks forward to when she comes here to visit me.'

'Thanks Al.'

'You know, my sister-in-law is one helluva cook. Makes her own *vedarai*, they're potato sausages. You should try try them!'

'Ah, no thanks Al. Not keen on foreign food.'

'Got two nephews. Daniel and Mathew. Bit on the wild side, just between you and me, running around the streets at all hours of the day and night. Nothing a clip around the ears wouldn't fix. Maybe we'll have a boy next. I'd love to have a son to go fishing with.'

'Nothing like a bit of fish for tea that you've caught yourself, is there Al?'

'No, you're right there Jim. Nothing like it in the world. Might even buy a place down the beach one day.'

Once everyone had moved out of their big house and into their own homes, Renata had more time on her hands. Later Petras bought a smaller house as he insisted that a big one was uneconomical, since it was just the two of them. One day whilst Petras was out having the car serviced yet again, she was putting his newly ironed clothes away in his wardrobe, when she found his bankbook, hidden under some old underpants. She looked at the withdrawals column and was astounded. There were fortnightly withdrawals for the same amount. Renata hadn't been a businessman's wife for nothing. She knew that it was a better strategy to watch and wait. A few weeks later, she casually asked Petras about their car when he came home.

'Do you think it's time to buy another car?' she asked innocently. This one seems to have so many things going wrong with it. You must be spending a fortune on repairs.'

'Durna boba - stupid old woman! What would you know about car maintenance?' he demanded in angry tone. 'We agreed that I'd pay the household bills and you'd pay for food and clothing, since we're both working.'

'No, you're the one who said that. I had no say in it!' Renata shot back. Now that she'd learnt a bit of English, she'd grown bolder. Her co-workers came from the Baltic States, but they all had English as a common language now, so the women were able to help each other with their problems, whilst they were on their tea breaks.

Renata had been able to save quite a bit, since she ate for free at the hospital and sometimes when one of the cooks was ill, she'd work in their place. At home she grew her own fruit and vege-tables, which she then preserved and her cupboards were lined with enough food if ever there was another war. She only need-ed to shop for meat and bread. The markets were where she felt at home and she soon got to know the Polish sausage seller and the stall where the bacon tasted like that at home. Chicken livers were cheap, so she whipped up her chicken liver paté with a dash of Petras's brandy or sautéed them with onions, just like Pierre had taught her back in Palanga. It was getting close to her and Petras's fiftieth wedding anniversary and she wondered whether they would go out to dinner. Neither really spoke much to each other, but at least it was a night out. Looking through her jewellery box, Renata remembered she'd left her rings by the phone in the hallway. She noticed a piece of paper torn out from the newspaper with an advertisement for the Asian Garden with a phone number. Wondering whether Petras had forgotten to book a table she rang the number.

'Hello, Asian Garden,' answered a polite young lady.

'Oh hello. I'd like to make a booking in the name of Baras.'

'No problem love, we know Peter Baras very well.'

'Do you? Well, it's our wedding anniversary this weekend and I was just wondering if we could have something really special?'

'You and your husband, right?'

'Yes, that's right.'

'Are you sure that's what you want? It might cost you quite a bit.'

'Well, it is our fiftieth anniversary, we want something special.'

As the young woman began to reel off a long list of their specials, Renata turned purple with rage. Shaking uncontrollably, she banged down the phone. She could well imagine this tawdry establishment knowing her wayward, good for nothing husband. Another little secret he'd been keeping from her. She'd show him!

Once Renata had calmed down, she decided she would wait and see what Petras came up with closer to their anniversary. She then went to his wardrobe and flung out his two best suits. Taking her big scissors from her sewing box, she proceeded to slash one sleeve and one trouser leg from each suit and then hung them back inside the wardrobe. That night, Petras asked her what they were having for dinner.

'Hmm, well since it's our fiftieth wedding anniversary, I thought we might go to The Asian Garden. What do you think my dear?'

Petras turned pale and stormed out, wondering how she had found out his little secret.

The next day, whilst Renata was the market and looking in Smith's Fruit and Vegetable stall for some green apples to make an apple strudel, she felt the hairs on her neck rise. She couldn't believe her eyes. In the midst of the crowd, she thought that she saw a familiar painted face. Agata! Surely it couldn't be? Remarkably well preserved. Yes, her hair was still in the same style and dyed the same flaming orange colour that she always had, back when she was walking the streets of Palanga. But now, Agata looked extremely well dressed and was accompanied by two, tallish youths who were also smartly turned out.

Renata's hair was completely white. She couldn't pinpoint the exact time it had gone grey, because she didn't have any mirrors to look at during the years they were on the run and living in the Displaced Person's camp in Germany. She only knew that when she had to undergo a medical before she was put to work in the Sydney Hospital for two years, to pay back her passage to Australia, she was horrified to see an old, dumpy woman in the mirror who resembled her grandmother Elena.

GAILA

Gaila constantly wished that she wasn't the child of refugees who had to flee from the terrors of Stalin, Siberia, Hitler and the Holocaust. As it was, once she started school she couldn't speak a word of English. She soon learnt because there was no other option.

'But mum, this feels too itchy and prickly, I don't want to wear it!'

'Be quiet, you ungrateful child! Your Grandma Renata knitted it especially for you.'

'But none of the other girls at school wear knitted dresses,' Gaila persisted with all of her six year old's logic. 'They all wear nice pleated shirts with jumpers and a white collar. They have white socks and black patent shoes.'

'I bet that none of the other girls will have such a pretty warm dress for winter,' replied her mother.

'See, your grandma's even embroidered the front bit.'

Reluctantly, Gaila let her mother slip on her white cotton singlet, then the blue knitted dress with the bright panel of colourful Lithuanian traditional patterns on the front, in different coloured wool. Thick woollen navy blue tights and sensible, stout lace up shoes completed the outfit.

Ella walked her daughter to school who was praying that no one would comment on her new outfit. What was wrong with her pinafore with the white blouse and cardigan?

'My legs are getting more and more itchy, and my neck is too!' Gaila started to complain again.

'Oh for God's sake, will you shut up? Stop your whining and be grateful instead! Gaila quickly sensed that Ella was losing patience, so remained silent for the rest of the way.

As soon as she walked into the classroom, the class bully started.

'Who's got a new dress? Where did you drag that out from? Home-made isn't it?'

Gaila kept her eyes down and hoped that by ignoring Jean, she would lose interest. But no, she was like a dog with a bone.

'Yuck! I wouldn't be seen dead in that sort of dress!' More voices joined Jean in her teasing.

Gaila's neck got itchier and she started to pull the dress away from her skin. She felt hotter and hotter and more embarrassed by the minute.

'Yuck! She's got fleas! Everyone, get away from her! I'm telling the teacher!'

Mrs. Mason looked up from her desk and beckoned Gaila with her bony fingers.

'Now, what's the matter with you dear? What seems to be the problem?'

'Ah nothing miss, I just feel a bit itchy.'

'Let's get you to sick bay, you might be coming down with something.'

Gaila followed Mrs. Mason down the corridor, past the staffroom, her head hanging in shame, away from the whispers of the mean girls.

She was motioned to approach the school nurse, who told her to strip off her clothes. Gaila stood in front of her, embarrassed in her cottontail underpants and white homemade singlet.

'Look at these red welts all over you!' she murmured sympathetically.

Gaila looked at her arms and legs and sure enough, they were covered with an angry rash.

'Hmm, you might be coming down with something, it's better that you stay here for the day.'

Gaila was dabbed all over with pink calamine lotion and allowed to rest in the little bed and given a few glasses of milk during the day. The nurse even fetched her lunch from her school bag. Gaila took only one bite of her salami sandwich and put it back in the paper bag.

By the end of the school day, the rash had gone. When Ella came to pick up Gaila, the nurse whispered to her, that she would have to keep a close eye on her little girl overnight, to make sure that the rash didn't re-appear. If it didn't, she would be allowed to return to school. It took quite a few times wearing the blue knitted dress and woollen tights for Gaila's parents to work out that she was allergic to wool. Grandma Renata sighed wearily.

'Nu va, well then! Now I will have to line all of your woollen jumpers with some sort of material, as well as every part of your blue knitted dress. Who's ever heard of anyone being allergic to wool?'

If it wasn't a problem with Gaila's clothes, then it was her lunch. Ella sent her to school with thick salami sandwiches, not the pure white triangles of white bread spread with Vegemite, the Australian yeast extract, that all Australian kids seemed to have in their lunch boxes. Gaila longed for plain cheddar cheese or strawberry jam sandwiches. She looked at them wistfully, wishing that her mother would make them for her. Her weekends were filled with Lithuanian Saturday School, scout meetings and folk dancing practice. Her school friends went off to play tennis, watch football matches or were allowed to go swimming at Bondi or Manly beach. Sometimes it seemed that she lived two separate lives, one on the weekends and another person on weekdays. Sometimes she'd even answer her mother in English, she was so desperate to fit in.

When Gaila was seven, she tried to dress up her big black tom-cat Voras in baby clothes to take him for a stroll around the garden. She'd named him Voras, because he looked like a big black spider. How she loved that cat! Whenever she could, she'd cuddle him and stroke his shiny black fur. Would he co-operate with a head-strong little girl? As soon as she got his head through the dress, he lashed out. Within minutes Gaila's arms and legs were covered in long scratches. As Grandma Rasa bathed her scratches, she said, 'Gaila, my dear, you have to remember that there is no medicine for stupidity.' Another time she tried to drag out the half-wild kittens that had been born under the rainwater tank. Again, Gaila was covered in angry red scratches along her arms with a few bites as well. And what did grandma say? Yes, her usual piece of advice. Gaila learnt a lot from Grandma Rasa because she had a system for day to day living, that she never forgot. If it was Friday, then it meant she'd be allowed to help make *sūrnikai* for dinner. Those soft diamond-shaped dumplings made from cottage cheese, flour and eggs, topped with a butter and breadcrumb sauce. They were her favourite.

'Why can't we buy fish and chips on Fridays like everyone else?' asked Gaila on afternoon.

'Because we can't afford it, that's why!'

If it was Monday, then it was washing day and Gaila would help Grandpa Bronius push the sheets through the wringer, put some blue starch in the rinsing water and hang them up on the clothes line. Mondays were tiring. Usually, all that grandma could manage for that day was milk and macaroni soup for dinner. Tuesdays were for ironing.

Therefore, Gaila was delighted that one Monday afternoon, she was given a holiday from her duties. Finally, she was allowed to go to play with her Estonian friend Eva, who lived in their street. The family owned a huge Alsatian dog called Brutus, who could be heard barking madly if any strangers approached the house. Grandma Rasa reminded Gaila to be polite and remember to say please and thank you if she was offered any refreshments. After opening the front gate, Gaila immediately went up to Brutus to pat him.

'Hello beautiful boy,' she said as she stretched out her hand. Unfortunately the dog only responded to Estonian, something that her friend Eva had neglected to tell her. Before she knew what was happening, Brutus had bitten her on the leg. Eva's mother came rushing out of the house as soon as she heard the screams. She took one look at Gaila's wound and called out to her husband Arvid to drive Gaila to the Sydney hospital. After five stitches in her leg and a tetanus shot, he drove a tearful Gaila back home. As soon as Rasa saw her grandma, she knew she was going to say her usual piece of advice. All Gaila wanted, was to be swept up in her grandmother's arms and made a big fuss of. Soothed and cuddled, reassured that she'd be alright and wouldn't get into trouble with her parents when they arrived home from work.

When Ella and Al had saved finally enough money, they bought a house a few streets away from her grandparents. All their relatives trooped in to inspect it. It was a deceased estate and there was a small, ugly shed at the back with a huge padlock that no one could open. The estate agent told Gaila's father that they were still trying to find the owner's key to the padlock. Al wasn't worried, since he planned to borrow some bolt cutters from work once they moved in. 'No worries, I'll have that shed open quick smart. No problem!'

Finally, Gaila was going to have her very own bedroom instead of having to sleep on the divan bed in the lounge room. Her father finally removed the big padlock with the bolt cutters. The posts were rotten and it looked as if the shed would collapse any minute. When Gaila looked across at grandma Rasa, she could lip read the sentence that was forming on her lips before she even said it to Al.

Once they'd settled into their house, Gaila found that she had become her mother's little helper. There were no grandparents to share the housework any more.

'Now that we have our own house, we won't have to eat those wretched *varškėčiai* on Fridays anymore,' Ella crowed triumphantly.

'Don't you mean *sūrnikai* mama?'

'*Sūrnikai, varškėčiai*, same thing. We're going to have fish on Fridays like everyone else!'

However, Gaila found that she sorely missed Grandpa Bronius making her a fresh radish sandwich, Grandma Rasa's meatball soup, her playmates and the familiar routines of the neighbourhood.

Instead, there was a Rabbit Man who would shout every Tuesday, 'Rabbits! Fresh rabbits!' as his horse and cart clip-clopped along their new street. He always looked gruff and unhappy and wore an old leather apron, but he could turn a rabbit inside out in a blink of an eye.

'Run out and buy me two rabbits before we go to visit Aunt Gerda,' called Ella from the bedroom where she was taking the curlers out of her hair and was putting on some bright pink lipstick. 'I'm going to stuff those bunnies with breadcrumbs and roast them for your father's dinner when we get home.'

Gaila always had an apple for the horse, which sometimes dropped his load right in front of their house. Ella was always extremely pleased whenever this happened, and would instruct Gaila to take the metal bucket and then water down the manure and spread it on their tomatoes and potatoes. Her daughter was mortified and was sure that the neighbours tittered at that strange foreign woman behind their net curtains.

'Willkommen, Willkommen!' boomed aunt Gerda as she crushed Gaila to her ample bosom. It was so soft that Gaila felt that she could sleep there forever. Her mother kissed her sister in law on both cheeks. 'Meine liebe frau,' cried Gerda, 'How haf you been?'

'Och, meine wunderbar, schöne, kleine Mädchen,' she gushed to Gaila, 'You haf grown zo tall since last month.'

She bustled about in her spotless kitchen with the shiny black and white lino tiles that her mother envied so much. They only had cheap speckled linoleum in their house.

'Schön zu sehen,' her mother greeted the other ladies sitting in the lounge room. They all looked the same to Gaila. Permed hair with slashes of red or coral lipstick, a dusting of Helena Rubinstein powder on their noses. They considered themselves ladies after all, gathered for their sumptuous monthly morning tea of delectable cakes like Apfel Strudel and Linzer Torte. They balanced their dainty, gold and navy blue rimmed cups on the matching saucers. Gaila dreamt of being like her aunt when she grew up, so she could also have such mouth-watering cakes and fragrant coffee.

'Tee, oder Kaffee?' Gerda asked Ella. Gaila knew she'd ask for coffee, because freshly ground coffee was a luxury undreamt of in their home, where Ella was accountable for every penny of her housekeeping money.

'Meine wunderbar, schöne, kleine mädchen,' Gerda smiled as she led her niece to her bedroom with its purple nylon quilt and her white lace-edged hand-crocheted doilies on the bedside tables. Once a month Gaila was allowed to play with the biggest and loveliest bride doll in the world. It sat like a queen propped up on her own pink nylon pillow in the middle of the double bed. She walked and talked too. Gaila often dreamt that it was hers.

From time to time, Gaila heard snatches of gossip with phrases like, 'Das ist so schön, nicht?' or, 'Das ist so schrechlich, ja? She was able to work out by their tones that 'schön' meant something good and 'schrechlich' meant something really horrible.

That morning, her uncle Simas, who was a giant of a man, came striding through the front door after his night shift as an orderly at Sydney hospital. As she ran up the hallway, he bent down to pick her up and threw her effortlessly up into the air. Ella called out cheekily in Lithuanian, 'How's my little brother?' They both chortled uproariously at their private joke.

Suddenly, her aunt's black eyes flashed angrily and her face contorted with rage.

'Sprechen Sie Deutsch! Sprechen Deutsch!' Gerda yelled at Ella, who could only gape at her.

'Raus, raus!' Aunt Gerda screamed at them, as Ella put her arm protectively around her daughter as they were shoved unceremoniously outside. She quickly took Gaila by the hand as they fled to the bus stop, where they could still hear Gerda yelling from her front door, 'Sprechen Deutsch!! Sprechen Sie Deutsch!'

'I guess we won't be invited back there for a while,' murmured Ella. As it was, the only socializing her family did was to go to their relatives' birthday parties. Sometimes if Al was feeling generous, he'd take them for a Sunday drive to Bronte or Bondi beach. If it was summer, he might buy everyone an icecream. But usually, on the weekends, Al would disappear off to his various Lithuanian committee meetings, coming home full of self-importance, if he'd been elected secretary or treasurer of his group. If Ella asked if they could go to Lithuanian Mass on Sunday, Al would tell her she could take herself and the children on the bus if she was that desperate.

'Anyway, you only want to go to that church, so that you can catch up on the latest gossip with your friends afterwards! Don't pretend to me that you are a good Catholic.'

Ella was lost in her thoughts and it wasn't until her daughter stood up to try to pull the cord to get off the bus, did she realise that they were nearly in Bankstown.

By the time they'd walked from the bus stop to their street, Gaila was tired and hungry. As they walked along to their house, they heard a familiar screaming match.

'You good for nothing son of a bitch! Why doncha do something around this place? You're a bloody disgrace. Why doncha just cark it and leave me in peace?'

Gaila and Ella could recognize Ada's screeching voice anywhere, as their neighbour yelled at Old Jock. He seemed happy enough. He had a comfortable bed, his favourite possessions around him, he was fed and watered regularly and was allowed down the street from time to time.

Yet to Gaila, he was like a monster from a nightmare. Unkempt, ungroomed, with a shock of matted brown hair and a permanent scowl on his face, Gaila always would make sure that she never walked on his side of the street. More often than not, Ada would have a cigarette hanging out of her mouth and her black hair tied up in a dirty scarf knotted at the back of her head. She'd yell and belittle Jock from dawn till dusk.

Sometimes they'd hear another neighbour yell out,

'Shaddup you old cow, people are trying to sleep here!'

Not to be outdone, Ada would reply with a string of curses so fast and vitriolic that there'd be spittle dribbling from the side of her mouth. Gaila didn't even know what those words meant, as they came out so fast and furious. All she knew that they were not a pleasant exchange between the neighbours.

'Whatcha gawking at?' Old Jock would yell at anyone who would walk past and dare to look at him while he'd take a swig from a bottle in a brown paper bag.

Grumbling and cursing, he'd sometimes be still in his pyjamas at three in the afternoon. Ella felt sorry for him. Yet at five, he'd put on his wrinkled shirt and pants, thrust his bare feet in a pair of scuffed shoes without any laces and stagger down to the local pub. After six o'clock closing, he'd sway and stagger back and fling himself on his bed.

Ada would squawk, 'So ya finally back now are ya? Got a skin-ful by the looks of yer.'

If Jock were lucky, she'd bang down some food in an old bat-tered tin pan by his bed.

Sometimes they'd hear Jock mumbling to himself or his little dog, who slept beside him. Old Jock and Skip were like peas in a pod. You know what people say about pet owners resembling their pets. Whenever Jock's harridan of a wife disappeared to the local shops, Ella would nip across the street with some leftover soup.

'Poor man! I wouldn't treat a dog the way that awful woman does.'

'But why does Mrs. McCraw make Jock live outside in a shed?' Gaila would question her mother from time to time.

'Because he's a drunk,' Ella would answer. Gaila didn't know what a drunk was. Other times she'd overhear their other neigh-bours refer to Jock as 'that old wino,' even though when Gaila thought about it later on in life, he would have been only in his early thirties. At that time, being an alcoholic was on par with being a drug addict. In their street, families hid their problems from their neighbours and friends or made excuses like, 'Poor Bob, or poor Joan, are just not themselves today.' Women with alcoholic husbands had to do the best they could with their lot in life. Many times Gaila would hear her mother talking to the neighbour, Mrs. Gabb. When you were a child, you tended to overhear all sorts of conversations. Often they'd discuss why old Jock was so thin.

'That woman only feeds him scraps,' Ella would declare self-righteously.

'Pfft,' Mrs Gabb.would reply knowingly, with a wave of her hand. 'Winos are always scrawny.' She was a rotund widow, who wore a variety of floral dresses sewn from the same pattern and made little cakes and biscuits, that Gaila and Ella were happy to sample whenever she'd hand them across their green picket fence. Both women enjoyed many chats over that fence, while Gaila played tea parties with her dolls on the front lawn. However, Mrs Gabb never saw the inside of their house, nor was Ella ever invited into her neighbour's home.

All they could afford were hand me down clothes and towards the end of the week, barley soup for dinner. Ella prided herself on making do with the meagre housekeeping allowance Al gave her. She discovered by accident, that dog bones were fifty percent cheaper than soup bones, had just as much marrow inside them and with a few extra potatoes, the soup would stretch further.

'But Mama, can I have some new shoes?' pleaded Gaila.

'Maybe later, now eat your soup.'

Ella, working at the cafeteria, was on her feet all day.

'Be a good girl now Gaila, and help me mend these socks.'

'But Mama! But I really need new shoes. These are pinching my toes.'

'No buts Gaila, they'll do you another winter. Help me with these socks. Watch me weave the thread in and out. Make the darn last. No, that's not neat enough! Unpick it and do it again!'

'But Mama, why don't you ever make Max and Paul help out?'

'Because they're boys, they'll look after papa and me in our old age,' Ella always replied.

When Ella thought Gaila was old enough, she finally agreed to let her go to one of the Lithuanian summer scout camps. Gaila was so excited that she was going to be free to spend a whole week with her friends, camping in tents, and singing around the campfire. She'd only been on overnight stays at her aunt's house up to then and had no idea what awaited her. Daytime was fine except for having to urinate in a roughly hewn toilet that looked like a park bench without the bottom seat. If it rained they got to splash the frogs! Then there were rumours circulating about how there was a big black snake nearby, which could slither from behind a branch and bite someone on their bottom. These tales were easily laughed off in the light of day, as Gaila and her friends debated about if it came to the crunch, would they really suck out the poison from another person's bottom to save her life? Most of the time they were kept busy with learning Morse Code or how to tie various types of knots. But once it got dark, it was a different kettle of fish. Terrifying, bloodcurdling ghost stories were told in their tent, scaring Gaila witless, with a torch the only source of light. Where had her friends heard such shocking stories of axe murderers, witches and haunted mansions? No one dared to go to the toilet at night by themselves, so if you were bursting to go, you had to wake up the person next to you and plead with them to come with you. Gaila discovered that it paid to be on the best of terms with everyone in her tent, because you never knew who'd agree to go with you. The torchlight cast eerie shadows amongst the trees and ever twig they stepped on, was a ghost coming after them.

One morning as Gaila was returning from washing her face and hands in a nearby steam, she overheard her cousin Mary telling the other girls that Gaila's parents had to get married.

'So that makes her a bastard!' she exclaimed spitefully. 'My mother told me, so it's got to be the truth!'

Gaila was mortified. What was a bastard? Why would her parents have to get married? Didn't people get married if they were in love? Too timid to say anything, she took a big breath, went into the tent and announced, 'Breakfast's ready! I've just heard them banging the pots together.'

The other girls would not look at her directly and Gaila felt that from that moment on, the easy-going relationship that she'd had with Mary had changed forever. She was determined that when she got home, she would go around to Grandma Rasa's house and ask her what Mary's spiteful words meant.

When Gaila was twelve, she was allowed to go interstate on a scout camp in Victoria. Once she was settled at Wonga Park, she noticed a boy from the Adelaide scouts looking at her. Her friends teased her mercilessly about her love-struck admirer. One morning, Gaila couldn't stand it any longer, so she marched up to him and said, 'Hey you! Why do you keep staring at me all the time?'

'Ah, um, is your name Gaila Kelmas?'

'Yes, so what's it to you?'

'I think that you're my cousin,' the boy stammered holding out a faded black and white photo.

Gaila peered at the photo. Yes, it looked like her all right. The photo was taken at Bronte Beach and she was standing in the shallows with a boy who looked about ten.

'Do you remember my parents and me visiting your family? My father and your father are cousins.'

'Really? I don't remember,' Gaila replied. 'My parents are going through a tough time. Dad doesn't have much to do with us. He's always going out somewhere.'

'Right! That explains it. My parents kept writing to him, but they never got a reply. We thought that he didn't want to keep up the friendship. Anyway, my name is Rokas.'

'Rokas? Is that Lithuanian?'

'Actually my parents gave me a litho name- Ernestas,'

'What's Litho?'

'You must be behind the times. A "Litho" is someone who was born in Australia, but their parents came from Lithuania, and we speak in a definite way.'

'So is being Litho, like when I put a Lithuanian ending on an English word?'

'Yep, you got it! Anyway, I got called "Ernie" at school, till I changed it to Rokas.'

'So Rokas, nice to meet you cuz,' Gaila replied and was thrilled to have a new relative in her life, especially a good looking Adelaide boy. Much more exciting than the Sydney boys she'd grown up with. She became the envy of all the other girls in her tent, who before the end of the scout camp, had scripted her a married life with Rokas in Adelaide with two children, a boy and a girl, living happily ever after, in the seaside suburb of Brighton.

'But we're cousins,' Gaila would protest and laugh.

'Yeah, so what? You can be kissing cousins!' her friends would shout delightedly at the top of their voices. They were happy to sit with the Adelaide boys at the campfire each night, since they were far more interesting than their own. On the last night, Rokas and his group performed a humorous song about Gaila's friends. Before everyone left to go back home, Rokas showed Gaila a gum tree, where he'd carved her name and his. He kissed her shyly on her cheek and waved farewell as he jumped on the bus that would take him back to South Australia. Gingerly, Gaila touched her cheek. Her first kiss! But did it really count if it was a kiss from a cousin? She'd have to ask her best friend, Julie.

After the camp, Gaila and Rokas started to exchange letters. For two years, every week, she'd get a letter from Rokas, detailing his favourite pop songs. Gaila would reply, writing about her favourite teachers and funny incidents in her classes, like when she singed her hair when she'd leant too close to the Bunsen burner in her science class.

When the weekly Lithuanian paper wrote that the next scout camp was being planned to take place in Sydney, Ella received a letter from Rokas' parents.

'Look Al, isn't that nice? Your cousin Mindaugas and his wife Magda are driving across from Adelaide for the big choir and dance festival before Rokas goes to the scout camp.'

'Oh well, I haven't seen him in years. But I'll be working. You organize it.'

Ella was daunted at the prospect of having to feed and house three more people. Rokas would have to sleep in the same room with Max and Paul. Mindaugas and his wife would have to sleep in on fold out beds in the lounge room. Gaila would have to bunk down on a stretcher in the dining room. From what she could gather, Al's relatives were much better off than her family. Mindaugas was an engineer and his wife was a teacher. Luckily, when they arrived, Magda pressed an envelope into Ella's hand and told her that the money was for any extra expenses.

That Christmas Eve stayed in Gaila's mind for the rest of her life. The twelve traditional meatless dishes on the table laid out on her mother's linen tablecloth with some straw underneath. Both sets of her grandparents came with food to contribute to the meal. Her uncle Vygis arrived with his family and her aunt's famous *vėdarai*, the potato sausages that melted in the mouth. Toasts were made and for once there was laughter in her house. When all the dishes had been washed, Gaila and Rokas sat on the front verandah talking about the forthcoming scout camp, reminiscing about the first time they'd met in Melbourne.

'What in the world are you two up to in the dark?' shrieked Magda.

'Oh, hi mum. Actually, Gaila and I were making plans to run away together!' replied Rokas in an offhand manner, as Gaila choked back her laughter and smacked his arm.

'What? You're both underage! You can't do that! You won't get very far! The police will bring you back home!' Magda shouted as she clutched at her heart.

Rokas caught his mother as she fell forward. Gaila ran inside crying for someone to call an ambulance. After the ambulance had taken Magda to hospital, Ella came out to talk to Gaila who was crying. Rokas, his father and Al were still at the hospital.

'Listen to me Gaila. Aunt Magda is not well. She has a very weak heart. Promise me that you won't upset her again. You must understand that Rokas is her only child. Promise me that you and Rokas will stay away from each other and not cause any more trouble.'

'But Mama, he's my cousin, not my boyfriend. We're just friends.'

'You and I know that my dear, but somehow your aunt has got this idea in her head that you and Rokas are boyfriend and girlfriend. Do you really want to be held responsible for another heart attack? The next one could be fatal. Could you ever forgive yourself?'

Gaila looked down at her feet. 'If that's what you want mama.'

'And that means no more letters, alright?'

When Al came home, he stormed in and dragged a terrified Gaila into the kitchen. Flinging open all the drawers until he'd found Ella's sewing scissors, he threw her onto a chair and started hacking off her long blonde hair. Ella kept shouting for Al to stop, but he was like a madman.

'Please daddy, don't hurt me, please,' Gaila kept whimpering.

When Al had finally finished, he pushed her down the hallway into her bedroom and shouted, 'That solves that problem, you little slut! You won't be having any boyfriends for quite some time now!'

When Gaila saw Rokas afterwards and told him what happened, he was horrified.

'Oh Gaila you poor thing. How can your father do such a thing? Your hair will grow back over the summer, but I don't think I can bear not writing any more letters. Can you?'

'No, but what can we do? We can't be responsible for another heart attack.'

'I've got an idea. I could ask one of my friends if you can write to me care of his address. Do you think one of your friends would agree to me writing to her address?'

Gaila thought about it as she tied a scarf around her hair and hurried over to Grandma Rasa's house once Al had gone to work the next day. She untied her scarf and blurted out the whole saga to her grandmother. 'What will I do? All the kids in my school will tease me.'

At the moment her grandfather walked in. 'Go on, tell him what happened Gaila.' said Rasa.

'Excuse us for a moment,' he replied as he took Rasa by the arm. When they came back, he pressed some money into Gaila's palm.

'I am truly sorry that my son has done this to his only daughter,' Bronius said carefully. 'Your grandmother will take you to her hairdresser friend nearby and maybe she can try to do something with your hair.'

The hairdresser took one look at Gaila and said, 'I know! I can make it into a short Audrey Hepburn style, what do you think?'

Gaila was quite happy with her new look and immediately thought of her best friend Julie who had short hair. She knew that Julie wouldn't think twice about being the go-between for her letters to Rokas.

'Hey, have ya see Galah's weird haircut? She looks like a guy!'

'Yeah, I reckon she must be butch. Ya don't wanna go anywhere near her.'

'See yous at recess for a smoke at the back of the oval, okay?

Gaila hid behind her locker door, not believing her ears. Why would they talk about her in such a cruel way? What had she done to deserve the group's anger? She took out her books for period one. English. She loved that class and the way the new young teacher Miss Moore encouraged everyone. Even that blockhead Jason, who stared at her at every opportunity. Wearily, Gaila sat down and took out her homework from the previous day. An argumentative essay about whether students should wear uniforms in schools. She'd put forward some very valid points for and against the topic and structured her arguments in the way Miss Moore had shown them on the blackboard.

'Who'd like to read their introduction this morning? Miss Moore asked pleasantly. Not one student put up their hand. 'What about you Gaila?'

'Um, I really haven't finished it Miss,' stammered Gaila in a shy, quivering voice.

'Well, just read out your first two sentences,' coaxed Miss Moore.

Gaila started to read. Sniggers and snorts of derision rippled through the class. Some people actually laughed out loud as soon as she read her first sentence. 'Uniforms are an excellent way of making students feel equal.' More laughter erupted.

'Yeah, you'd know of course, wouldn't ya, you stupid galah,' sniggered Sharon, the class bully. Gaila went beetroot red. She hated the way that she made fun of her name. She was going to shorten it to "Gail," as soon as she could. Why did she have to be the only one in her class who didn't have the latest brand name casual clothes to wear when it was Casual Clothes Day? Ella told her many times that they couldn't afford store bought clothes. Gaila tried to continue reading her essay. 'Due to a lack of money, many students can't afford the expense of wearing different clothes every day of the week.'

'Yeah, we know that you for one, can't afford it!' yelled out Ben, who thought he was the best-looking guy in the class.

'That will do Ben!' reprimanded Miss Moore. 'See me in my staffroom at recess. You can come on yard duty with me and pick up some papers.'

Gaila slumped back into her seat, and buried her head in her hands. Luckily the bell rang for period two. As she was leaving the room, Sharon gave Gaila a big shove and she went sprawling into the corridor, her folders scattering over the floor.

'Sorry Gay-lah!' yelled Sharon, and went off to Science.

Gaila fled to the girls' toilets and into the nearest cubicle. She was mortified. How she wished that she could change her name to Gail Kelm. No one could pronounce her name properly. Gaila Kelmas was pronounced differently by all her teachers. The worst offender was her Maths teacher, Mr. Bench. When he went through roll call in her first year at high school, he called out 'Galah Kelmass!' From then on the teasing began, 'Galah, Galah where's your ass?' the bullies would shout as she walked past with her friend Julie. She wished that Julie were in her class. Maybe they could have a chat at recess about Sharon and Ben. As Gaila closed the toilet door behind her, she gasped. In thick black texta, someone had scrawled 'Gaila the galah is a bitch' on the back. Tears poured down her face. She fled into the next cubicle but the same sentence was there. Stunned, Gaila checked the other ten cubicles. Each door had the same sentence scrawled across the back.

Slowly, Gaila made her way back to the lockers, got her books and walked out of the school. She didn't care if she got into trouble on Monday. She hoped that no one would be home. Walking like a zombie, she began to construct a letter in her mind, that she would write to Rokas. Their system of writing to their friends' addresses was still working. Perhaps he could give her some advice about how to cope with her classmates' bullying. Passing the local library Gaila had a brainwave. She walked in and asked the librarian whether she could borrow the Simplicity pattern book. She was sure that she could trace a dress pattern onto butcher's paper and then once she saved up enough pocket money, she could buy some material and make herself a modern dress. She would ask grandma Rasa to teach her how to sew clothes on her Singer sewing machine. Later on in life when Gaila had plucked enough courage to go to her high school's twentieth re-union, she was relieved to see that she didn't look so bad after all. Sharon by then was an obese blimp with five children, having married Ben who had lost most of his hair and was covered in tattoos. As for Jason, he looked as if he was spaced out on drugs.

When Gaila finally got home from the library with her Simplicity pattern book, Ella was excited and in a good mood for once. She was rummaging through her wardrobe looking at all her dresses. Finally she put on a knitted maroon dress with a scalloped hemline and pink daisies around the neckline. Renata had made it as her going away outfit and Ella thought that it still suited her.

'Your father's taking me out for my birthday tonight,' she told Gaila happily.

'You'll have to keep an eye on Paul, make sure he does his homework. The two of you can cook your own tea or heat up some of those left over bacon buns or cabbage rolls.'

Circling Victoria Street like hungry wolves, Ella and Al shook off the rain and stepped into a small German restaurant. Even though it wasn't what she had hoped for, Ella was pleased that Al was making an effort for her birthday. A skinny pimply waiter led them to a table at the back near the kitchen.

'No thanks, mate. We'd like to sit next to the window,' Al said quite firmly.

Ella wasn't sure why he insisted on a window seat, because there certainly wasn't much to see in Darlinghurst. It wasn't as if they were in some expensive restaurant overlooking Sydney Harbour. As they were perusing their menus trying to decide whether to have veal schnitzel or roast pork with sauerkraut, a shiny red sports car pulled up outside.

An attractive woman with a handsome gentleman strode in the door. Heads turned. Al nodded to the couple and summoned the waiter with a flick of his fingers.

'I know them. Tad and Elvyra. They can join us at our table.'

The woman with the bouffant hairdo, nodded at Ella, smiled seductively and seated herself opposite Al. As she took off her fur coat, Ella nearly choked on her glass of wine. Even though it was winter and raining, the woman's low cut shimmering dress was completely out of place in a suburban restaurant. Taking her napkin, the woman arranged it artistically around her ample cleavage.

The waiter's eyes nearly popped out of his head as he came up to take her order.

'What are you having for dinner, sweetie?' she lisped to her companion, and batted her impossibly long lashes. Her eyes were made up with black eyeliner, like Cleopatra.

'I'll have the roast chicken thanks.

'Good choice!' said Al, 'I'm a breast man myself!' He laughed uproariously at his own joke.

Tad joined in the laughter. 'Ha, ha! Well how about that? I'm a leg man!'

The waiter finally took their orders and reassured the women that the fish was fresh and that the owner's wife made the soup and cakes herself.

Whilst the discussion centred around the menu, Tad revealed that he was Polish. 'I used to love my mother's *kartacze*, her potato dumplings.'

Ella looked up with interest. 'Really? Tell me what they're like.'

'They're oval shaped, made from raw and mashed potatoes with meat inside.'

'They sound like our national Lithuanian dish, the one we call *cepelinai.*'

'Your national dish? The Poles have been making *kartacze* for centuries!'

'Pan Tadeusz! I can't believe it! It's ours, along with our *koldūnai* dumplings.'

'You, madam, must mean our *pierogi*, now that's one of Poland's national dishes!'

'What? That's nonsense!' replied Ella, who was sure that she knew all about traditional Lithuanian dishes. After all, her mother was a *cordon bleu* cook in Palanga.

'Oh for goodness sake! Everyone calls those stodgy dumplings something different!' pouted Tad's buxom friend. 'Let's drop this stupid argument! I need a light for my cigarette!'

Both men rushed to find their lighters in their pockets, vying for Elvyra's attention.

'Nice little sports car you've got out there Tad,' remarked Al, smoothly changing the subject.

'Oh that! That was just a tiny little present for my pussy cat, wasn't it Vera, darling?'

'Mm, yes sweetie pie, it certainly was,' simpered the woman as she kissed her benefactor, leaving the imprint of her bright red lipstick on his cheek, as her matching scarlet talons blazed in the candlelight.

Al held up his wine glass and looked at the woman sitting in front of him. 'I'd like to propose a toast to our new friends, Elvyra and Tad!'

Ella was taken aback. She was expecting Al to congratulate her at that point on her birthday, but he was still too busy drooling at the woman who'd taken out her breasts for dinner.

At ten p.m., Gaila was jolted awake by the front door slamming and her parents shouting. She pulled the quilt over her head, so she couldn't hear the hateful words flung carelessly all over the house. She remembered when she was in primary school and how she used to threaten to run away to grandmother Rasa's house when she couldn't bear the fighting. Her father would yell at her that he'd help her pack her suitcase as he'd fling it onto her bed.

'How could you humiliate me tonight of all nights? I thought that you were going to wish me happy birthday, or give me a present!' sniffed Ella in between sobs.

'I took you out for dinner, didn't I? What more do you want?'

'At least you could have bought me some perfume or flowers. Some men, believe it or not, actually buy their wives birthday presents!'

'They're a waste of money! Be thankful for what you got. A nice meal and wine.'

'Oh yes, that. And did you have to keep staring at that cheap looking tart, Al? It was embarrassing!'

'You're the one who's embarrassing Ella. Look at yourself. It wouldn't hurt you to smarten yourself up. That ugly knitted dress of yours is ancient!'

'With the tiny amount of housekeeping you give me, what am I supposed to do Al?'

'You could learn to sew or you can always find yourself a second job! Anyway, I don't have to stay here and listen to your hysterics. I'm going out!'

Gaila heard the door slam as her father left in a cloud of aftershave. She heard her mother sobbing. Tiptoeing into the bedroom, she noticed her mama sitting forlornly in bed, wearing her faded pink nylon nightdress, her eyes swollen with tears. She thought back to when she was about five and had seen Ella crying for the first time. When she's asked Grandma Rasa why her mother was in bed crying, she was told that her mother had just lost a baby. At that age, Gaila could not understand how anyone could lose a baby. It was only much later when she was studying biology, did she learn about miscarriages.

'Mama, are you all right? Do you want me to make you a cup of chamomile tea?' she asked hesitantly. Chamomile tea was Grandma Renata's remedy for everything.

'Thank you Gaila. Yes, that would be lovely. Don't worry, sweetheart, go back to bed.'

When Gaila got back to her bedroom she found Paul sitting on the floor with a woollen blanket wrapped around him.

'I swear that I'm going to kill that bastard one day!'

'You'll do no such thing Paul, it's not worth sitting in jail for the rest of your life.' Gaila could see that Paul was growing into a gangly sixteen year old. He would be tall like the rest of the men in their family.

'I wish that Max had knocked dad out for good, that time he took a punch at him!'

Gaila looked at him sharply. 'What are you talking about?'

'You were at grandma Renata's helping out when they were sick last year and Dad noticed some strange little plants growing in amongst mum's tomatoes.'

Gaila was intrigued. 'What sort of plants?'

'I think that dad took them over to the guy next door to ask him. Old Vince laughed at him and asked dad if he was going into the marjoram business.'

'Did he mean marijuana?'

'Yes, I'm pretty sure that's what dad said when he got back, and then he waited for Max to come home.'

'Just think, no one has told me about this. Why didn't you tell me? Does mama know?'

'Dad told me he'd beat the hell out of me if I told you or mama, or anyone.'

Suddenly the pieces of the puzzle were starting to fit. Gaila had to know more.

'Okay. Paul, then what?'

Paul huddled deeper into his blanket, reminding Gaila of when he was two years old sucking his thumb and holding onto his favourite blue blanket called 'Blankey Bear.'

'Anyway, Max came home from work and dad started to yell at him that he knew that he was growing and smoking marijuana and took a swing at him. Then Max turned round and punched dad so hard that he fell to the floor. Honestly Gaila, I thought that he'd killed him. He said that he could have made thousands of dollars from those plants. Yelled that he leaving and that he'd never come back to Sydney. Never again!'

Gaila put her arm around her younger brother. 'You poor thing, you've kept this to yourself all this time?'

Paul trembled and at last the tears began to fall. He was relieved that the secret he'd been carrying was out in the open. 'I know I shouldn't say this, but I'm glad Max is gone.'

Gaila understood what he meant. From the time Max was a toddler, he'd been given whatever he wanted for birthdays and Christmas. Paul and Gaila were lucky to get second-hand, repainted bikes and what not. They knew that he was their parents' favourite. When Max demanded a motorbike for his eighteenth birthday, he got it. Gaila had to learn to cook, bake, clean and mend clothes at a very early age. She often felt sorry for herself back then, but now she was glad to have these skills. Since she was six years older than Paul, she also had to help her mother by changing his nappy or give him his bottle. When Max was born, she had to take him for walks, put him down for his naps, babysit both boys during the school holidays when her mother worked, as well as do the housework and get tea on the table. Sometimes she felt as if she was the mother.

One would think that growing up with such a lot of attention, Max would have turned out to be a decent human being. In high school he ran around with all the naughty boys, smoked marijuana and got into trouble. Yet, whenever there was a phone call from the headmaster, her parents would always excuse Max's behaviour. Finally, he dropped out when he was thirteen and somehow got a job on the wharves. God knows where he was now. Maybe she would ask Mama in a few days after everything had calmed down. She noticed Paul had fallen asleep on the floor. She didn't want to disturb him. If he did wake up, she'd lead him back to his bed like she used to do when he was little and came to her when he'd have a bad dream.

'Mama, do you know where Max is?' Gaila finally plucked up the courage to ask Ella when her mother was in a good mood and her father was out somewhere. They were both rolling out the dough to make *kibinai* savoury pastries for supper.

'Yes, I do, but don't let on to your father that I know,' replied Ella.

'Why didn't you tell us mama?'

'It was better that way Gaila. Knowing you and your big mouth, you would have told Paul or let it slip to your father that you knew. Promise me that you'll never let on to your father that I told you.'

'How did you find out, mama?'

'Max sent me a letter to my work address. He's working in one of the gold mines in Kalgoorlie.'

'That's so far away, mama. Western Australia is thousands of miles from here.'

'Is he okay?'

'Well of course he is Gaila. He wrote to say that he's met a nice girl there.'

'Max? A nice girl? Where could he possibly meet a nice girl in a mining town?'

'Don't you criticise Max to me Gaila. He's a good boy. Loves his mother.'

'Has he sent you any money mama? I've heard that miners earn heaps over there.'

'No not yet. But I know that he will. Soon. He won't forget his mama.'

'I swear that I'm going to throw myself off The Gap,' sobbed Ella to her mother on the phone a week later.

'Don't tell me. Let me guess. I bet that good for nothing husband of yours is playing around again!'

'It's worse this time Mama. Do you remember Elvyra? The one whose first husband was killed in that awful train accident a few years ago?'

'What about her?'

'One of the choir ladies told me that she'd seen Al and Elvyra getting out of her red sports car at two in the morning and going into her flat.'

'Sounds like a familiar story Ella. You know very well that your husband started going out at all times of the night and day, even when Gaila was a baby. Leopards never change their spots Ella, surely you know that. Funny how you ended up marrying a man just like your father!'

'But I was really was in love with him, mama. I swear to God I was. I thought that he was so brave to warn his family that the Russians were going to deport people in Kaunas to Siberia. I really thought that he'd change once Max was born. He always wanted another son. Said that I forced him into marriage, when I got pregnant with Gaila.'

'Brave? Al? That's a lot of rubbish! His parents told me that they were in Alytus when the Nazis were retreating. Certainly not Kaunas. One of their friends warned them the night before that the Russians were coming, so they left that same night.'

'Why didn't you tell me this before, mama?'

'Would you have listened to me Ella? And did you know that even when he was in the DP camp, he'd hide in someone's wardrobe so as not to have to face the latest girl he'd jilted. Oh yes, your father Petras has had some long chats over the years with Al's father.'

'What's wrong with me mama? Why doesn't Al love me? I've tried so hard to be a good wife. If he didn't like the dinner I made, I'd make him another one. I try to look nice for him when he comes home from work, even though the housekeeping he gives me is a pittance. I always have his cold glass of beer ready. I'm not frivolous.'

'Maybe that's where you went wrong Ella. You've worked most of your life. You should have kept some of that money hidden away somewhere.'

'Maybe it all started when I got depressed after Paul was born. You know, Bronius and Rasa virtually brought him up. Bronius would wash his nappies and Rasa would give him his bottle and make dinner for everyone. I was depressed for a quite while mama.'

Yes, yes, I remember, Ella. But every woman gets the baby blues. I did too. That's part and parcel of being a new mother. As for Al, you're supposed to support each other in sickness and in health.'

'Don't preach to me, mama. Your own marriage has been a sham for a long time. Do you think I've forgotten how papa treated me? It was as if I didn't exist.'

'I'm sorry Ella. Yes, I was a doormat back then. But what options did I have?'

'You could have gone back to Ventuva and lived with Grandma Kristina and Jonas. I loved her, mama. She taught me so much.'

'What? Me? Go back to Ventuva and be humiliated by all the gossip mongers? Let me tell you that I was a fine lady in Palanga. I had the respect and admiration of all the important people in town. Today, women have options. You can get a divorce, I couldn't.'

'But what will people say? None of the women in the choir will talk to me, they'll think that I'll be after their husbands once I'm divorced.'

'Ella! Do you really want to live like this for the rest of your life? Answer me!'

'I, I suppose I could find out what my options are. After all, Paul's in high school. Gaila will start university next year. She can always get a part-time job and pay me for food and board.'

'You know you can always come home to us. Haven't you suffered enough?'

'Thanks, mama. You're right. As usual. I might ring Emilia, you know my friend who works with me. She had a really nice lawyer, when she went for her divorce. She'll advise me.'

A few weeks later, when Al came home from work, and inserted his key into the front door, he noticed an unfamiliar stillness, as soon as he stepped inside the hallway. There was no loud pop music coming from Gaila's bedroom and Paul wasn't shooting goals at the basketball ring in the back yard with his friends.

Slowly he walked into the kitchen. There was only one chair, with a plate, knife, fork, spoon and coffee mug at the table. His eyes scanned the room. On the stove, stood one frying pan, one saucepan and the kettle. Luckily the fridge was still there. He stood there scratching his head. Walking into the bedrooms, he noticed that neither Gaila nor Paul's beds were there. In his bedroom, there was a single bed. Ella had gone and left him. He sat down, his heart racing. He clutched the bottle of heart pills and swallowed one. Even Ella's dressing table was gone. In the living room, he saw his favourite arm chair with the reading light and a small table. There was a hand written note propped up against an empty beer glass.

This is goodbye, Al.

I've had enough of your lies, whoring around and spending money on yourself, instead of our family. I'm sick and tired of your emotional cruelty to our daughter, whom you have called 'clumsy cow,' instead of her real name for most of her life. Your coldness when you shut me out all those years ago when I was depressed after Paul was born. Your horrible temper towards Max. Yes, I know all about it. Max wrote to me. Your uncontrollable anger towards our children when things didn't work out for you at work. The constant excuse of your poor old leg when you didn't get the promotions that you thought you were entitled to. The lining up of Max, Paul and Gaila at the foot of our bed telling them that you were going to die, all those times when you just had a bad cold. That was really cruel. I have tried to be a good wife to you, but obviously the more I tried, the more you got away with doing whatever you wanted. I have discussed this separation with Gaila and Paul. Neither of them want to live here with you. Well that about sums it up Al. I have had enough. You'll be hearing from my lawyer soon. I hope that you'll be very happy with Elvyra or some other tart that I'm sure you have lined up elsewhere.

Bye, Ella.

'Shit! Shit! Shit! How did that bitch find out about Elvyra?' yelled Al, at no one in particular. He peered into the fridge. Ella had left behind some *koldūnai dumplings*, a bit of bacon and half a carton of sour cream. He'd fry them up. That would be fine for his tea. Tomorrow, he'd ring up a lawyer. The house was in his name, he'd make sure that Ella got nothing. In any case, he could always marry Elvyra. She'd be willing and she had a flat. He'd spent enough on her, buttering her up. Buying her perfume, dresses, flowers and dinners at the expensive restaurant that she liked at Double Bay. If that didn't work, there were any number of women who'd be very happy to have him in their beds or make him a few cabbage rolls. It was a smart move on his behalf that he'd joined the drama group last year. There were trips interstate and the big festivals every two years. He might even go and stay with Max in Western Australia and have a holiday. Al let out a huge burp and settled in front of the TV. At least Ella didn't take that. He lit up a cigarette and thought that the divorce could be a blessing in disguise. He could sell the house and move in with Elvyra. They could go on a few holidays to Fiji or Tahiti. He'd always dreamed of seeing those hula dancers. At least, he wouldn't be the bad guy in this break up. Yes, his wife left him. He could imagine telling all his co-workers tomorrow. That and his bad leg. He was bound to get lots of sympathy, maybe even a few days off. He wouldn't have to pay maintenance for Gaila once she eighteen. As for Paul, a few trips to Luna Park or McDonald's would put him back in his good books again. He might even watch him play basketball. Have a chat to the other fathers, make them feel sorry for him.

After her parents split up, Gaila decided to move into a house with some girls she'd got to know at Sydney University. She still visited her mother and grandparents on the weekends and also discovered the power of long hair, a mini skirt and boots. Sometimes she wore the long cardigan that Renata had knitted for her. It was made from cream wool and had front panels with maroon tulips. Actually it was only after Gaila started her uni course that she could afford a pair of jeans. All her previous clothes had been made by Ella or Rasa from Simplicity patterns, with materials from bargain basement fabric stores. Studying politics brought her into conflict with her grandparents' beliefs and way of life. She was passionately against the Vietnam War and participated in many moratorium marches. One weekend, Petras hit the roof one day when he saw Gaila's photo when she was marching with other protestors, on the front page of a Sydney newspaper. He lectured her about the evils of Communism and why their family ran from the Russian invaders.

Gaila couldn't even begin to imagine the horrors her family had been through, all she could see was the horrific result of napalm bombings on the poor Vietnamese people on TV. She tried to explain it to her grandparents one evening over dinner.

'How do you think your mother got a bullet wound in her leg?' shouted Petras.

'Calm down old man,' said her grandmother, who begun to call Petras 'old man' whenever she was displeased with him.

'Many men in our Ventuva village were freedom fighters, brave partisans,' Renata tried to explain. 'If they were caught, the Russians would torture them, cut their tongues out and worse. Then they'd string them up in the village or town squares and force the people to file past. All the time watching for anyone who'd break down. My sister Julia's boyfriend was one of those brave men. My other sister Virginia's husband, Marius, was deported to Vorkuta in Siberia for being one of the Forest Brothers.'

Gaila listened politely, and later, she decided to write an essay on 'Soviet Imperialism in the Baltic States' to show her grandparents that she understood her Lithuanian background. This time she got a distinction, unlike her other grades, and was praised for being a Maoist of all things, 'Because,' as her tutor explained, 'the Maoists are against Soviet Imperialism.' Gaila couldn't link the partisan stories that her grandmother told her with what was happening in the Vietnam War. Years later, she found it somewhat ironic that her radical, bearded, Maoist tutor had become a clean shaven, suit wearing, conservative member of parliament.

It was also at this time that Gaila's English lecturer was thrown over The Gap to his death by a group of thugs who hunted down homosexuals for fun. There were many heated discussions about this tragedy at the university cafeteria after lectures. In fact, many afternoons or mornings began to slip by, until Gaila's friends worked out a rotation system where one of them would listen to lectures, take notes and come back to dictate them to the group. Feminism made another huge impact on Gaila. Her group decided to make a point about the Miss Sydney University contest by talking her into taking part in her grungiest jeans and baggiest t-shirt.

'Who won the comp, Gaila?' asked one of her friends later in the day, as they sat smoking their roll your own cigarettes in the cafeteria.

'Some bimbo with a plunging neckline and a tiny skirt.'

Her group felt totally satisfied with their efforts and celebrated by making a huge peace sign on the lawn, by lying next to each other.

Some days, they'd listen to rock groups play at lunch time concerts and many of them went on to become famous in Australia and overseas. Next, cooperatives became the latest thing and one even started up by the Student Union which introduced a lunch system whereby rolls and salad items were bought in bulk and then students would form orderly lines and make their own rolls for lunch and pay what they could afford. That suited Gaila's budget very well and she announced to Jana that she'd be saving lots of money by not having to make lunch at their share house, where people just helped themselves to whatever was in the fridge, regardless of whose food it was. Needless to say, there were never any orderly queues for the new scheme and it only lasted a fortnight, because someone embezzled the takings.

Gaila had always loved English in high school and it was around this time that she wrote her first poem, which formed part of a long Spenserian tale of unrequited love as part of a literature essay. Overnight, she had fallen in love with Heinrich, her German lecturer, who of course didn't know she existed. He wasn't handsome in the classical sense, but his soft, hypnotic German accent and his patient explanations of German writers like Kafka, fired up Gaila's imagination. She drooled over him during lectures, fantasizing how they'd get married and then live in some picturesque little German town, like Passau on the banks of the

Danube River. Of course nothing came of it and she fell in love many times at uni.

Her best friend at this time was a Latvian girl called Jana. The two girls were a direct contrast to each other. Gaila with her long blonde hair and Jana with her long dark hair. Sometimes, they would go on double dates and were happy with this arrangement, until her second year, when Gaila fell for a tall, good looking Estonian student called Mike, who had a body to die for. They went out for about a month and she declared to Jana that she was really and truly in love and that Mike was the 'one.' Instead of Jana saying her usual, 'That's great. I am so happy for you,' she turned away with a guilty look and confessed that she was in love with Mike as well and that he'd asked her out, because he was planning to break up with Gaila. Of course Gaila was totally heartbroken and didn't speak to her friend for a long time after. When Jana and Mike broke up, they became friends again and commiserated about men and their fickle natures.

'What would you like to do for your twenty first birthday?' Ella asked her daughter. 'You know, I can arrange for the Lithuanian Ladies Auxiliary to make the food smorgasbord style and because I'm in the choir, I can get the hall at a reduced rate. Invite all your uni friends.'

'Thanks, mama, but I would really like to go backpacking with my friends around New Zealand.'

Gaila didn't want to admit that she felt embarrassed about Ella going out with a new man each week. Why wasn't she like other mothers? All of a sudden, she was getting dressed up and being taken out every weekend by all the widowers or divorced men in the Sydney Baltic community. Sometimes, Ella would announce happily to her daughter that some friend at work had set her up on a blind date. For heaven's sake! Gaila was supposed to be the one going on dates, not her mother! She didn't really want to make small talk at her twenty first birthday party with another one of her mother's admirers she didn't care for, and then have to put up with all the ribald teasing about her mother and her boyfriends.

'What would you say, if I told you that the trip would be our present to you?' suggested her grandmother Renata, who had noticed Gaila's turmoil every time she met one of her mother's admirers.

'Grandpa and I are not getting any younger, and God knows, you can't take it all when you're lying in your coffin.' She stared stonily at Petras who was glaring at her and shaking his head in disagreement. She was not going to let him win this battle.

Gaila hugged her grandmother gratefully and immediately rang her three best friends. Jackie, Jana and Nina all agreed to come with her. They were sure that their parents would help them out with some of the expenses towards their trip as well.

'I've got a bit saved up from waitressing,' admitted Gaila, who worked at a café close to Sydney University. when she wasn't attending lectures.

'That might last you a week in New Zealand,' scoffed Renata. 'Besides, you'll need a small tent and sleeping bag and sturdy walking shoes, as well as your airfare.'

After a small party at home with her family and her close friends, where her sixteen year old brother Paul embarrassed her, by vomiting on the verandah, after drinking almost half a bottle of vodka, Gaila started to plan her trip. She wrote down everything that she would need. Making lists like Grandma Rasa, gave her a sense of control over her life.

'I can't believe we're finally in Auckland!' exclaimed Jackie after their plane landed.

Gaila consulted her list. 'We need to get the shuttle bus into the city centre, since our backpackers' hostel is in Queen Street.'

After unloading their gear in the room that they were going to share for a few days, the girls started exploring their surroundings.

'Let's go to Albert Park first,' suggested Nina, who had arranged to meet an ex-boyfriend who was studying at Auckland University.

Derek was waiting for them under the Clock Tower. He took the last drag on his roll your own Drum cigarette, threw it down onto the pavement and squashed the butt under his foot.

'Hop into my chariot ladies, I am all yours,' he said with a flirtatious grin, as they squeezed into his battered Mini Minor. Since he was part Maori, he was always keen to show visitors some of his heritage.

About three kilometres later, they were at Mount Eden. From the top, they could see the whole of Auckland.

'Look! Can you see the old Maori fortifications, the terracing and the storage pits over there,' pointed out Derek.

'Where did your people originally come from?' asked Jackie who was interested in ancient cultures.

'They came from Maungakiekie, one of the largest settlements. I know it's a bit hard to pronounce. Its English name is One Tree Hill. If you like, you could do the coast to coast walk tomorrow.'

'That would be excellent,' agreed Jackie, who'd consulted her tourist information pamphlet. 'There's a walkway, isn't there Derek?'

'There sure is. Just follow it From Waitemata Harbour around to Manukau Harbour. It'll take you girls about four hours.'

Where are we having lunch?' asked Jana, who liked to have her meals on time.

'I'm going to take you to Parnell Village. You'll be able to see Auckland Harbour from there. We can have a cheap lunch at one of the pubs there.'

Just before they reached Parnell, the girls gasped in surprise. Thousands of roses were blooming in a huge public garden and the perfume was intoxicating.

'I just love this Derek. Thank you, thank you for bringing us here,' said Gaila, whose grandfather Bronius used to graft roses for a hobby after he retired. After demolishing his meat pie and chips, Derek lit up another cigarette and said that he had to go.

'I've got to leave you here ladies. Got an architecture lecture to catch. Enjoy your lunch.'

Once he was gone, Nina was bombarded with questions.

'He is gorgeous Nina! Why in the world did you let him go?' asked Jackie.

'I first met him at Sydney Uni, but then he had to go back to Auckland to help look after his two little brothers, after his parents were killed in a head on car smash in Rotorua.'

'Oh, that's so sad,' replied Jackie who'd taken a fancy to him and the intricate tattoos on his arms. 'But I thought the Maoris were a tightly knit community.'

'Oh, they are, but his grandparents were elderly and his two brothers were quite a handful. He thought that he should do the right thing and go back. Got a part time job stacking supermarket shelves at night, to help out. Sometimes, he earned extra money when he got phoned up to dance the Haka with his cousin's Maori dance troupe, you know, if one of the guys was sick.'

The girls pondered their own lives as they ate their toasted sandwiches for lunch and then set off to walk back to the hostel.

They were planning to go over to the Bay of Islands after doing the coastal walk and a hike through the Pohutukawa forest up to the summit of the island.

By the time they'd returned, the girls were totally exhausted. Only Nina was still fired up, with tourist maps spread out in front of her.

'How about we hitch a ride to Paihia?'

'What's so great about Paihia?' asked Gaila.

'For a start there's a great backpackers' hostel near the harbour, and Derek's aunt lives there. She's an artist. I'm sure that she'd give us a bit of lunch or dinner.'

The girls started out the next morning and soon a truck pulled up alongside of them.

'Need a lift somewhere girls?' drawled a tattooed, suntanned man in his forties.

'Um, we wanted to get to Paihia,' said Jana. 'Are you going that way?'

'Near enough,' replied the driver. 'I've got some stuff to drop off in Waitangi. Paihia is about a twenty minute walk from there. You might want to check out the Waitangi National Reserve whilst you're there. There are some nice waterfalls along the track.'

Nina and Jackie climbed into the back, whilst Gaila and Jana chatted to the driver as they drove through the rolling green landscape.

Three and a half hours later they were in Waitangi. They thanked the driver and sat down on the small wharf and shared their rations of nuts and dried fruit. They decided to take the truck driver's advice. Adjusting their backpacks the girls started their trek. Walking through the mangrove forests they gazed at amazement at the old trees. They stopped at Hutia Creek for a drink of water and finally got to Haruru Falls.

'Isn't this amazing? Who would have thought that these falls were here?' exclaimed Jana.

'I'm starving!' announced Nina. 'Let's go to see Derek's aunt.'

The girls trudged along, their backpacks growing heavier by the minute. By the time they got to the little township of Paihia they could hardly drag one foot in front of another.

'We're just not that fit, are we?' said Jackie. 'Now where does this aunt of yours live?'

'Not far from the hostel,' replied Nina.

Once they'd registered at the backpacker's hostel, they set off to find Maisie's house.

Nina knocked loudly on the door. A young woman with face tattoos opened it.

'What do yous want?'

'Hello. We're looking for Maisie Rewa,' said Nina very politely.

'Oh! You mean Big Maisie? She's living in Russell now. We bought this place off her last year. She said it was too much for her to keep up on her own. Go down to the wharf and buy yourselves a ticket for the ferry across to Russell. She lives next to that old Duke of Marlborough Hotel.'

'Okay, thanks.' Nina was disappointed.

'Well then girls, what do you think? Do we have enough?'

They counted out their money and agreed it was within their budget.

'We should be able to get a student discount on our ticket,' suggested Gaila who had inherited her thrifty nature from grandmother Rasa.

Soon they were on the ferry to Russell which lurched up and down with the light swell. When they got off, they asked for directions for the hotel.

'It's staring yous in the face!' said the gruff captain. 'The Duke of Marlborough Hotel is at the end of this jetty! Bloody tourists!' He spat derisively onto the pier.

It didn't take them long to walk off the pier and to knock on Maisie's door.

'What a surprise Nina!' Maisie exclaimed. 'Why didn't you write and tell me you were coming?'

'Um, I wasn't sure whether I'd be welcome. You know, since Derek and me broke up.'

'That's not your fault, girlie,' said Maisie as she crushed Nina to her bosom. Her walnut face it up. The myriad of wrinkles looked as if they were going to burst through her cheeks. 'How about I put the kettle on and show you some of my paintings?'

The girls stared in amazement at Maisie's sketches of old Maoris with face tattoos and her delicate watercolours of the harbour at dawn and sunset.

'These should be in a gallery,' remarked Gaila. 'People in Sydney would pay good prices for these paintings.'

'I can make do with whatever I sell at the market here and over in Paihia,' replied Maisie.

'Anyway, I've met another artist who's staying at the hotel next door where I do a bit of cleaning. Saw him sketching outside the other day. He'll be coming over shortly to borrow some of my brushes.'

The girls envisaged some old eccentric artist, but were astounded to see a handsome dark haired man striding towards them with an easel. Butterflies somersaulted in Gaila's stomach. All of a sudden, she didn't know what was happening to her.

'Myles, come and meet my young friends. Nina you introduce them. I can't remember all their names. Must be getting old.' Maisie repositioned her long grey hair back into bun at the back of her head, securing it with a green pearly shell clasp.

Nina introduced her friends. Myles shook hands with them, but found his hand lingering longer in Gaila's warm hand.

'Hi, I'm Myles. Maisie's taking me under her wing for a few days, to refine my brush work.'

'If I was younger, I'd be teaching him a lot more,' cackled Maisie.

The girls looked away, embarrassed. They weren't used to their elders talking in this way.

After numerous cups of tea and cheese sandwiches on Maisie's front porch, the girls were loaded up with chocolate biscuits, tea and four packets of crumpets.

'You'd better get on that last ferry girls, otherwise you'll be camping on my porch for the night! I'll see you tomorrow, when we come across for the weekend market at Paihia. We'll be setting up there, bright and early.'

Gaila and her friends had lost track of time, she realized that she was extremely pleased that she was going to see him again.

'So, who's got the hots for Myles?' asked Nina cheekily.

'Yeah, we saw you blushing!' chorused Jackie and Jana.

'Um, yeah he is pretty cute,' admitted Gaila.

Their good-natured teasing continued until they got off the ferry and trudged back to the backpackers' hostel. As soon as they got closer to their room upstairs, Gaila sensed that all was not as it should be.

'Who left the door open?' gasped Jana. 'Look! Someone's been through our backpacks!'

'I, I'm sure I locked it,' said Nina, taking the key out of her pocket. She hastily checked her backpack. 'Oh no, this can't be happening! There's a $50 missing from my bag!'

The others checked their belongings.

'Oh my God, oh my God! All my money's gone!' cried Gaila, bursting into tears.

Jackie checked as well, but wisely, she'd kept most of her cash hidden in a money belt tucked into her baggy t-shirt.

'What are we going to do?' moaned Gaila. 'That money was my twenty first birthday present. I can't ring up my grandparents or my mum and ask them for more, they aren't very well off.'

'First things first! We have to go and report the theft,' said Nina, swinging into action.

The receptionist gave them a bored looked and went on smoking her cigarette.

'Yeah, that sort of thing happens all the time,' she said nonchalantly. 'Gotta be careful nowadays. Did you lock your door like I told yous to, when yous checked in? You can report the burglary to the police, but they'll tell yous, that whoever took your cash, is bound to be miles away by now.'

'Yes, I'm sure we locked the door,' replied Nina. 'Um, can I use your phone to call my parents?'

Nina called her parents, who reassured her that they'd go to the bank as soon as they were able and deposit some more money into her account for the rest of her trip. She went back to the others to report what the receptionist had told her. Gaila just kept on crying, heartbroken that her trip of a lifetime was going to be cut short.

'I'll just have to fly back as soon as I check with the airline.'

'Look, let's not panic. I will ask Maisie what she can come up with,' suggested Nina, who felt responsible. She couldn't remember whether she had locked their door or not.

The next morning they walked desolately over to the Paihia market, where Maisie and Myles had set up their stall. Paintings, postcards and greetings cards covered the trestle table.

'Good morning girls! Why are you all so glum on such a lovely day?' called out Maisie, waving at them.

In between sobs, Gaila told her what had happened. Myles, hearing her sad story, came over and put his arms around her.

'Hey, that's really bad luck. Can't trust anyone nowadays. How about you give me hand selling my paintings?'

Gaila nodded. At least it would keep her mind off losing her money. By lunch time, Myles had sold four paintings. In those few hours, Gaila learnt that he was an agricultural scientist working in Nelson, at the Agricultural Institute which had been set up by his great-great uncle.

'But as you can see, painting is my first love,' he admitted to Gaila. 'I wish I didn't have to go back to Nelson tomorrow. I'd really love to live here and paint instead.'

Maisie overheard the last bit of his conversation.

'You wouldn't be able to earn a decent living here in this small village,' she said. 'Keep it as a hobby, that's my advice.'

'I've never heard of Nelson, what's it like there?' asked Nina.

'Oh you Sydney people! There are other places in the world you know!' Myles laughed good-naturedly. 'Why don't you all come back with me and I'll be your tour guide?'

'Thanks, but we've made plans to go to Wellington next,' said Nina.

Gaila turned away, disappointed that she couldn't go with her friends.

'Look Gail, I know that we haven't known each other for very long, but you are very welcome to come back to Nelson with me tomorrow,' said Myles. 'I'm sure that my uncle Ed won't mind putting you up in the sleep out room at the back of his house.'

Gaila hesitated, not sure what she should do. 'I, I don't really know, if I should. What will your uncle think about it? I mean, you've just met me.'

'Don't worry, Uncle Ed is used to me bringing people home. I, I don't mean I bring back women home all the time, if that's what you're thinking. I mean, I make friends easily and he likes the company of young people.'

'But where are your parents?' asked Gaila.

'Oh, they live in Sydney. They're always on about how I should be grateful that Uncle Ed offered me a job in Nelson.'

Gaila finally agreed to Myles' suggestion and parted with her friends the next day, but only after Myles had written down his address and telephone number, because they told him in no uncertain terms that were going to check up on Gaila every few days. Just to make sure she was alright.

'Girls! I promise. I'm not Jack the Ripper!' laughed Myles.

On the way, Gaila asked Myles about how his Uncle Ed had come to be in charge of the Nelson Agricultural Institute.

'Just before the war, Uncle Ed's father, Thomas, was in charge of the Seed Research section there.'

'And what about before that?'

'Before that, his father David Smythe left a vast fortune and land to the city of Nelson with which to establish a research institute, because he was interested in the development of agriculture in New Zealand. You see, the land around Nelson reminded him of his ancestral home in Yorkshire.'

'Really? Land was important to both our families. My grandparents came from a tiny village in Lithuania,' said Gaila. 'But no one in our family is rich. They came to Australia with just a suitcase each.'

'Must have been hard for them,' Myles sympathized. 'One of my other ancestors was a convict, who was transported for stealing a loaf of bread to feed his children. Anyway, if we want to get back to Nelson, we'll have to make an early start tomorrow, it will take us a few hours to get there.'

Gaila wondered whether Myles was pulling her leg. A few hours, make that twenty-four hours! The next morning, Maisie waved them off with a huge packet of cheese and chutney sandwiches, a flask of strong black tea and a few apples and oranges.

'You'll need a little bit of sustenance on your journey,' she said as she hugged them goodbye at the bus stop to go to Albany. Three hours later, Myles and Gaila emerged and stretched their legs.

'Look! There's the bus to the Auckland train station!' yelled Myles. 'Quick! If we miss it, it will take ages for another one to come along!'

At least that was a short trip thought Gaila, as they arrived at the station. Surely it wouldn't be much further. However, she was in for a huge shock! The train trip to Wellington took ten hours! She dozed on and off, leaning on Myles' shoulder as the scenery whizzed past. Myles had his sketchpad out and from time to time, showed Gaila his drawings of mountains and people he saw along the way. It was four o'clock by the time the train pulled into Wellington.

'Are we there yet?' asked Gaila hopefully.

'Ah, not quite. We now have to catch a ferry to Picton on the South Island.'

'Good grief,' whispered Gaila, 'I'll be dead by the time we get there!'

'No, you won't. I'll look after you!' laughed Myles. 'Look! There's Picton, we're nearly there!'

Gaila woke up with a start. She'd fallen asleep again against Myles, lulled by the gentle rocking of the waves and hoped that she hadn't been snoring.

'Just as well that the water's calm today,' Myles told her. 'Otherwise, you'd be turning a most unattractive shade of green or heaving over the rails.'

Once they'd got off the ferry, Myles announced that there was one more bus to catch and then they'd be home.

'Are you really sure? Not pulling my leg are you?'

'Trust me! We're nearly there!'

Sure enough, Gaila saw a road sign that said Nelson. She felt sick with fatigue and was trying very hard not to fall asleep again.

When they finally arrived in Nelson, they were greeted by Uncle Ed.

'Hullo, hullo! What have we got here?'

'Hi Uncle Ed, this is my friend Gail from Sydney. I told her that it would be alright with you if she stayed with us for a few days.'

'Not a problem. I bet both of you could do with a good feed first. Lucky I've got some beef stew left. Made a mountain of it yesterday. Thought you'd be back soon enough.'

After supper and in the back room, she actually felt more relaxed and happier than she had been in a long time. Her parents' divorce had taken a toll on her, and for years she had always felt responsible for looking after her younger brother Paul. She knew that her other brother Max was doing all right in Western Australia.

But after two more nights of eating Uncle Ed's stew, Gaila offered to cook. She missed fresh vegetables and fruit.

'Look, it's the least I can do to say thank you for putting me up,' she told Myles and his uncle.

The three of them fell into an easy rhythm, and she liked the cheerful relationship that Myles had with his uncle Ed. They always included her in their bantering and whatever else they were doing. Once Myles and Ed had gone to work at the Institute, Gaila would make her way to the shops to see what bargains she could buy with the money Ed gave her to make dinner each night. For her first dinner, she bought a cabbage, carrots, tomatoes and some lean minced pork and veal.

'What are you making us for tea my dear?' asked Ed curiously.

'Cabbage rolls, just the way my mother does,' answered Gaila as she plunged the cabbage leaves into boiling water. 'Have you got a bit of rice somewhere? I forgot to buy some this morning.'

'Here you go, do you want me to cook some for you?' offered Myles. 'I can cook rice.'

'Thanks, but I usually just put a few spoons of uncooked rice into the meat mixture, it will cook with the meat.'

Myles watched Gaila turn a few basic ingredients into a meal he'd never eaten before. His mother usually boiled the life out of cabbage or made an Irish dish with cabbage and potatoes called *colcannon*. Before serving, Gaila went outside and picked a few red geraniums and arranged them in a little vase she found under the sink.

The next night she made a goulash and served it with cauliflower and broccoli polonaise.

'Who'd would have thought to combine cauliflower and broccoli together? Looks like a mash doesn't it?' said Ed admiringly. 'I just love that melted cheese on the top.'

'We usually just boil some frozen peas and carrots,' admitted Myles.

'Are you sure you don't want to can stay here with us forever?' said Ed with a twinkle in his eye. 'That roast chicken you made tonight with apple sauce and roast vegies sure beats anything me or Myles can turn out! I'd give you a job as a cook any day!'

Ed wasn't young any more, but he wasn't blind. He certainly noticed the way his nephew's eyes lit up whenever Gaila walked into the room. After work, Myles would often go for a drive with Gaila or take a walk around Nelson. Slowly they revealed their lives to each other.

'Do you know that one Guy Fawkes night my brother and me nearly burnt down the church hall next door to us?'

'Oh my God! What were you doing?' exclaimed Gaila.

'Oliver and me were making sky rockets and the grass caught alight. Luckily my Dad and the neighbours ran out with hessian bags and put it out, I couldn't sit down for days after the hiding he gave me!'

In her mind's eye Gaila saw her father hitting Paul and her with his strap. 'How old were you?'

'About ten.'

'Well, during the school holidays, I had to babysit my brothers while Mum and Dad went to work.'

'How old were you then?'

'Twelve. My parents figured that at that age I should be able to do the vacuuming, the washing and look after my brothers. Paul was six, but Max was only four. I must have got distracted by something and didn't realize that I'd forgotten to turn off the stove after breakfast. When I smelt smoke, I realized that Dad's precious coffee percolator had a hole burnt at the bottom.'

'Bummer!'

'You said it! I couldn't sit down for days either after Dad belted the daylights out of me!'

The next night, there was a phone call for Gaila.

'Hi! Just checking to see if you're still alive or not!' laughed Jana. 'Jackie and Nina say "hi!" too.'

'Thanks. So how's Wellington?'

'Really great. We're staying at the Waterloo Hotel by the docks. It's a backpackers' hostel. On Bunny Street! Can you believe it? What a funny name for a street! The train station is just opposite.'

'So what am I missing out in Wellington? Myles and I just passed through it on the way to Nelson.'

'Well we've been to Katherine Mansfield's house, the writer you studied. Then St Paul's Cathedral.'

'Gothic style, right?'

'You'd love it Gaila. It's got the most beautiful stained glass windows. We've also been swimming at Oriental Bay. Tomorrow we're going on the ferry to Matiu/Somes Island. It used to be a POW camp during World War One and Two. Imagine that!'

'Well you girls have certainly been busy. I miss you all, you know.'

'And Gaila, guess what?'

'What Jana? Tell me.'

'And, we met these three really cute guys from England. They're earning some money working at the pub we're staying at.'

'Well, well, well! Don't tell me, but I'm willing to bet $5, that you fancy one of them! Right?' Gaila asked slyly.

'Mmm, maybe I do,' replied Jana cheekily. 'They're planning to go to Sydney next, but they need to work a bit longer to save the airfare. If not, they reckon they'll get a cheap fare on a freighter. So tell me, how are things working out for you with Myles? Any developments we should know about?'

'Actually we're getting on really great, but there's nothing exciting to report yet.'

'Okay then. If you don't hear from us, we'll see you back in Sydney, okay?'

After a week in Nelson, Gaila thought that she should really get back home to Sydney. She didn't want Myles and Ed to think that she was taking advantage of their hospitality. Again, she and Myles had to make the trip to Wellington to fly back to Sydney, because even though Nelson had an airport, they only had flights within New Zealand. At the departure lounge, she felt her throat tighten as she tried to hold back her tears from Myles.

She took a deep breath and said, 'I guess that this is goodbye. They're calling my flight. Thanks for everything Myles. I will repay you for the buses and trains and ferry when I get back to work in the café.'

She held out her hand. Instead of shaking her hand, Myles gathered her against his chest. 'I don't know why, but it feels like we've known each other forever. You'll write to me won't you?' He kissed her cheek first, then swept her off her feet with a passionate kiss. Gaila felt her head whirl as she kissed him back. She let out a contented sigh.

'Oh Myles, I was hoping that you felt the same way as I do. But if I stay here any longer, I'll never get on this plane.'

They parted reluctantly and Gaila felt as if her heart would break. How could it be possible that she had fallen in love with someone she'd only known for a few weeks?

Myles watched her long blonde hair swish behind her and knew that he didn't want anyone else to have her but him. He would have to make some difficult decisions and knew that he'd have to stand up to his father.

A few weeks later, it was as if Gaila's holiday had been just a dream. She'd started on her librarianship course, and from time to time she would meet her friends at one of Sydney's pubs and they'd reminisce about their New Zealand adventures.

To her great surprise, Gaila received a beautifully hand painted card of the Russell foreshore in the mail.

Hi Gaila,

Just writing to let you know that I've quit my job in Nelson and that I'm coming back to Sydney. You were right in telling me to follow my dreams. I've enrolled in a Fine Arts course. I'll have to go back to live with Mum and Dad in Concord until I find a part time job.

Uncle Ed still talks about you, saying what a delightful young lady you were. (And I agree with him, of course!) Anyway, I was hoping that you'll go out with me. I know that there was this spark between us. I hope that I'm not too late and that you haven't got yourself a boyfriend. You didn't mention one to me, but you never know. I want to be sure that you're free to see me. As soon as I've settled back in Sydney, I'll give you a call.

PS. I hope that you like the card, it reminds me of the first time we met at Maisie's house near the pier.

Lots of love,

Myles. xxxxx

As soon as Gaila finished reading the letter, she let out a big whoop and danced around the room. She rang Jana hoping that she'd be home, so that she could tell her the good news.

'See! We knew that he really, really liked you,' she said. 'I bet you $10 that there'll be wedding bells before the end of the year!'

'Aren't you getting ahead of yourself? I mean, he's just asked me out, he hasn't proposed.'

'Oh he will,' replied Jana. 'He's not a user, he's a keeper, I can tell.'

'You are doing what?' Ella yelled, almost choking on her sauerkraut, when Gaila told her that Myles had proposed to her one evening at Doyle's restaurant.

'You're making a big mistake, mark my words!' Ella said shaking her finger at her daughter. 'He's not one of us. Aren't any of the Lithuanian boys here in Sydney good enough for you? You know very well that Mrs. Kustas and I have been planning for you to marry her son Vince. How can you betray me like this?'

'Mama, I was born in Australia, not Lithuania! Besides, Vince isn't interested in me one bit. He loves guzzling beer, smoking and playing poker.'

'But Gaila, we don't know this Myles character or his parents, or where they live. What kind of people are they?'

'Oh mama, don't be so old fashioned. Agnes and Edward are Catholics just like us.' She didn't want to tell her mother that she felt awkward and inadequate when Myles had first introduced her to his parents after they became engaged. Their smart home in Concord contrasted with her grandparents' little house in Bankstown.

'Well one thing is for sure. I am not going to the wedding if your father and that tart Elvyra are going to be there. I won't be humiliated in front of the whole community. And you can be sure that your grandparents won't go either. They'll support me, you'll see!'

'But grandma Rasa and grandpa Bronius said that they'd come.'

'I don't care. They never did approve of me marrying Al.'

'Please listen to me, mama. We only want a small wedding. Just our two families and our closest friends. Not the whole litho community. Myles and I will organise it. His mother said she'd make my wedding dress and the cake.'

'Besides, if Myles' parents are strict Catholics they won't approve of me. I'm a divorcee,' Ella said with a worried look. 'And as for your wedding cake, your grandmother Renata will have a fit. She'd definitely want to make a huge *Napoleonas* for you.'

'Mama, don't worry, it will only be a small wedding, I promise. If you don't want papa there, we won't invite him, ok. We haven't seen him for years. Please Mama, don't get yourself all worked up.'

'It's not what I dreamt of for my only daughter. I wanted you to have a big, white wedding, with lots of bridesmaids, with your father walking you down the aisle, our Lithuanian priest officiating. You know, the works! But who would have thought that my life would have turned out to be such a mess! I certainly won't come to your wedding if your father's invited. What will the other Lithuanian ladies in the choir say?'

'Mama, enough stressing! I don't care about that sort of thing. Myles and I were thinking of having a marriage celebrant down on the beach at Watson's Bay. Just casual. I don't want some big white meringue wedding dress. Then maybe a few canapés and cocktails at Doyles after.'

'I can't afford to pay for a big reception at Doyles, you know that.'

Renata came in and sat down. 'Why don't we invite Myles and his parents over for dinner here? I'll make some traditional Lithuanian dishes and then we'll all have a friendly chat about your wedding reception. Maybe we could agree to just pay for our own guests. How about that?'

A few days after Myles' parents had been over for dinner, Gaila received a card in the mail. She opened it up to see an unfamiliar script.

Dear Gail,

I am sending you this card to welcome you into our family. Even though you are a foreigner, at least you and your family are Catholics and we can see that you love our son Myles very much. We are sorry that your parents are divorced, but after your grandmother's dinner, we can see that your mother is a decent woman. I want to tell you again, that you are very welcome at our house at any time. Even though we were disappointed that Myles gave up his well-paid job in Nelson, we understand that he must follow his heart and make a life together here in Sydney with you. Please call us Mum and Dad. Wishing you both every happiness on your wedding day. I hope that you will like the dress I am making for you and don't worry about the wedding cake. I was not offended when your grandmother said that she wanted to make a special one for you. I am sure that it will be very nice.

Lots of love from
Agnes and Edward Smythe.

Gaila was sorry that Jana and Eric were unable to make it to her wedding. Their honeymoon in London sounded so romantic. Who would have thought that they'd both find Mr. Right in New Zealand, of all places? Myles and Gaila ended up having a simple wedding ceremony with a celebrant at sunset at Watson's Bay. They even wrote their own special vows. Myles' brother, Oliver, was his best man, and his sister Eileen was one of the bridesmaids along with Gaila's friends Nina and Jackie. They didn't invite Al, because Ella got so worked up that Gaila thought she'd have a heart attack. Anyway, he hadn't bothered to contact either Paul or Gaila since the divorce and besides, they didn't know exactly where he was living.

Myles' parents didn't want to stand in the sand with their finery, so they sat on chairs overlooking the sea along with Ella and her family. Gaila didn't know whether she was seeing things or not, but for one minute, she thought she saw a red sports car. Then she blinked and it was gone. She wondered whether her father had really been there. She knew that Myles' parents were disappointed that they didn't get married in a church, but after all it was their wedding. In the end, it was just the two families at the reception. A few champagnes and nibbles. Myles and Gaila were still on a tight budget, so they drove across to the Barossa Valley in South Australia for the honeymoon, staying in a delightful, family run hotel, set amongst the vineyards. Afterwards, they spent a few days at another hotel overlooking Glenelg beach, eating fish and chips on the foreshore at sunset. That was the first time Gaila had tasted shark or 'flake' as the locals called it. Her cousin Rokas had rung her to wish her every happiness for her married life, but said that he didn't want to intrude on her honeymoon, when she asked him if he wanted to meet them for a quick coffee in Jetty Road.

They agreed to catch up when he was recording his next album in Sydney later in the year.

'Are you happy darling?' asked Myles as he kissed her, while they were strolling along the Glenelg jetty, watching the fishermen and some high-spirited teenagers diving off the end. 'One day I'll buy you a huge diamond engagement ring to replace the amber one you have now, to show you just how much I love you.'

Gaila kissed him back. '*Aš tave myliu* - I love you. And I just adore my beautiful ring that we discovered at that pawnbroker's shop at Kings Cross.'

'I agree, your ring is totally unique!'

'Do you think that we can come back here one day, Myles? It's so peaceful compared to the hustle and bustle of Sydney.'

'Hey, maybe someday, when we have our first child, I'll buy you a diamond eternity ring. Now, tell me. Do you regret not having a big church wedding?'

'Myles! Don't you ever think that! I want you to know that I was very happy with my blue, chiffon dress that your mum made. A posy of native flowers from mama's garden meant much more to me that a big expensive bouquet from some fancy Double Bay florist.'

They still had a long drive back to Sydney where Myles had been successful in obtaining a position lecturing in Modern Art, whilst Gaila worked as an library assistant at the Sydney University Library. Feeling queasy some months afterwards, Gaila discovered that she was pregnant and gave birth to a tiny girl she called Alana and a few years later, a very active little boy called Ray appeared in their lives. During the time she was at home with her babies, Gaila completed a jewellery-making course and found that she was able to contribute to the family finances in a way she enjoyed.

There was always lots of excitement whenever Alana and her family flew down to Sydney from Queensland for a visit. Where had all those years gone when her children were babies and their lives were a never ending round of nappies, teething and childhood illnesses? Ella would just say, ' And this too, shall pass,' whenever Gaila rang her for advice.

Now, she fussed about getting their rooms organized and launched into a frenzy of baking sweet treats for her grandchildren, as well as huge quantities of bacon buns and *koldūnai* that she stacked into her big freezer.

On a hot summer morning, Alana was helping her mother make *vinegretas* before meeting her friends, the Wardles, at the Royal Botanical Gardens.

'Are we putting any diced beetroot in this potato salad?' she called out to her mother who was busy chopping up hard-boiled eggs.

'Do Zoe and Jack like beetroot?' asked Gaila.

'No they don't, sorry mum. They won't eat beetroot at all!'

'Hmm, must take after Hugh's side of the family. All Lithuanians are born loving beetroot, that's a well-known fact,' replied Ella in a teasing tone.

'What about dill?'

'No probs mum, they like dill. I always use it when I miss you and dad.'

'Ok then, we'll give the kids their own small bowl of potato salad without the beetroot and we'll put in the beetroot in ours, right?'

'Thanks, mum. It will taste awesome with the cold chicken and your bean salad when we get home today from the park.'

After Ella and Alana had finished making the potato salad, it was 30°C outside and it was only ten o'clock. Alana was glad that the two families had stayed in touch from the time when she lived in Sydney. The Wardles were going to put their bikes on the train since they lived in the Blue Mountains. Alana's friend Jill confided to her, that it would be easier to cope with her four energetic sons on the train for two hours, rather than have them fighting amongst themselves whilst she was trying to drive. By two o'clock, the temperature had climbed to 43C and Jill was complaining that they should have met at Manly Beach, even though it would have meant putting all their bikes on the ferry at Circular Quay. Alana disagreed, since she didn't want her children sunburnt on such a hot day and afterwards she'd have to have them all troop sand through her mother's house. She noticed that Zoe was totally over-whelmed by the four garrulous Wardle boys kicking a soccer ball. Even Jack's personality changed once he was with the Wardles.

'You're not playing with us! You've got girl germs!' one of the Wardle boys sneered at Zoe.

'Yeah! Why don't you go back to your Barbie dolls, you baby,' sniggered Jack.

'We don't like stupid little girls!' yelled the youngest Wardle.

When Jill finally decided to leave, Alana was relieved and thought to herself that she no longer had much in common with her. The four boys had been very rude to their mother, demanding that she buy them icecream and drinks the whole time they were there.

When Alana finally got back to Manly Beach, she was exhaust-ed, so Myles suggested that he could take Jack to see the latest *Star Wars* movie.

'Awesome!' yelled Jack. 'Can dad come with us?'

'Wouldn't miss it for the world, buddy,' replied Hugh. 'Hans Solo is still my favourite.'

'My friend told me that Finn the Storm Trooper was the best,' answered Jack.

Zoe was too young to go to such a film, so Gaila put on the *Ice Age* DVD that she knew was one of Zoe's favourite movies.

Peace reigned for the next two hours while Gaila and her daughter chatted and read their Tarot cards. Alana was happy that she'd drawn out the Sun card for her future, knowing that it was a good omen. When Gaila saw the Death card in her own reading, she made light of it, telling her daughter that the interpretation meant a new beginning for her.

The following day, Gaila, Alana, and Zoe decided to have morning tea at Rose Bay. Then Alana wanted to go into some of the dress shops that had fifty percent off sales, whilst Gaila tried to keep an eye on Zoe who was getting more and more boisterous. Finally, Alana bought a smart, black cocktail dress to wear whenever she was called upon to do any wedding photography.

Afterwards, Gaila's son Ray joined them for dinner. At eight, Hugh's father came over with his holiday house keys because the next day, Alana and Hugh were off to stay overnight at Bondi Beach to catch up with all their old school friends there.

'Come with us, have a break!' Alana said to her parents.

'Thanks sweetheart, but we reckon that we'd just be like shags on a rock. You enjoy yourself and have a good time with your friends. Besides, we've got a gallery to run,' replied Myles.

The next morning, the formidable Denise and her fifth husband Enrico Fernandez were on Gaila's doorstep at 8 a.m. Zoe was overjoyed, telling the speechless Gaila how she'd only met her long lost great-aunt recently.

'She's going to take me for a swim in her pool at her big Vaucluse mansion and then take me to Bronte Beach to see my little cousin Chloe at their beach house. Won't that be great?'

More and more plans were made. On Monday, Hugh's dad, Bob, wanted to take Zoe and Jack to Shark Bay. At times like this, Gaila felt like she could do with a personal assistant. She typed up a timetable and stuck it on the fridge.

Finally, Denise brought back Zoe at 10 a.m. the next day, after Gaila had phoned her twice to ask when they were coming back. Zoe was firing on all cylinders. She revealed that they'd been shopping at one of the big shopping malls and her aunty had bought her new sneakers, a fairy dress, a new Barbie, a Barbie quilt cover, Barbie stickers and a huge packet of lolly snakes, and that she wouldn't need any dinner. When Denise finally said that she had to go, Zoe put on a tantrum, screaming how she was going to miss her new aunty. Denise smiled smugly at Gaila, then climbed into her Mercedes and with a royal wave, drove off.

Somehow Gaila had anticipated this scenario, even though it was the first time she'd met Denise. So she lead Zoe into her garden to look for the little toys that Myles had hidden amongst the cactus plants. By then Zoe had calmed down, so they had macaroni cheese in front of the TV as a special treat and watched the new *Cinderella* DVD that Denise had bought. Later they played dress ups and pretended that they were super rich ladies having afternoon tea on a yacht on Sydney Harbour. Gaila detected a touch of Denise's snobbery in granddaughter's speech. Then it was time for Zoe's bubble bath where she reprimanded all the toys floating there. After her bath, Zoe's eyes were drooping.

'Grandma, I've had it! Can we please just go to bed now!'

Gaila smiled, as she heard her daughter's voice. Then she snuggled up with her granddaughter in the queen size bed. Zoe found her second wind. So they had to sing all Zoe's favourite songs. When Myles returned from his Rotary Club meeting, he carried a sleeping Zoe back to her own bed. Turning to Gaila, he said with a cheerful wink, 'So, did my two favourite girls have a lovely day?'

'I'm exhausted Myles. Absolutely exhausted! Looking after kids is much harder at our age!'

Myles went out to the kitchen and made Gaila a cup of valerian tea. 'That should put you to sleep in no time,' he laughed as he snuggled in beside her. ' I still love you, even though we're not so young anymore.'

The next day Zoe announced to Gaila at breakfast that she loved her new great-aunt Denise more than anyone else. 'Just because you're my grandmother, doesn't mean I have to love you! Aunty Denise buys me heaps more things than you! So!'

Gaila reigned in her emotions, knowing that if she replied hastily, all hell could break loose. Instead, she breathed deeply, vowing that she wouldn't let a four year old get to her.

'I'm glad that you love your great aunt Denise,' she answered calmly. 'Buying you lots of things does not necessarily mean that she loves you more than we do.'

Zoe, seeing that she didn't get the reaction she'd hoped for, went into the lounge to watch the morning children's programmes. Gaila heard the front door bell chime.

'Myles, is that you? Did you forget something' she called. No one was there, but Gaila thought she could smell smoke.

A few months later Myles was driving to the clinic for his annual check-up. Halfway there, intense pains sliced through his chest, and he broke out in a cold sweat. Praying that he would reach the clinic in time, he tried to slow down his breathing. As he staggered to the counter, he managed to splutter out to the receptionist that he was having chest pains. Immediately, the nurse called the doctor who ordered an ECG and a test for diabetes. They took his blood pressure, temperature and Doctor Marr listened to his heart. He was asked if the pain had travelled to his arm or if he felt nauseous.

'The ECG looks normal,' said Doctor Marr, 'but by law I have to call an ambulance to take you into hospital for further blood tests to see if there's any damage to your heart.'

The receptionist rang Gaila, who, fearing the worst, drove as fast as she could to the clinic, after locking up the gallery.

'We've called an ambulance, but there won't be one available for an hour and a half,' the nurse announced. 'They said that you could take your husband into Sydney Hospital yourself, but Doctor Marr disagreed.'

'Mr Smythe, I know from experience, that unless a patient is admitted to hospital by ambulance, that there can be a lot of waiting around,' advised the doctor.

Gaila was truly thankful that the clinic was on the way to BALTIK, since all of the major hospitals were on that side of Sydney. She followed the ambulance into the emergency department, praying the whole time that Myles would be fine. She didn't want to imagine what she'd do if she lost him.

In the ambulance, the two paramedics were calm and efficient. One of them, a cheerful tall man called Dylan ran another ECG along the way and gave Myles a tiny aspirin that dissolved in his mouth, then told him what to expect in the hospital's emergency room.

Once Myles was wheeled into a cubicle, the hospital staff set up another ECG and took a blood test to check whether the enzyme was present to indicate a heart attack. Other tests were also done to check the state of his liver, pancreas and kidneys. The freezing air-conditioning in the building made him shiver with the contrast of the 40C summer heat outside. An orderly brought him a warm blanket. He closed his eyes and tried to push the thoughts of open-heart surgery out of his mind. Gaila prayed silently as her husband fell in and out of his drowsy state. 'Oh God, please don't let Myles die now,' she whispered to herself.

As if in a fog, Myles felt Gaila stroking his hand, reassuring him that he'd be fine. An orderly wheeled him into the radiology section to take an X-ray of his chest. More waiting. Gaila went into the Accounts office where she was given a bill for admittance to the hospital, and felt relieved that they had kept up their medical and ambulance insurance. Doctor Marr bulk billed for all his consultations at his clinic, and in Sydney especially, that was a huge saving.

A nurse asked Myles whether he could make it to the toilet by himself for a urine sample and thoughtfully provided another hospital gown for modesty's sake. Gaila glanced at her watch, noting they had been in the hospital for six hours. A new doctor who'd just clocked on, told her that there was one more blood test and ECG to do. On the small TV screen overhead, Gaila and Myles watch numerous travel shows about stately Georgian mansions in England, a walk around Dublin's Phoenix Park and a tour of Scotland based on an old travelogue by someone called Black. They talk about their children and the funny things they used to do when they were kids.

'Do you remember screaming "WHAT ARE YOU DOING?" at the top of your voice at Alana when she was about six?' asked Myles.

'I certainly do. I recall screaming "PUT THAT DOWN NOW!" even louder,' recalled Gaila.

'Oh yes, and then Alana turned to me and said she was just doing a little op. Smiling at me in her nurse's uniform, as if butter wouldn't melt in her mouth.'

'Can you believe that her little scissors were poised precariously over Ray's anatomy?'

'So I said to Alana, "No sweetheart, your little brother certainly doesn't need an operation today". I surprised myself at my calmness that day Myles, I can tell you.'

'Ha, ha, I admire you for that honey. Didn't Ray tell you that Alana said that it wouldn't hurt him one little bit?'

'Oh God! Our little Ray might have had nothing left, if I hadn't come a long in the nick of time. I guess he didn't realize that I saved him from a fate worse than death.'

'There's one thing that my mum always used to say 'Parents should never assume that things are fine when there is silence in a house, especially if you've got little kids.'

'Do you remember when Alana was sixteen and she wore her flip flops for her driving lesson?' asked Gaila. 'You sat next to her and said "What are you doing in those?'

'Chill out dad!' she told me, 'you know, in that bored teenage voice of hers.'

Gaila laughed. 'Oh yes! Then I heard an almighty crash! Bang! Right into our neighbour's Holden's bumper bar! Terrible. She confused the accelerator with the brake!'

'Sorry dad, it was a mistake! Too right it was Gail, a very expensive mistake. She didn't get any pocket money for a month after that!'

'Do you remember the time you decided to repaint our back deck, Myles?'

'Sure do. Came home from Bunnings and I started to paint, didn't I? The first coat was great. Clear and shiny. After it had dried, I thought I'd pop on another coat.'

'Yep, I was admiring your workmanship through the kitchen window, when I saw that the second coat looked rather white,' recalled Gaila.

'What are you doing? Yes, you yelled that at me through the kitchen window,' laughed Myles.

'And you yelled back that the first coat was fine, it would dry out fine and that I should stop stressing!' replied Gaila.

'Well, no, it didn't dry to a lovely finish. We couldn't work out what had happened. Perhaps the paint was faulty. Anyway, that's what I thought.'

'Did you remember to stir the paint?' Gaila asked.

'No, I'd forgotten. Remember how I spent days trying to sand back the areas that were white?'

At 6 p.m., a volunteer interrupted their reminiscences and brought them some sandwiches and tea. It was the first thing Myles had eaten or drunk since breakfast. Finally, a new doctor appeared, telling them that it wasn't heart attack, but probably an anxiety attack. Gaila was so relieved that she broke down and cried. Only then did she ring Ray, then Alana in Queensland. She certainly didn't want to worry them earlier on.

'Just as well you were been admitted on a Monday morning,' the doctor told them. 'If it had been a Friday night or on the week-end, you would have been here much longer. I suggest that you take a holiday as soon as possible.'

Gaila and Myles were grateful and thanked the medical staff as they left. They knew fully well, that on the weekends the doctors and nurses had countless drug overdoses and addicts out of control to deal with. Gaila thought that it was time that they went on a holiday. She'd seen so many big cruise ships come through Sydney Harbour, perhaps one day it would be their turn. That weekend she saw a competition for a cruise to Fiji in Sunday newspaper, so she thought that she would fill out the entry form and send it off.

Once Gaila had returned to work at BALTIK, after winning the competition, she arranged to have coffee with her best friend, Vizma.

'So tell me, what did you and Myles enjoy the most on your Pacific cruise?' asked Vizma, who was struggling on a post-graduate scholarship in Linguistics.

'Hmm, I have to say it was the food and the nightly entertainment,' Gaila replied, her eyes sparkling. She launched into her description.

'Tropical fruit was cut up in bite sized pieces every morning. You just strolled past the fresh muffins and croissants, all types of bacon, sausages, eggs and then I'd always linger at the huge display of smoked salmon.'

'Mmm, I just love salmon!' cooed Vizma, whose Latvian-born mother was well known in the Sydney multicultural network for her bacon buns and hospitality.

Gaila continued. 'You wouldn't believe it, but each morning we saw a little old lady dressed in black, piling on as much of that smoked salmon as she could fit onto her platter. You know the type you use to serve the Christmas turkey. Then she'd stagger back to her table. Her husband's eyes would light up, thinking that he'd get at least half of it.'

'Well and did he?

'No way! The old lady started shovelling the salmon into her mouth, whilst giving her husband a smirk now and then. She slapped his wrist with her butter knife, when he tried to spear a piece with his fork.'

'How greedy!' remarked Vizma.

'And do you know what she said to him? More for me! Can you believe it? Everyone was watching her, wondering how one little lady could eat so much!'

'I suppose that no sooner had you'd finished breakfast, it would be morning tea time?' laughed Vizma.

'You bet, it was hard to take. There'd be mounds of macaroons, fruit tarts, scones, donuts, and more tea and coffee.'

'Mmm, my guess is that a teensy, weensy, little fruit tart with fruit on the top is healthy, right?'

'You bet! Then before you knew it, it was lunch time!'

'Make me drool some more Gail! What did they serve for lunch?'

'Ok, are you ready for this? There were two varieties of soup, hamburgers, bratwurst and sauerkraut. Pizza, tortellini, gnocchi, spaghetti marinara, turkey breast wraps, all kinds of salads, four types of salad dressing, fried cat fish, grilled flounder. Chips, mashed potato, potato bake, roast beef or pork. Ruby jellies, quivering puddings, and kiwi fruit topped cheesecake squares all beckoned.'

'It sounds like food porn to me. I bet you needed a stroll after all that!'

'At three, Myles and I would go to the pool. Most people would be working on their suntans or reading their trashy novels, but the food court was usually packed once more with people stuffing their faces with afternoon tea.'

'Cruising sounds like an ideal retirement plan to me. I suppose after all that food you wouldn't need any dinner would you?'

'Oh yeah, it was a hard decision. Myles and I would agonize whether to go back to the food court for a smorgasbord of culinary delights or whether it would be better to go into the formal dining room with our fellow travellers, where there was portion control.'

'Portion control? Gail, you've described anything but portion control!'

'True, but you will love this next bit! Remember the little old lady I told you about?'

'The smoked salmon fanatic?'

'Yep, that's the one! Just as we were sitting down one night in the dining room, a familiar looking, little old lady keeled over at the next table. She was carried out on a stretcher.'

'Oh that's a shame. What happened to her? Heart attack?'

'Some sort of gastric attack. Ate too much smoked salmon. Anyway that's what the other diners told us afterwards. And guess what her husband said after they carried her off?'

'What?'

'*More for me*! Can you imagine that? *More for me*! I tell you, we all laughed so much that we nearly choked on our dinner!'

Vizma and Gaila laughed till tears ran down their faces and ordered another coffee. Vizma thought to herself that she might like to go on a cruise one day.

'And what about the nightly entertainment?' asked Vizma as she and Gaila started on their second latté. Gaila smiled as she told her friend about a musician whom she had dubbed "The Silver Fox".

'There was this Italian guy who played the keyboard every night in one of the lounges. He really thought that he was the handsomest man on the ship. He'd fling back his mane of silver hair and he used to flash his impossibly white teeth at the crowd.'

'A bit up himself was he?' remarked Vizma.

'You know, he smiled that white smile so hard, that women would giggle, and I mean giggle like a bunch of schoolgirls. Then he'd flex his fingers at his never-ending supply of admirers. He told us that he'd spent eighteen years playing on various cruise ships.'

'Oh God, what a boring life! Was it the same repertoire every night?'

'Sure was. Silver Fox would relax the crowd with "Memories", "Moon River", "Unchained Melody", "O Solo Mio" and then launch into "It's Now or Never".'

'I bet that got a few Elvis onto the dance floor!'

'You could request a song. But one night this woman sidled up to him in this really tight, black skirt that hugged the curves of her bottom with a vengeance.'

'Out for a good time, was she?'

'Absolutely. Her black hair flashed wildly about her face, then while he was playing "That's the way I like it", she gyrated right in front of him.'

'A bit of a dancing queen was she?'

'Mmm, you could say that. She was out to score with Silver Fox, that was pretty obvious to everyone, but he refused to acknowledge her.'

'Oh, so what did she do then?'

'Well our dancing queen led her daughter onto the dance floor and they danced up a storm to "Crocodile Rock", without any success.'

'This sounds like a TV reality show Gail. Did you go back the next night?'

'Vizma! Everyone went back the next night. Dancing Queen and the Silver Fox were on everyone's lips. This time, she wore very tight black pants and a tiny shimmery top with a mass of dazzling gold bangles! As soon as Silver Fox launched into 'Pretty Woman' she went up to some random guy and made him to dance with her.'

'Change of strategy obviously!' Vizma was really enjoying her chat with her friend.

'Well, you should have seen Dancing Queen bump and grind against Random Guy. He didn't know what hit him.'

'Do you think that he was aware that he'd been chosen as her hapless victim?'

'Maybe, maybe not. Dancing Queen looked as if she was out to demonstrate her repertoire of bedroom moves to the Silver Fox. I can tell you, she left nothing to the imagination! We could actually see the sweat pouring down this guy's face and running down the back of his shirt.'

'Don't walk away, hey!' sang Vizma and Gaila together, laughing.

'Don't laugh Vizma, because at that exact moment, the Dancing Queen shimmied up to Silver Fox. His eyes finally locked with hers.'

'So, did she get what she wanted?'

'I guess, because she danced triumphantly off the dance floor, tossing her mane and laughing like you wouldn't believe.'

'I bet that you all went back the next night to see what was going to happen next!'

'We sure did, but I'd better get back to BALTIK or Myles will think that I've been run over by one of those red Hop On and Off double decker tourist buses.'

Gaila had always loved working alongside her husband, in their small gallery tucked away in The Rocks area of Sydney. Years ago, before they had decided to rent the gallery space, Myles used to sell his vibrant, eye-catching paintings at the weekend markets, while she tried to sell her jewellery, in the hopes of catching the eyes of the thousands of tourists, who would flock there every weekend. One morning, a middle-aged woman in a brightly coloured caftan, bought two of Myles' watercolours of the Opera House and three of Gaila's chunky necklaces. She left her business card and said that they shouldn't waste their time at the markets. Instead they should consider having their own gallery.

'Do you really think so?' asked Myles. Privately he thought that they couldn't afford to give up their day jobs just yet. Maybe if they both worked part time, it could be done.

'Sure do,' the woman drawled. 'I've got to move back to San Francisco to look after my elderly folks, who can't manage any-more. The lease on my little place is coming up soon, if you're interested. It's just around the corner in George Street, you're wel-come to take a look when you're finished for the day.'

After packing up their unsold items, Gaila and Myles wandered up to 'Auld and Older', the shop that the woman had told them about. They saw a jumbled assortment of old plates, clothes and bric-à-brac in the window.

'It would need a major renovation and then we'd have to paint all the walls white, and after all that, it might be okay. We'll need a lot of natural light if it's going to be a gallery,' remarked Myles, who could see that from its location, it could become a successful business venture.

For a few years, Myles and Gaila kept working part time, until they decided to resign from their jobs. BALTIK gallery's paint-ings, picture framing and jewellery brought them a reasonable income, after they'd paid the rent. Alana was always trying to help, by advising her mother to sell her jewellery online as well.

'Come on mum, get with it!' Alana would joke.

'Why can't you sell your stuff online? I could create an awesome webpage for you, with some great photos, you know I could.'

Even though Alana had an excellent business sense as a photographer, Gaila tried to explain to her that most women wanted to try on jewellery, hold it against their skin, to see if the shape and colour suited them. Besides, she liked meeting the tourists who came in everyday from all corners of the world. Some would buy her jewellery, but many of the people who came off the huge cruise ships that berthed almost in front of her gallery at Circular Quay, would just take a cursory glance at the gallery's paintings and jewellery. They were too eager to be off on their Sydney walking tours, or the children bustled their parents out of the gallery impatiently, for their Taronga Park Zoo excursions. Others would just come in for a chat.

'Will they let us walk the koalas and ride the kangaroos?' were just some of the unusual questions that children asked Myles. Adults often asked Gaila if Australians kept their pet kangaroos in dog kennels. Sometimes, she'd put on a very serious face and tell them that yes indeed, her kangaroo and dog slept in the same kennel side by side. If Gaila had a dollar for every time she had heard that funny question, she'd be a millionairess. The more learned tourists would often point out that the Gallery's name BALTIK should be spelt with a "C". That was one of Myles' brain waves and it had certainly paid off. More often than not, once the customers had pointed out the so-called spelling error, they might buy a small painting, a touristy card of Sydney's landmarks, or one of Gaila's pendants or earrings. How often did she have to listen to them complaining amongst themselves that they could buy much cheaper jewellery during their cruise ship's sale days or that jewellery was one sixth of the price in Asia. Then there were those smug young mothers who informed her that babies' amber teething necklaces could be bought so much cheaper online from China. Worse by far, were the stingy, self-righteous husbands who'd complain to Myles, that their wives had enough baubles, to sink a god-dammed cruise ship! Then they'd wink conspiratorially at Myles, daring him to disagree with them.

'Never mind, hon,' the wives would whisper to each other, 'we can always pop into those cute little craft shops when we get back to the States.'

Sometimes Gaila couldn't but help overhearing bits of conversation, like the recent one between two women. One was complaining about a relative from overseas who'd stayed with her for seven weeks and didn't lift a finger to help out even once, because she had fake nails. The other one remarked, 'Honey, visitors are like fish, they go off after three days!'

Nearly every day, Gaila and Myles caught the Manly ferry together to travel across to Circular Quay. On other days, Gaila would work on creating her exquisite pieces of silver jewellery in the studio room they'd built onto the back of the house. Luckily, Gaila didn't get seasick, because if the swells were heavy, the ferry would heave up and down near The Heads and some passengers would turn a most unattractive shade of green. She never got tired of seeing the Opera House as they turned towards Circular Quay, its roof like the sails of an old sailing ship. On the way to BALTIK, they'd stop for a morning coffee at one of their favourite cafes along George Street.

'Hi Gail, how's business?' the café owners would greet her as she'd walk past. Some days if there weren't many customers, Gaila would slip away to have a coffee and catch up on the local gossip at Darling Harbour with her friend Vizma, who worked at the Maritime Museum. She'd become friends with Vizma, or Vi, as she was commonly known, when they had worked at Sydney University Library. They had bonded over their common Baltic heritage and striking resemblance to each other.

Once a month, they would volunteer at the Wayside Chapel, feeding the homeless. Gaila would entertain Vizma with a description of Myles, who in his very polite BBC voice, would sometimes give convoluted directions to tourists looking for that 'Oprah House,' or when they asked for the nearest McDonald's.

'Amazing!' she'd remark to Vizma. 'Can you believe that these people have just to come from a cruise ship's all-you-can-eat buffet breakfast? Where can they possibly fit all that food?'

'Ha, ha! Do you remember that time we flew to Bali for a holiday?' said Vizma.

'I sure do!' replied Gaila, recalling the sumptuous buffet breakfasts at their hotel.

'You know, back then, I had never been overseas, let alone to an Asian country.'

Their hotel, opposite Legian Beach, was very attractive from the outside, but once inside there was a strange smell coming from the drain at the bottom of their bathroom floor. Vizma, who was a seasoned traveller, proceeded to pour some disinfectant down the drain and explained that the hotel's sewerage system was very basic and told Gaila blithely that as long as they used the hotel's toilets and restaurants they wouldn't get sick. Having been forewarned by the hotel manager about not eating anything that was uncooked or already peeled, they set off on their walk into Kuta Beach to explore the shops. The day was hot and humid, so within an hour, they knew that they needed to buy a cold drink and sit for a while, to recover in a cafe that had overhead fans or air-conditioning if they were lucky. They ordered a Coke each and a bag of Krupuk, the local prawn crackers. That way, they reasoned, they'd be drinking from a bottle that hadn't been tampered with. Both had been warned about the water bottle scam where locals filled up used bottles with water from their taps and glued the caps back on so it would look like you were buying pure water. As anyone knows, Coke has caffeine in it, which is a diuretic, so by the time the two women had finished their drinks, they were in desperate need of a rest room. The café owner pointed them towards a door marked WC. Once Gaila got inside, she nearly died of shock. There in the middle of a concrete floor, was the first squat toilet she'd ever come across. It was basically a hole in the ground. Next to it was an ancient concrete sink full of water with an old saucepan next to it. No toilet paper. She did what she had to do and came outside with a disgusted look on her face.

'So now you know why so many tourists get Bali Belly!' Vizma chortled.

'Well at least our gallery's toilets are clean,' Gaila replied, and went on to tell Vizma about the young mothers who would drag in squirming children into her gallery, approaching Gaila at the counter and asking in hushed tones if they could use the restroom.

'My kid's busting to go, and if we can't use your WC this second, he'll wet his pants!' The problem was, that their gallery had to share the toilet with four other shops and those owners weren't as charitable as she was, when she'd hand over the key to a grateful parent.

'Why don't you just direct them to McDonalds?' they'd say, shaking their heads in annoyance. 'We haven't got time to keep going in there and mopping up all these tourist kids' messes off the floor!'

One afternoon, as Gaila was putting out some of her Tiger Eye necklaces for her window display, she heard a frantic whisper, 'Excuse me! Excuse me miss!'

Gaila looked up from the display and saw a stately elderly woman, dressed in a well- tailored black and white linen suit, hobbling towards her with an intricately carved walking stick.

'Good afternoon madam, how can I help you?'

'My purse has been stolen, right out of my handbag!' the old lady said in an upper class English accent.

'In this gallery?'

'I'm not sure. You see I'm going all the way round.'

'I beg your pardon?'

'Got on in Southampton. England you know. Going all the way round!'

Gaila was quite perplexed, but she continued to be polite. 'How can I help you?'

'I need to contact Barclays, to get some money. Only half way round, you know.'

'Oh, I see. Would you like me to phone a branch of Barclays?'

'That is ever so kind. Thank you. Would you dear?'

Gaila looked in the telephone directory for a Sydney branch of the bank. Fortunately, there was one in Oxford Street, but it would be a long hike for the old lady in front of her.

'I've located a branch madam, but you'll need a taxi to get there.'

'Give me the phone dear.' The woman caught her breath before launching into a lengthy conversation.

'Oh, hello old chap. This is Lady Broadford. Yes, I'm on the Queen Victoria cruise ship that's just docked in Circular Quay. It's huge, one of the biggest in the world. Yes, I'm a passenger on it. They even upgraded me to my own suite. I travel a lot. What?

Why am I ringing? I've lost my purse. Yes, that's right. No, I don't know where I lost it! There are pick pockets everywhere! I'm an old lady. Yes, of course I'll need a new credit card today and some travellers' cheques. Maybe some cash as well. We sail tomorrow. Yes! That's why I'm ringing you, young man! You can do that? Brilliant!'

The old lady turned to Gaila. 'They're sending round a taxi in a few minutes. You just have to know how to deal with those little bank clerks. Tiresome little people.'

Ten minutes later, a taxi appeared outside BALTIK and Lady Broadford hobbled out. 'Goodbye dear,' she said, waving at Gaila in a stately fashion. 'You've been ever so kind. Do look me up when you're in England next. Come in July. My rose garden is ever so lovely at that time of the year.'

When she had gone Gaila and Myles dissolved into fits of laughter.

'Oh my dear,' Gaila said to her husband mimicking the old lady's accent.

'Shall we take a trip to England next year? Do you fancy going on the Queen Victoria? All the way round?'

'Oh darling, yes! But won't it be frightfully expensive?' replied Myles in his best imitation of Lady Broadford's accent.

'Of course darling, but I'm sure that our friend the duchess will pay. Oh, won't it be ever so nice, to be in England again!'

In the middle of that month, Gaila's family were all gathered on her front patio, looking at the sun set over Manly beach. As she sipped on her glass of chardonnay, Gaila smiled fondly at Alana who'd flown down again from Queensland to take the wedding photos for an old school friend. Paul and Gemma had flown in from Hobart and her son Ray and his family had come as well.

Hugh came up and put his arm around Alana. 'You haven't forgotten what we agreed on before we came here have you?' he whispered to her.

'What was that?' Alana whispered back.

'We agreed that we'd go and visit all of my side of the family,' Hugh reminded Alana. His family was five times larger than Alana's, and he wondered how they'd fit everyone in before they flew back to Noosa .

'We could spend a day with each of them or we could all meet on the foreshore here overlooking Manly Beach and have a barbeque,' suggested Alana, who wanted to spend more time with her mother and friends in Sydney. Just the airfares to and from Queensland put a dent in the family's budget. Then there were more renovations scheduled for their home, which was a typical Queenslander, wooden two-storey house in Noosaville. They'd bought it because the river was across the road and Hugh thought that it would be handy for walks and kicking a football with Jack. Once Jack saw a carpet python slithering across the grass and ran home in a panic. From that day onwards, Hugh always went with him.

'But Aunty Gemma promised me that we were going to have a girls' day out!' Zoe yelled out as she pulled up her aunt off the deck chair to dance with her around the patio. Gemma had promised to look after her whilst Gaila and Alana went off to have foils put in their hair at the Manly Beach Salon.

'Come on Aunty Gemma, get up and dance with me!' Zoe sang her favourite song and turned cartwheels across the lounge room.

Ray's three year old daughter Ruby was half asleep on the bean bag, with Mr. Meow, Gaila's black cat, curled up protectively beside her. It had taken Ruby a while to get used to him. At first she wasn't very keen on the way he rubbed himself against her little legs, or tried to get her to play with him by pawing at her wrists.

'No, no, no!' she'd scream. 'Go away!'

'You can always borrow Angie,' Zoe told her uncle Ray. 'She's really good with little kids.'

'I'm not sure whether your cat would like to fly from Noosa to Sydney in the cargo hold of a plane,' joked Ray. 'She'd get very lonely, wouldn't she?'

Gemma had suggested to Elle that she buy Ruby a toy cat to play with, but Mr. Meow persisted with his affections and won Ruby over in the end. If no one was watching, she'd slip him a bit of Gaila's chicken liver paté or a bit of salmon under the table.

Gemma certainly knew how to handle little children. She'd had plenty of experience in her previous job as a primary art teacher, in the little country school where she'd first met Paul. It was only after the government had closed down their school and many others, did they decide to open up their bookshop. She remembered Gaila telling them how she'd found Mr. Meow a long time ago, lying helpless in the park across the road from their house. He'd obviously crawled there, after being been hit by a bike rider on the promenade. When Gaila first peered at him, he felt a jolt of recognition. He reached deep into her mind, and was sure that he knew this woman from before. Gaila reminded him of his beloved Kristina, especially her eyes, which were the same shade of topaz blue. Her blonde hair was the same colour as well.

At first, Gaila thought that this beautiful black cat was going to die in her arms, but she scooped him up and drove him to the local vet who set his broken leg in plaster. After that, they had adopted him and christened him Mr. Meow, because he'd whimpered so pitifully. He took up residence on Ray's bed, but sometimes he'd jump onto Alana's as well. During the night, Gaila would sometimes feel a heavy sensation on the back of her legs as she was sleeping on her left side. Then she'd hear Mr. Meow licking himself or his deep purring and somehow, she'd feel instantly comforted. Myles would only get annoyed if Mr Meow settled in between them.

'That's it! You're going back to your beanbag!' he'd admonish the protesting cat, who felt it was his duty to protect his mistress. Oh, yes! He'd been quite happy to move into their house, earning his keep by overseeing Gaila at work in her studio or guarding his new home. Mr. Meow was deliriously happy to have somehow found his old mistress again. He perched high up on the pillars of a sandstone fence, spitting at any passing by dogs who displeased him.

It was soon after this visit to Sydney, that Alana and Hugh noticed that Zoe had developed almost a new personality. If you asked her what she wanted for breakfast, she was more than likely to say, 'Bumble bees on toads.' Other mornings she might request 'Gizzards of gnats and donkeys' toes.' It was the same at lunch and dinner. After three months of this behaviour, Alana decided to ask her friend Amanda who was a child psychologist and specialised in sand play therapy, to see if she could find a solution.

As they approached her apartment in the main street of Noosa, Alana tried to explain to Zoe why they were going to visit Amanda.

'She's got some really great toys for you to play with and likes helping children.'

Having been welcomed inside, Alana greeted Amanda, who was in her thirties and smartly dressed in classic vintage clothes that she'd bought at one of the Sunday markets. There was a photo of her and her three children at Noosa's Main Beach on her desk. Her office shelves were lined with hundreds of different figurines ranging from Snow White to Shrek. A square coffee table, filled with sand at the bottom, covered with a clear glass top, was in the middle of her consulting room.

'Hi there Zoe, how's school going?'

'It's okay, I guess. Is that photo at Main Beach in Noosa?'

'Yes it is Zoe. Do you like going there?'

'Yes I do, but mum and dad prefer Sunshine beach near the Surf Club. It's not as crowded there. Sometimes we go to Pelican Beach to see the fish and the pelicans, but Jack can't surf there.'

'Well it's lovely to see you and your mum again. My children are at still at hockey practice. Why don't you take some figures that you like off the shelves and make a picture in the sand of your family for me?'

Zoe considered her options, taking her time to decide whether her father should be Darth Vader or Superman. She chose the former. After all he loved Star Wars. Her mother was nice to her most of the time, but when she was angry, she scowled like a witch. Zoe took the Wicked Witch of the West off the shelf. Her brother Jack was bossy and teased her a lot. She looked around the shelves. She chose a vampire with blood dripping from his teeth.

'I'm ready now.'

'Not quite Zoe, what about a figure for you?'

Quick as a flash, Zoe picked up an exquisite miniature Cinderella doll with dainty glass slippers and cautiously approached the sand table. She propped Darth Vader and his sword on a small rock, then placed the Wicked Witch on his right. Both figurines looked as if they were going to strike Cinderella. Then she positioned the vampire standing over Cinderella, whom she'd sat with her head in her hands.

Amanda frowned. 'Um, Alana can you just come into the other room for a minute? Zoe, just keep playing with the figures, okay?'

Alana sighed and followed her out.

'Look Alana, I'm a bit puzzled. From Zoe's representation of your family, it seems to me that she feels that she's being picked on.'

'What? What on earth are you implying? That all of us give Zoe a hard time?'

'Hey, I didn't say that. It's just that the figurines Zoe has chosen and the positions she has placed them in, are an indication of how she feels at the moment.'

Alana took a deep breath. 'Can I ask you something?'

'Sure, go ahead.'

'When we go back into your office, could you ask Zoe what she had for breakfast today?'

'Bumble bees and toads,' Zoe replied with a cheeky grin.

'No dear, I mean what did you really eat for breakfast?'

'I've already told you!' replied Zoe crossly and folding her arms, she scowled at Amanda.

'What about dinner last night? What did your mummy make?'

'Daddy made us barbequed bats' wings, a scoop of maggots and snail shells,' replied Zoe.

'What an active imagination you have Zoe!'

'That's it? Just an overactive imagination?' queried Alana.

'Yes, that's what I think for the moment, but if Zoe doesn't grow out of this phase, and mind you, she is only five, you may want to bring her in for a few more sessions until we get to the bottom of what's bothering her,' counselled Amanda, in the other room. In the mean time, I suggest that you enrol her in a drama group and the after school art classes at the Noosa Regional Gallery. They also have Family Day every month, so Jack could come with you to participate in the activities they run there. It will be lots of fun, I promise.'

Once Alana and her daughter were outside, Zoe asked, 'Was I a good girl mummy? Since we're in Hastings Street, can you buy me an ice-cream? Please!'

'Okay, let's go across the road to the Bay Village Food Court, but then we'll have to stop off at the Noosa Junction supermarket to get some things for dinner.'

As they strolled about the area with their macadamia nut ice-creams, Alana looked in the windows of the expensive boutiques, wishing she could buy another pair of shoes.'

'Look mum! There's the "Secret Princesses" book my friend Jessica has!'

She dragged Alana into the bookshop. 'Please mum, can you buy it? You can read it to me before bed. Please!'

Alana wearily agreed and then realised that Jack would complain that it was unfair, if she hadn't bought him anything.

'Zoe, what book do you think that Jack would like?'

'Anything by Andy Griffiths, mum! "The Day My Bum Went Psycho" is his favourite.'

'Okay. Now, how about we go and buy some chicken schnitzels and a bag of coleslaw? You and Jack can help me make grandma's potato salad for tea.'

'Yummy! Caterpillar shoulders and kookaburra slaw! My favourite!'

Zoe hummed "Kookaburra sits in the old gumtree" to herself, as she played happily with her Barbie doll in the back seat. She was busy creating more exciting adventures in her mind and the secrets she would share with her secret friend Misty, once she got back to her bedroom.

Once the children were asleep, Alana told Hugh what had transpired at Amanda's office. He was tired having just driven back from Brisbane from his architects' conference.

'Why don't you ring your mother and ask her what you were like at Zoe's age?'

'Hi mum, how are you and dad going? You two should take a break from BALTIK. Why don't you come and stay with us for a week? Next year? Okay. Um, mum, do you reckon that I was a difficult kid, when I was about Zoe's age?'

'No, Alana. You just loved playing dress ups and getting the neighbours' kids and your friends to take part in your mini plays. You had a vivid imagination and an incredible feel for acting. Remember when we got you your first guitar, you wanted to be a pop singer?'

'Yeah, that was fun. What about Ray?'

'Ray always loved sport, just like your uncles Paul and Max. Couldn't get enough of playing cricket, football and basketball. Remember that basketball ring he had on the back of his bed room door? He'd keep shooting goals from every angle of the room.'

Alana felt relieved and when she asked her mother what was new in her life, she discovered that that Gaila's friend Jasmine was coming for a visit. Her mother sounded very pleased.

Every April without fail, Jasmine would fly to Sydney to visit Gaila and Myles. She'd moved to Hong Kong when she had married a wealthy stockbroker from Canberra.

258

'You realize, don't you, that your mum has always been jealous of you,' Jasmine blurted out, after she'd drunk a few too many glasses of red wine during lunch.

'What? What do you mean?' gasped Gaila, as she took their plates over to the dishwasher.

'When I used to live in Sydney, your mum often told me on our way to choir practice, that she resented your marriage lasting longer than hers and that you had a career and your own money.'

Gaila sat there, stunned, by Jasmine's revelation. The thought had never crossed her mind to be jealous of Alana or Ray. Yet, whenever she thought back to her relationship with mama, she remembered that Ella certainly didn't want her to marry Myles. The fact that her husband was a profound romantic, who often bought her flowers or a box of chocolates just for no reason, must have made her mother reflect on her own unhappy life with Al.

'Maybe you're right Jasmine. After I got married, mama would periodically find fault about my appearance or the way I was bringing up Alana and Ray.

'Oh really?'

'Yeah, if it wasn't about the way I dressed them, then she'd be on and on about how our kids don't speak Lithuanian, what a shame it was, bla, bla, bla.'

'But I remember you or Myles taking your kids to Saturday school, the scouts and basketball.'

'We did, but after a while, they told me that it was boring and that they didn't want to go.'

'I thought that Ray still plays basketball with the Sydney Litho team?'

'He does. He really got inspired to play again, after we took him to see Lithuania win bronze at the Sydney Olympics. He even got some of the players' autographs!' 'Good on him! Anyway, this is my theory for what it's worth. If you really sit down and think about it Gaila, our mothers didn't have all the opportunities that we had.'

'True. Mama was only little when the second world war broke out, and while I was happily writing stories and doing my homework in primary school, she was probably dodging bombs and bullets.'

'You have to admit it Gaila, our parents have had to cope with a lot in their lives.'

'True. By the time they came out to Australia, they'd managed to escape from the Russians and the Nazis.'

'My mama always had to defer to her father as head of the family,' added Jasmine.

'Mum's brother, Simas, was always given a lot more personal freedom than her. I think that she carried those old traditions into her marriage too. Dad's word was law. My brothers and I lived in dread of mama warning us of what would happen, when dad got home and heard about us being cheeky to her or naughty at school.'

'Same. I can't ever recall my father saying that he loved my brother and me. He was a harsh disciplinarian and we got a belting if we ever stepped out of line. I think it must have been the same, for most of us back then,' replied Jasmine.

'Well, I vowed that that would never happen in my marriage and that my children would not be smacked into submission,' replied Gaila. 'Myles and I would tell our kids that we loved them at every opportunity and we still do. Mama always bowed to dad's wishes. If he didn't like what she'd made for tea, she'd make him something else, and it had to be meat based, because according to dad, men had to be fed meat every day.'

'You're kidding me! I knew that I would never be a doormat, that's for sure,' replied Jasmine.

'Nor me. In our family, every Sunday night, we'd have a chat about what sort of meals we'd be having the following week, so Fridays became kids' night. Easy food, you know, like build your own hamburgers, tacos or a take aways like fish and chips or pizza. Myles cooked a stir-fry on Thursdays and pancakes every Sunday for breakfast.'

'Well, our mothers didn't have cake mixes, frozen vegetables or ice-cream, did they?' recalled Jasmine. 'All of our Lithuanian meals were really hard work.'

'Mama had a mincing machine and we also had to grate zillions of potatoes for those *cepelinai*,' replied Gaila recalling how while she was grating potatoes, she'd often grate quite a lot of a bit of skin from her fingers as well.'

'Or *kugelis*,' recalled Jasmine. 'Do you ever make that potato bake?'

'It's a bit too heavy for my taste,' replied Gaila. 'I think I made it once or twice early on in our marriage, because Myles wanted to taste it. Mum used to make it a lot in winter, because it was cheap and filling. That and all the other traditional Lithuanian dishes.'

'What about *Skilandis*?'

'Skill what?'

'My grandmother used to make a big *Skilandis*. It's like a haggis, but it's minced pork in a pig's stomach.'

Gaila laughed. 'Don't really fancy that. It sounds like too much work to me. Can you imagine me going to my butcher and saying, Hey Bob, got a pig's stomach for me?'

'I guess not. Aren't we are lucky to have vacuum cleaners, automatic washing machines and clothes dryers?' admitted Jasmine.

'Mama would be on her hands and knees scrubbing our old linoleum floors with a brush, and when I was seven, she said that I was old enough to do it. Afterwards, we got a proper mop thank goodness. Since I was the eldest, it fell to me to do a lot of the housework and mind my brothers during the holidays when mum had to work.'

'We weren't well off when I was a kid either,' admitted Jasmine. 'We wore our cousins' hand-me-downs, but at least we didn't have to run into air raid shelters at night or leave our home at a moment's notice like our parents did.'

They took their glasses outside and Gaila opened a bottle of non-alcoholic apple cider.

'Dad always kept telling me, that if I didn't win a scholarship to Sydney University, I would have to work in a factory or in a supermarket', mused Gaila.

'I know what you mean. A few stints in cafés and big department stores during the school holidays, made me realize that I didn't want to stand around on my feet all day long.'

'Oh, I think that Mum was proud once I got into uni, but she couldn't understand that I had a lot of platonic male friends,' replied Gaila. 'She didn't believe that men and women could just be friends, so she'd hint that I must be getting around, as she called it.'

'You're kidding me! What a thing to say to your own daughter! Unbelievable!'

'Exactly! I can tell you that I was really shocked, that my own mother could even think I was like that, but that was the way her generation had been brought up in the old country. Young girls stayed at home until they were of marriageable age and then were married off as soon as possible, or as soon as a young man showed any interest.'

'Did your mum ever hint to you that Mrs. So-and-so's son in the Lithuanian community would make you a great husband?'

'All the time! It was hilarious! Fortunately we knew these guys much better than our mothers and their matchmaking friends!' laughed Gaila, as they finished eating their lunch.

That night, the apparition returned to torment Gaila. Over and over again, unseen hands clutched at her, as she tried to escape a raging inferno. She thrashed about, forcing herself to fight back, but it felt as if she had been drugged and dragged down into the bowels of Hell.

'No! Get away from me!' she shouted at her invisible tormentor.

Myles tried to wake her, but she fought him, and it was only until he removed the tangled quilt from her and began to soothe her, did she open her eyes.

'Gaila, shush. It's okay, it's only me, Myles. You're safe. I love you. Shh, shh, darling.' Myles held her in his arms and rocked her like a child, perplexed and shocked by his wife's terror stricken face.

'It was here, in our bedroom again!' Gaila tried to explain the inexplicable, as her breathing slowly returned to normal. She rubbed her eyes with her fingers, trying to banish the grotesque image that she battled with in her nightmares.

Myles went into the kitchen to make his wife a cup of herbal tea. He saw that it was 4 a.m., the usual hour when her night terrors occurred. He wondered whether they should make an appointment with a psychologist. He made a mental note to look up someone near their gallery who could help his wife explain, what she was unable to describe to him.

Later that morning, instead of her usual quick shower, Gaila decided run a warm bath to shake off the unease that engulfed her. Pouring some bath salts into the water, she inhaled the scent and felt calmed by the smell of pine forests. Examining herself in the foggy mirror, she was shocked to see a tousled, frightened, wide-eyed woman staring back at her.

Paul was still in bed when he heard his phone ringing at 8 a.m.

'Hi Myles, what's up? Who's died?'

'Relax mate, no one's died. Gaila's been having those terrible nightmares again. Look Paul, I'm really worried. She can't, or won't tell me what's bothering her.'

Paul opened the bedroom window and saw Hobart's cloudy skies. Hoping the day would turn out to be sunny, he plugged in the coffee maker.

'Do you want me to talk to her?' he asked. 'Can she describe what's in her dreams?'

'That's the problem Paul. All she can tell me, is that someone she calls The Evil One, tries to harm her in these dreams, and that there's always a fire.'

'I'll have a chat to Gemma when she gets back from New York. They've chosen one of her silk quilts to put on display in their gallery.'

'Was that the one she based on a Renaissance painting? Gaila told me about it. I'd love to have that one hanging in our gallery.'

'Yep, that's the one. She got really inspired by it. Not her usual Estonian folk art style.'

'So how come you didn't you go with her?'

Paul would never admit to anyone that money was tight nowadays. He pretended to everyone that their bookshop was going really well and that the books flew off the shelves. In reality, he was scouring stores like Target and buying the latest best sellers at discount prices, then marking them up.

'Hey, I would have loved to have gone, but you know, someone's got to run the bookshop.'

'Ok, I won't hold you up Paul. I'm ringing from my study. Gaila won't be going to the gallery with me today, she's decided to work on some jewellery in her studio. That nightmare took a lot out of her.'

'Okay talk to you soon. Hopefully, we'll be able to fly over to see you at Christmas and afterwards, maybe we could all stay at your friend's holiday house in the Blue Mountains.'

'Sounds good, I'll get Gaila to ask her friend. I'll talk it over with her later. Bye.'

Paul knew that Gemma would really love a trip to Sydney again. Apart from the MONA gallery in Hobart, Gemma wasn't really happy with the number of galleries that they had in Tasmania. He was sure that Myles would agree to display a few of her quilts to sell at BALTIK. It had been six months since he'd seen his sister. Then, maybe he could find a way to talk to her about her weird dreams. He couldn't really talk to her about them on the phone. He'd have to bring it up on a one to one basis, over a coffee and a big slice of cheesecake in one of those George street cafes that Gaila loved to frequent. When Gemma returned from New York, they could make the final arrangements.

Paul finished his toast and honey, had a shower and wondered how in the world he could help his sister. Locking the front door securely, he began his daily climb down the steps to his bookshop in Salamanca Place. As he waved to the daily joggers, he glanced back at his house in Battery Point, glad that it had been heritage listed along with the others. Funny how old buildings fascinated Gaila and himself. Both of them had chosen to live in old houses and renovate them. He thought how fortunate he was, being married to Gemma who shared his passion for antiques. Opening up his bookshop, he glanced at his wife's colourful Estonian style quilts on the walls and plugged in the coffee maker. Filling it up, he took a tablespoon of espresso coffee and placed it onto the filter paper. Friends had asked Paul why he didn't buy a modern coffee machine, but he told them that he liked old things.

He then went across to the antique bookcase in the shape of a horseshoe in the middle of the store. Flipping open a book, Paul started to read about the meanings of dreams. His love of books had come from his mother, who'd read to him when he was little. It was sad that he and Gemma weren't able to have any children, but that was the way things were. He was looking forward to spending some time with his sister in Sydney. Too bad that Max had not bothered keeping in touch with the family. For a few years they had exchanged Christmas cards, but now, who knew what he was doing or where he was.

Gaila looked proudly at the twelve dishes spread out on her best white linen tablecloth for Christmas Eve and was reminded of the Christmas Eve when her cousin Rokas and his parents came to stay at her home in Bankstown. In the middle of her table, she'd placed a big white aromatic candle set in a wreath of pine needles and pine cones, tied with red ribbon. There were no meat or dairy dishes according to the old Lithuanian customs, but since Sydney had fabulous fresh seafood, she'd bought smoked trout and salmon, freshly cooked tiger prawns, fresh oysters and had also made several salads. She admired her *kisielius*, the fruit pudding for dessert and the tiny poppy seed biscuits. An empty chair stood at the table as a mark of respect for the deceased members of her family.

She missed Myles' parents who had been killed instantly, many years ago, in the 1977 Granville train disaster. The Christmas tree twinkled with fairy lights in the corner of her dining room and the smell of fresh pine needles permeated the house. She'd even managed to get some straw to play the traditional games with her grandchildren. Myles would soon be home from BALTIK, stopping off to buy a few extra bottles of wine before he came home. Sometimes, he'd be late, especially if there was a last minute rush as people raced in to the gallery, to buy a piece of jewellery or a framed photo of the Sydney Harbour Bridge or the Opera House. She prayed that the ferry wouldn't be too crowded. Gaila checked the presents under the tree, hoping that Alana and Gemma would like the jewellery she'd created for them. Silver was expensive, but the delicate twisted wire and lapis lazuli earrings would look fabulous. She'd experimented with making jewellery from silver plated dessert spoons and forks, but people had complained that the earrings especially, were far too heavy to wear all day. She'd fashioned a silver plaited ring for her son just like the one she'd made for Myles when they celebrated their tenth wedding anniversary.

Alana had arrived from Noosa two days earlier with her family. Gaila was immensely proud of her tall, lithe, attractive daughter with shoulder length honey coloured hair. They'd already been over the road to Manly beach and Alana had gone running both mornings. She liked to keep up her fitness routine wherever she was. Jack and Zoe, were bursting with excitement as they admired the huge Christmas tree against the bay window.

'Cool! Santa's left some presents here for us!' they shouted. Hugh, their father, was ready for an icy cold beer as he joined Ray and his wife Elle at the bay window. They looked out across to

Manly beach where Rod the surfboard man was busy stacking up the boards he rented out each day, rain, hail or shine.

'Hey, I heard that the surf will be good tomorrow,' commented Hugh.

'Can I come with you, can I, can I?' pleaded Jack, who at eight years old, was already a competent surfer. He had been invited to join a surf school in Noosa and was hoping to become a professional surfer when he was older.

'As long as I can come too,' joked Paul, 'And your aunt Gemma. But we'll have to go to church first, remember?'

Throughout their Christmas lunch of seafood and cold chicken and salads on the beach, Gaila's family laughed and shared happy memories of previous Christmas meals. Everyone had their favourite memory of Christmases past, but whenever she thought back, there'd always been some sort of culinary disaster at their house. It first started a few years ago, after they stopped going across to Bankstown to spend Christmas with her mother and grandparents. She and her younger brother Ray used to take it in turns to cook lunch. Sometimes Gaila roasted a duck in the ancient oven and since Ray was the family's weber wizard, he could turn an ordinary joint of meat into a mouth-watering meal. Sometimes there'd be a Christmas card on Ella's mantelpiece from their brother Max in Kalgoorlie. If there wasn't, Ella would make the usual excuses, telling them that he was far too busy working seven days a week in the goldmine to remember to send cards. 'He probably doesn't know what day it is in that dark mine,' she'd say with a wave of her arm.

One year, Myles decided that he could be a weber wizard as well. 'How hard can it be?' he'd say nonchalantly whilst sipping on a Coopers Ale. 'You just chuck on the meat and forget about it.' As soon as he had some spare time, Myles went on an inspection tour of all the barbeque shops, and ended up buying his Weber barbeque, just in time for Christmas Day at home.

'Mum, remember when we had your friends over to join us for Christmas lunch and Dad was chomping at the bit to show off his master chef barbeque technique?' reminisced Alana.

At one o'clock the table was all set to go with salads and the ham, when Gaila asked Myles what time he'd put on the turkey. 'Oh about six, this morning,' he replied airily, 'so that it could cook nice and slow.'

'What?' Gaila yelled at the top her voice, startling the guests who were still devouring the last prawns on the platter. Myles turned pale and rushed out the back door. Fifty dollars worth of turkey had turned into a charred voodoo doll. Now it had become part of their family and their children often recalled the time Dad burnt the turkey to a crisp. Mind you, no one was laughing that particular Christmas Day as they ate ham and salad.

Another Christmas featured the same Weber, but this time there was also an extra one from her friends, Vizma and Frank. Myles had decided to cook a variety of expensive gourmet sausages he'd bought in Potts Point. Blessed with the gift of ESP, Gaila had cooked a whole fish in the oven beforehand as one of the main courses, and was minutes away from serving up lunch. That morning she couldn't help herself from reminding Myles not to put on the sausages too early.

'We don't want to witness another cremation,' she told him cheekily.

'Stop nagging me,' he replied. 'I'm not stupid!' Time dragged on, their guests had devoured all the dips and smoked salmon. Gaila asked Myles how the sausages were coming along. 'Don't keep telling me what to do. I'm onto it!' he snapped. Soon the two webers were lit up, blazing away merrily in the back yard, but as most people know, the charcoal takes a while to settle, before the meat can be grilled. Two o'clock came and went, and people were getting merrier and merrier as they drank more and more rum punch.

Finally, Myles decided to throw the gourmet sausages onto the two webers nevertheless, reasoning that they were going to be barbequed anyway. Unfortunately, he didn't realise that the weber was unlike an ordinary bbq that could be turned down to regulate the heat.

'Ha ha! I remember that time, dad,' Alana laughed. 'We were not very impressed with your expensive gourmet sausages that all looked the same shade of black!'

'And what about the time we had those strange Japanese exchange teachers staying with us?' laughed Ray. 'I was only little then, but I remember Kuro and that other guy Kenta.'

'What a pain in the backside Kuro turned out to be!' added Alana. I guess it was my fault since I wanted to study Japanese. Then we had to host the students from my sister school in Osaka.'

'But Gaira, the hotel will not have a hair dlyer!' Kuro would announce imperiously as he tried to wheedle his way out of looking after one of his sick male students.

'Yes Kuro, the hotel will have a hairdryer!' Gaila had replied as calmly as possible.

'No!' shouted Kuro and stamped his foot, which was encased in a sock and sandal. 'It is not my job to spend all my time in Sydney looking after sick students. Also I do not want to miss excursion to the Jenolan Caves in The Blue Mountains. Gaira, you know that I am very interested in stalagmites and staragtites!'

Kuro was very proud of the knowledge he'd gleaned on his previous trip to Australia. He loved the excursions to the nearby towns of Leura and Katoomba. There was no way that he was going to give up another trip to the Pinnacles of the Three Sisters at Echo Point.

'But you have been there before,' Myles had pointed out testily.

'Does not matter! I am in charge!' countered Kuro. 'I will ring up that silly woman from headquarters and she can look after the sick boy.' He then shuffled down the passage way in white socks and sandals like a geisha.

Only five years before, Kuro had seemed like a polite and caring young man. But he had only stayed for three days and was then put up in a hotel. This time he came with a P.E. teacher named Kenta who was a mild mannered middle-aged family man who would just shrug his shoulders as soon as Kuro started throwing his weight around. Kuro reminded Myles of a big spoilt brat. He tried his best to explain the theory of 'in loco parentis' to Kuro, where in Australia, a teacher was expected to act in place of a parent at school or on an excursion, even more so if they were overseas and a student became ill.

'Not in Osaka!' replied Kuro smugly. 'I am always the boss in in my high school in Osaka.'

After two weeks, Kuro was starting to get on everyone's nerves. When he first arrived, he was overjoyed to see his hosts again and kept pointing out to Kenta all the places he knew and said quite confidently, 'You will see. We will have bbq steak every night!'

Gaila's family had to take countless photos of both of them pretending to help out with cooking, washing and drying the dishes and sweeping floors.

'Australians like guests to help out,' he would say after each photo. The problem was that he did no such thing, he just took photos to show everyone back in Osaka, that he was being helpful. Myles and Gaila were working in the gallery and their two children had the usual sporting commitments. Feeding six people quickly turned into a nightmare.

'No! I don't care for pasta,' Kuro would announce imperiously whenever they had something for dinner he didn't like. 'All Australians eat steak.'

Kuro went on his excursion. By the time he returned in the afternoon, the poor exchange student was in Sydney Hospital with severe influenza. Later that night, the International Exchange Co-ordinator rang Gaila to discuss the situation. She just told her what Kuro had said.

'That's it! I've had a gutful of that man,' said the co-ordinator. 'This has happened before. There's no way that Kuro will travel on any more exchange trips to Australia.'

She must have informed Kuro about her decision on the last day, because he started to shed crocodile tears in their lounge room.

'But Gaira, it was a misunderstanding a very bad misunderstanding. You know me. I am really a very good man!'

Gaila was counting the hours before he got onto the bus and was taken to the airport. Kenta bowed to them and his eyes were wet with tears. 'Thank you Mr and Mrs Smythe,' he kept repeating over and over again as he bowed to them. It was the only sentence that he'd learnt, but it was much appreciated, more than they appreciated Kuro's antics.

'But Gaira I have no hair dlyer!!' accompanied by a shuffle of feet down the passage, became one of the family's sayings when someone did not want to do something.

Gaila heard the phone ringing as soon as she came in the front gate. She was tired after working all day at BALTIK and the ferry ride from Circular Quay to Manly had been rough. Although she never got seasick, this time she felt her stomach heave as the swell tossed the ferry up and down.

She grabbed the phone as soon as she got in the front door. 'Hello.' She recognized her mother's voice. She was crying and Gaila thought she heard her say something about her grandmother Renata.

'What did you say? Mama, speak slowly! I can't understand what you're saying. Did you just say grandma's been taken away?'

'Grandma Renata's in the ambulance.'

'What happened? Is she alright?'

'I called triple zero!'

'That was very good of you mama. I'll be there as soon as I can.'

Myles was still in Hobart for an Arts conference at the MONA gallery, so Gaila rang her brother Paul to tell him the news. Gemma answered the phone.

'Hi. Paul and Myles are still at the gallery,' she informed Gaila. 'I'll tell them to ring you as soon as they get back from the conference dinner. I'm sure she'll be fine.'

Gaila got into her car and started the long drive to her mother's house. A pain shot through her chest as she tried to stem back the tears. She cursed the peak hour traffic, hoping that she would not get held up for too long on the Sydney Harbour Bridge. As she looked up, she saw a line of people walking right on the top. 'I could never do that,' she said to herself. Heights terrified her. She envisaged herself falling down, down, down into the cold waters of the harbour. Just the other day, she'd read an account of a navy diver being bitten by a shark in the waters near the Marine Museum.

What if she had to organise her grandmother's funeral? Gaila wasn't sure that her mother was capable of doing it. She'd become very indecisive in recent months and would often forget simple words, grasping the air with her hands saying, 'You know, the thing that you put the dishes in, so they get clean.'

'The dishwasher?'

'Yes, that's what I meant.'

Once, Gaila found her mother's purse in the refrigerator. 'So that's where it was,' her mother said. 'I've been looking in every bloody corner of this bloody house.' Her mother, who'd never sworn in her life, had started to swear quite a bit lately. Gaila wondered if Ella had got into that habit after keeping company with a man who wanted to marry her. Angelo was a very traditional man who expected to be waited on hand and foot once he'd moved in with her mother. Renata had put her foot down saying that she was too old and set in her ways, to have tenants and told Ella that she had saved her from another unhappy relationship. Ella had never forgiven her mother and Gaila recalled the bitter fights both women had over Angelo.

'He was a much nicer man than Al,' Ella would tell Gaila and anyone else who would listen.

By the time Gaila had reached her grandmother's house, she had calmed down somewhat. However, when she got to the front door, she saw that it was open.

'Mama, where are you?' she called, walking from room to room. Her mother wasn't there. In a panic, Gaila raced into the garden and around both sides of the house. Nothing. She ran into the street. Daylight was fading and she starting to worry that an accident may had happened. She envisioned Ella lying on the road with all her bones broken, or lying in a coma.

Suddenly she saw old Mrs. Kilpatrick waving to her from across the street.

'Yoo, hoo! Over here, dear!'

Mrs. Fitzpatrick had lived in the street for as long as she could remember, her front yard was overgrown with weeds and littered with catalogues. Gaila quickly crossed the street.

'Hello there Mrs. Fitz. Have you seen my mother by any chance?'

'Your mother? Of course I have. We're having a nice cup of tea. Ella's had a big shock poor thing. We all saw the ambulance pull up outside her place. Not nice is it, seeing your poor old mother being carted away to the charnel house, is it?'

'I believe it's called a hospital.'

'Same thing. Once they take you to hospital, you're lucky to come out alive. Just the other week, my good neighbour Bert got pneumonia and died. He only went in to get a pacemaker. Then there was my best friend Frances. She went in to have a hip replacement and died on the operating table! Then there was …'

Ignoring Mrs Fitz's tales of woe, Gaila went over to her mother who was sitting on a faded brocade armchair sipping a cup of tea. She was staring up at the ceiling, as if there was someone up there.

'How about I make you a nice hot cuppa Gail? asked Mrs Fitzpatrick, delighted that she had some visitors for once. She bustled about in her tiny kitchen and opened a packet of chocolate Tim Tam biscuits.

'How's that son of yours going?

'Really well. Ray has his own export company now and his wife Elle works part-time there.

'What about their little daughter?'

'Ruby goes to a childcare centre on the days when Elle is at work. We mind her if she's sick or when they want to go out.'

'How's your daughter? In Queensland now, aren't they?'

'Hugh's doing really well as an architect and Alana is busy with her photography business.'

'And how are those little grand kids?'

'Really good Mrs. Fitz. Jack and Zoe have both started school.'

'You must miss them, dearie'.

'Yes, we do, but I'm driving up there during their holidays to look after them, so they won't have to be stuck in a holiday program for the whole two weeks.'

'That's nice. How did you get your hubby to agree to that? My Tom would have never let me travel anywhere by myself.'

'Myles is quite happy for me to drive up to Noosa, he's quite capable of running our gallery while I'm away. I've done it whenever he's gone interstate or overseas on business.'

'You are a lucky one then.'

Ella looked up at both of them. 'Who's Lucky?'

'It's fine, Mama. We can go home now.'

'Home? But Palanga's so far away. We'll have to fly there. It will take ages,' replied Ella.

'She's in shock,' Gaila thought to herself, as she thanked Mrs Fitzpatrick and steered her mother out the door and across the street back into her house.

'Mama, listen to me. How about I stay with you here tonight?' she whispered gently to her. Her mother looked blankly at her, not comprehending what her daughter was saying.

'No, you can't. That thing is still in the house.'

'What thing?'

'You know, that awful thing,' her mother replied.

Gaila's skin went clammy. Her worst fears were now a reality.

'Tell me Mama! What are you talking about?'

'He comes into the room. You can't stay there, he might hurt you too.'

Gaila tried to calm her breathing. There was no way that she was going to tell her mother that something evil haunted her own dreams.

'Is there anything we can do about him?'

'We have to find a little book. There's something in there that my grandmother Kristina wrote down.'

Gaila gasped. This was the first time in years that Ella had mentioned her grandmother.

'Can you remember where you put this little book?'

'I hid it, so it will be safe!' replied Ella triumphantly.

Gaila groaned. It would be a job and a half to find some little book in her mother's house. Even then they may not find it, but fortunately, Ella didn't throw much away. She still had her old photographs from Ventuva and the seaside resort of Palanga, somewhere in amongst her great grandfather's candlesticks and small wooden carvings of old weather-beaten men. Ella called them 'the worriers.' At first Gaila thought they were soldiers and remarked to her mother that they didn't look like soldiers at all, just tired old village peasants. Ella had explained that they were traditional carvings that were placed at crossroads all over Lithuania, and that her grandfather Jonas was a woodcarver.

'Come on Mama, how about you come and stay with us for a few days,' cajoled Gaila.

Finally Ella agreed and as soon as Gaila reached Manly, her mother tapped her on the shoulder as soon as they had come in sight of the ocean.

'Stop the car!' demanded Ella.

Gaila stopped the car. They got out and she waited for her mother, who gingerly put one foot in front of the other. Clutching her daughter's hand tightly, Ella walked up and down the promenade. 'Promise me that you'll scatter my ashes here. Your grandmother has always wanted hers scattered in Ventuva. Promise me you'll do that.'

She remembered how she and Al used to bring Max, Paul and Gaila to the beach in summer, in the shade of the striped tent and canvas chairs, wilted tomato and cheese sandwiches for lunch, waiting that eternal hour before the kids could swim, worrying about sharks, until the council installed the shark nets.

'The sea air always does one good, you know,' Ella was speaking to no one in particular.

They saw a group of surfers, lined up like a squadron of fighter jets.

'Haven't had a decent ride in yet, what about you?' Ella heard them call out to each other.

Out of nowhere, a trio of dolphins appeared, jumping in and out of the sea.

'Dolphins always bring you good luck. Warn you about any sharks nearby,' remarked Ella to her daughter.

Later, she walked along the shore, slimy seaweed clinging gently around her ankles, feeling happy and relaxed that she was propped up by her daughter and her memories.

'Oh my God, Gaila! Just look at that woman!' she shouted. 'Wearing a bikini at her age! Should be ashamed! What a tart!'

'Mama, she only looks about thirty, she's not old.'

'Shameless woman! She wouldn't be allowed on the beach in Palanga, I can tell you that right now! Unless of course she went to the women's beach. She wouldn't need that tiny scrap of a bikini there!'

Finally, they got home. After Gaila had made her mother comfortable in the spare bedroom, the phone rang. It was her vet.

'Hello Mrs. Smythe. I'm sorry to tell you that your cat's been brought into the surgery.'

'Oh no! Is he all right?'

'One of his hind legs is broken. Car accident, by the looks of it. Do you want me to amputate it or put him down? After all, he's nineteen years old.'

'No, please don't put him down. Do what you can to save him.'

'We'll try, but don't get your hopes up.'

She must really get a new mobile phone. She kept putting it off, knowing it was another expense that she couldn't afford at that moment. She would get a new one as soon as a few more paintings were sold. Gaila went back to her mother to tell her about Mr. Meow, all the time feeling uneasy and hoping he'd pull through.

'You'll get over it. It's just a cat. Get another one!'

'But mama, he's part of the family.'

'You'll save heaps on cat food! Then you can go away for months, instead of just one week.'

How could her mother just dismiss nineteen years with Mr. Meow? Nineteen years of loyalty, love and friendship. Whenever she was ill, he'd lie by her side, snuggling close, to comfort her. Purring Gaila to sleep, or nudging her awake she'd remember to drink. As soon as he'd see Myles and Gaila coming down the street, he'd stroll down the steps to greet them. No matter what the weather, Gaila would see him there or sitting high up on the sandstone pillars.

After a second phone call from the vet to say that Mr Meow hadn't survived the operation, she had to remind herself that she wouldn't have to feed him that night. In those last minutes of his life, she desperately wished she was there with him, blaming herself for not having a new mobile phone and not being able to rush to the surgery in time.

'Don't blame yourself,' he'd told her over the phone. 'I just want to tell you that there was nothing we could do. The shock to his system was too great.'

'I will be over to collect him,' Gaila replied. 'I want to bury him under a rosebush. He deserves respect.'

Before she could tell her mother that she was off to the vet's, the phone rang again.

'Is that Mrs Ella Kelmas?'

'No, it's her daughter Gail Smythe.'

'I regret to inform you that Mrs. Renata Baras passed away this evening due to a cardiac arrest,' said an official sounding voice.

'Oh no! Thank you for letting me know.' Gaila went into the lounge room with the sad task of trying to explain to Ella that her mother had died.

'Your mama's gone,' she told Ella gently and put her arm around her.

'Gone?' Ella asked plaintively. 'She should have come back from shopping in Palanga by now.'

Gaila made her mother a cup of valerian tea and poured herself a glass of chardonnay. As she put the bottle back in the fridge, she watched her mother staring blankly into space and finally nodding off to sleep in the armchair.

By the time Myles returned from the gallery, Gaila was a mess. Two deaths in one day! How was she going to cope? Myles did his best to soothe his wife, ' Remember, how we managed to get through my parents' funeral, before the kids were born? We'll get through this together.'

He rang Paul in Hobart to tell him the sad news about Renata.

'Oh Myles, how awful. You two just hang in there. Gemma and I will fly over, as soon as we can get a flight.'

After a private cremation for Renata, they sat huddled around Ella's ancient dining room table and waited till she was settled. After their meal, Gaila went to make mugs of tea and coffee. Paul's eyebrows furrowed as he watched his mother fumble with her mug.

'Where are my cups with the gold trim? Where are those nice almond crescent biscuits that I made?' complained Ella.

'Mama, I don't know where they are. There are just these plain ones in your biscuit tin,' answered Gaila gently. She knew that Ella hadn't baked any biscuits for years.

'Do you know where Grandma's will is?' Paul asked his mother.

'Will I what?' asked Ella.

'Do you know where Grandma's last testament is kept?' repeated Gaila gently.

'In a big tool box.'

'Where is it?'

'Somewhere in the tool shed,' Ella replied vaguely.

Paul went outside to the tool shed but found nothing. It had to be somewhere. Then he pushed open Renata's bedroom and started looking through the bedside drawers and then in the wardrobe. Nothing! Then he saw a piece of paper on the linoleum.

He walked back into the lounge room, scanning the note, but he couldn't believe what he was reading.

'Oh no!' Paul slumped in his chair.

'What is it Paul? What's wrong? Give it to me. Let me have a look!' Gaila snatched the piece of paper from his hands.

'It says the usual. Being of sound mind, bla, bla, bla ... I hereby leave my house and estate to my wife Agata Ivanovitch, and my two sons Kestas and Joseph Baras.'

'What? That's a load of rubbish!' exclaimed Gaila. We know that our uncle's name was Simas and our mother's name is Ella. They're the only children Grandpa and Grandma had.'

'Mama! Who in the hell are these characters? And who's Agata?' yelled Paul.

Ella cowered in her seat. 'I don't know, I don't know,' she sobbed.

'Listen you two, calm down. You're upsetting your mother. Do you think it's possible that these people somehow got your grandfather to change his will?' Gemma spoke up for the first time.

'Paul, look! It's just handwritten. Surely that can't be legal, can it?' exclaimed Gaila.

'I don't know! I'm not a lawyer! Look at these witnesses' signatures. I can't make them out, they're a bit faded.'

'What's going on?' asked Myles who'd just come back from the gallery.

'Do you think that Grandma Renata found it?' exclaimed Gaila. 'Could that have caused her heart attack last week? She told me that she had to go and show it to a lawyer. I thought that it was just about her own will. Obviously grandma didn't get around to making a new one after Grandpa Petras died last year. That bastard! How can he get away with this?'

'Slow down, Gaila. Slow down. We don't know anything for sure yet. Either you or I will have to take this so-called last testament to a lawyer. Otherwise mama will have nowhere to live, if this will were to hold up in court!'

'Mama, do you know why grandma didn't make a new will once grandpa died?'

'Is my grandpa dead?' Ella cried out in alarm, then stared back into space.

'I can see that I will definitely have to stay on here,' said Paul. 'One of us will need to look after mama, the other will have to go and find a lawyer to sort out this mess. Gemma will look after the bookshop, won't you Gemma?'

'No problem Paul, do what you have to do here. I can manage. Look Gaila, your grandma was really old. She wouldn't have known anything about Australian laws. I'm sure that back in Lithuania, if a husband died, then the house would go automatically to her or the kids. Anyway, that's what used to happen in Estonia.'

Ella looked bewildered as she tried to follow her children's conversation. She thought back to happier times with her children crowding about the dinner table, laughing as they snatched the last *koldūnas* or piece of poppy-seed cake, before she'd away clear away the empty plates. She knows that she can never tell them, nor name her grief at her life now, waiting for the next dose of painkillers to ease her pain. She smiles at them and then is transported back to when she was nine as she romped about her grandmother Kristina's garden in July's heat. Ella blinks at the memory of her wedding day to Al. Her father, gruff but proud, in the only suit he possessed, her mother in her new linen dress that crumpled around her as she stood up in the stifling church, as it climbed to forty degrees.

'Do you kids remember that holiday we had on a farm?'

Paul and Gaila stared, astounded at their mother's question. Yes, they could remember that hot summer, running about the paddocks and the dams. The yabbies they were hoping to catch were buried deep in their coffins of mud. The farmer's old kelpies who just managed to raise their rheumy eyes from the dust at the cockatoos that screeched day in day out. How they all used to laugh around the dinner table telling knock-knock jokes or playing charades with their father. That was when they were still a family, before their father and mama divorced and Al had married Elvyra, whom he left after only two years, to take up with yet another woman.

Paul wanted to tell his mother that he was sorry, so sorry for not coming earlier. Too busy with his life and his bookshop in Hobart. He cleared his throat.

'Mama, do you think that an aged care facility might be the best for you in the long run, now that grandma Renata has passed away? You certainly need a break from looking after her for so many years.'

Ella nodded and smiled. 'Thank you dear, but my home is here. I have to get stuck back into the housework and my garden. There are cucumbers to pickle, jams and *kvasas* to make.'

When they'd all gone home, Ella locked her doors and stared at the bottle of painkillers. Opening up a bottle of mineral water she started to take them, one by one. Then she lay down on her bed.

With just a suitcase in their hands, they had stumbled off the ship, blinking in the cold morning light.

'But, but they told us that it was hot in Australia,'

'Bloody Balts! Don't want them here. Do we, mate?'

'Why doncha speak English? Cat got ya tongue? Stupid foreigners!'

She went to sleep. No one was going to cart her off to an aged care facility. And that was how Gaila found her mother, when there was no answer to her repeated phone calls the next day.

In her will, Ella had stated that she wanted the Lithuanian Choir to sing in the church and that she be buried in her national costume. A wreath of flowers was to be put on top of her coffin and the Lithuanian flag draped over it, and the wake had to be held at the Lithuanian Club. Whilst Gaila and Paul tried to honour their mother's wishes, Gaila was adamant that she would keep her mother's national costume and amber necklaces. There was a young Lithuanian priest from Melbourne conducting the service. As soon as the small choir started to sing 'Jezau, pas mane ateiki' tears rolled down Gaila's cheeks. 'Jesus come to me', she tried singing the words of the old hymn, but ended up sobbing, as she remembered the funeral of her grandfather Bronius, who'd passed away three months after Grandma Rasa. Sixty years of marriage. Imagine that. Her Grandfather Petras' big expensive funeral that he'd paid for in advance with a pre-paid plan. Important members of the Lithuanian community, speaking on his behalf, praising his work in helping to build the club, his generous nature, promising to assist his widow. Now Grandma Renata was gone too. Myles put his arm around Gaila and on either side, Alana and Ray held each other's hands. Paul and Gemma with their heads bowed with grief. Paul blaming himself for his mother's death.

People she only vaguely remembered came up to her at the wake to offer their condolences.

'*Nu va, ką padarysi*? Well then, what can you do? And it was such a shame, your mother leaving your father like that. Such a nice man.'

'Why don't you come and join us at the choir now that you don't have to look after your mother? I bet that you have a nice soprano voice just like hers.'

'Why don't you join the senior folk dancing group? You used to be such a graceful dancer, just like your mother. You can catch up with my kids. Surely you remember them?'

'Why don't your grand children come to Saturday school? You should bring them along.'

'*Ačiu ponia*. Thank you madam,' Gaila managed to stammer out to the well-meaning ladies but found herself at breaking point. Fortunately Myles stepped in and ushered her away to join the rest of their family at a table laden with all sorts of traditional Lithuanian food prepared by the Ladies Auxiliary.

'Gaila, don't cry. They wouldn't know what our father was really like. We know what our mama went through. We know.' Paul had his arm around her and was trying his best to comfort her.

The rest of the day passed in a blur. Only when Gaila was getting ready for bed that night, did she realise that her brother Max hadn't been there. That night, her familiar nightmare returned, only this time, she saw her mother stretch out her hands towards her, begging to be saved from The Evil One.

Gaila did not know how she was going to cope after the funeral and was very relieved that Alana had offered stayed on, helping her go through Ella's things, sorting out what should be kept for the family and what would go to charity. As Alana was leafing through some of the novels, she came across a note she'd never seen before.

'Mum, what sort of money is this?'

'Oh my God! It looks like an old pound note! This dates back to just before we changed over to decimal currency!'

'We'll have to check every book now mum! This looks like grandma's banking system.'

Over several days, Alana and Gaila went through at least hundred books and found five hundred pounds, neatly slotted throughout the pages.

'I am so glad you are here with me,' Gaila whispered softly to her daughter.

'I'll take them to one of the coin dealers near the gallery and check their value. It could help towards the lawyer's fees.'

'Mum do you want to keep this big book? Um, but it's written in Lithuanian.'

'I can still read Lithuanian Alana. I didn't go to Saturday School all those years for nothing. Let me have a look. It does feel rather heavy.'

Gaila opened the book about the history of Samogitia, but she thought it rather strange that there was a hollow in the middle. Wedged inside, was a smaller leather bound book. She opened it carefully. The smell of old rose petals and another herb she couldn't identify, assailed her senses.

Turning over the yellowed pages, she tried to decipher the un-familiar words and thought that maybe she'd found her grand-mother's book of Lithuanian recipes.

In the middle section she found a drawing of a circular amulet with the following words written below, *'Turn circle turn, turn to the East. Turn circle turn, turn to the West. Turn circle turn, turn to the North. Turn circle turn, turn to the South.'*

'They don't make any sense,' she said aloud to herself.

'What did you say, mum?' asked Alana, who was looking a pile of white starched linen handkerchiefs she'd discovered in a shoe-box.

'Nothing sweetheart, this looks like grandma's little recipe book, that's all. I'd like to keep it. When I've got time, I'll look up the words and see if I can translate them. I can't seem to make head or tail of them. I'll put it away in my studio when I get home.'

'Look at these beautiful monogrammed handkerchiefs!' Alana held them up to the light.

'One says, Virginia, another Julia. Who were these women? Do you know, mum?'

'I think that they were my mother's aunts. I'll check through her photo albums tomorrow. Thanks for all your help today. I don't know what I would have done without you here.'

Gaila hugged Alana and breathed in her familiar perfume. If anything happened to her children or grandchildren, she didn't know what she and Myles would do.

She had finally decided to see someone about her nightmares and found a psychologist in central Sydney, that way no one would know. The following week, as Gaila made her way to Castlereagh Street, she hoped that this Dr. Dobson could find a solution.

'Ah, Mrs. Smythe. I'm Dr. Dobson, but you can call me Eric. Please take a seat over there. Now tell me, what's been troubling you?'

'I've been having nightmares for quite a while now.'

'Can you tell me about them?'

'I see a man, but he's almost like a spectre. I can't really see his face. And there's a fire burning all around me.'

'Have you ever been in a fire?'

'No, I haven't, that's what so weird.'

'How long have you been having these nightmares?'

'Not long after my parents split up.'

'How did you feel about that?'

'I felt relieved. My parents fought a lot.'

'What did they fight about?'

'Money. Dad going out by himself.'

'Times were tough, were they?'

'Yes, sometimes all we had was soup for tea, until dad's wage came in at the end of the week.'

'Parents still alive?'

'Mum's passed away, but my dad's still alive.'

'I see. Were your parents born here?'

'No, they came out with their parents from Lithuania as refugees, after the Second World War.'

'Hmm. Obviously they would have been traumatised by what they had to go through.'

'I guess so. They always used to tell us stories about the war and the old country.'

'Research has shown that children of refugees often take on their parents' wartime traumas.'

'Really? Do you think that's what might be wrong with me?'

'We'll get back to that later. Would you say that you have a happy marriage?'

'Myles and I have had our ups and downs, like any other couple. But yes, I would say that on the whole, we are very happy.'

'What about his parents?'

'Both have passed on.'

'Children?'

'We have two. A boy and a girl.'

'No problems with the births?'

'Alana's was difficult. I had to have an epidural and a forceps delivery.'

'I see. Any post-natal depression?'

'I don't think so. I had the baby blues in hospital for a while. But everyone has those don't they? Ray's birth was normal.'

'Any other operations?'

'Really doctor, I can't see how this is going to solve my nightmares!' Gaila felt flustered as she rose from the chair. She wanted to get away from this interrogation as quickly as possible.

'Please bear with me Gail. I am just trying to establish what hardships you have been through.'

Oh, okay. Um, I had to have a hysterectomy a few years ago. I had very heavy periods, you see. Excruciating back pain.'

'I see. Any other operations?'

'Um, yes. After the hysterectomy, a year later I got a bowel prolapse and a year after that, a bladder prolapse.'

'Hmm, I see. So would you agree that your body has been through a lot in recent years? You do realise don't you, that anaesthetic takes a good three months to leave your system?'

'Ah no, I didn't know that.'

'Anything else you'd like to tell me?'

'Ah well, um, I had my gall bladder out last year.'

'Nothing since then?'

'No.'

'Now, I have got a full picture of your medical history, I'd like you to consider my next suggestion. I'd like to hypnotise you to see if you've suffered any post-traumatic stress.'

'Is that really necessary?'

'It could shed some light on your nightmares.'

After Gaila agreed, he turned on a tape recorder. 'So that you can hear for yourself what transpires,' he reassured her.

Eric Dobson was astounded that once Gaila was under, she started to speak and cry in a little girl's voice. Unfortunately he couldn't make head or tail of what she was talking about, but he could hear the sheer terror in her screams.

When Gaila came out of the hypnosis, she asked straight away, 'What did you find out?'

'I'm sorry Gail, I couldn't understand it. It sounded a bit like German to me.'

'Can I listen to it?'

'Sure go ahead.'

Mesmerized, Gaila trembled when she heard the torment in the frightened girl's voice.

'Oh! She sounds really terrified, doesn't she? I wonder what she's saying? One or two of the words sound similar to standard

Lithuanian, but they are slightly different. I can't make them out. All I can recognize is the name Kristina.'

'Do you know anyone by that name?'

'My great-grandmother was called Kristina.'

'Do you have any German ancestry?'

'Yes, my aunt Gerda was German. She was married to my Uncle Simas, but they were killed in an accident when their tourist bus went over a cliff on the Great Ocean Road.'

'That's in Victoria, isn't it?'

'Yes, it was on the bend before a town called Lorne. Their bus was run off the road by a jeep that was travelling in the opposite direction. It was going well over the speed limit.'

'I'm sorry to hear that. Did they have any children?'

'Two boys, Helmut and Hans are younger than me.'

' In touch with them?'

'No, they were at least eight years younger than me.'

'Well Gail, you've obviously had a lot of tragedies in your family.'

'So what does all this mean? Why was I speaking in a foreign language?'

'Do you believe in re-incarnation?'

'No, we were brought up as Roman Catholics.'

'It's a strong possibility that you may have lived before, in another time. I'll have to consult with my colleagues and have someone identify what language is on the tape. Only when it's been translated, I'll have an answer for you. I'll have my receptionist ring you when I have the transcript.'

Gaila was totally overwhelmed and tried to process what she'd just been told. She automatically paid the receptionist, who told her that she'd ring her as soon as they had the results. Slowly, she walked out of the office and into the glare of the sun. Adjusting her sunglasses, she looked in the shop windows, before she made her way to her gallery in the Rocks.

'Did you have a nice morning shopping darling?' Myles greeted her as she walked in. 'I'm just getting organised for our opening this Friday night. Do you like the way I've arranged all the paintings? By the way, have you ordered the champagne and the canapés?'

Gaila blinked. She'd completely forgotten about it.

'Um, sorry I forgot. I'll get onto it immediately'

Myles shook his head. Gaila seemed to be lost in her own thoughts lately. Hopefully she'd be back to herself by Friday.

When they finally got home after the opening, Gaila checked the letterbox and picked up a letter addressed to her, with a strange stamp on the envelope. She tore it open and began to read.

Dear Gaila,

I don't know if you can read Samogitian or not, so I'm writing this letter in standard Lithuanian. I hope that you or someone can read it to you. I am your cousin Dana and your mother was my godmother. I found your address in the pile of letters my grandmother Virginia had. She was your grandmother Renata's sister. They had a stepsister called Julia. I am sorry to tell you that they are both dead now. Grandmother Julia died last year, a few years after her husband Kestas was killed whilst he was working on the new railway line. He was crushed under a load of sleepers that had fallen off the truck. Then my grandmother Virginia died two months later. Those two had spent all their lives together, and

I truly believe that Virginia could not bear to live by herself once Julia died.

Now that our country is independent once again and there's no Iron Curtain, I would like to meet you if you ever come to visit Lithuania. I looked after my grand-mothers until they died, and before that I looked after my uncle Darius, who was born a dwarf. I remember wearing his shoes so that I could go to school! He passed away not long after grandma died. She used to tell me that when she'd come to Australia, she would bring you a present from great grandmother Kristina.

You are very welcome to stay with me. I live in a town not far from Ventuva, though sometimes I think that I'd like to move back to the village. My husband can pick you up from the airport in Palanga. He'll recognise you because we have seen photos of your husband and chil-dren that your grandmother Renata sent us. I feel as if I know you already.

Please write back and tell me that you will come. Or maybe we could email each other? I have enclosed a photo of me and my family. Let me know when you de-cide to come and visit us in Lithuania.

Your cousin,
Dana.

After receiving Dana's letter, Gaila decided that in the near fu-ture, she would indeed like to visit Lithuania, but first she needed to know what was on that tape in Dr. Dobson's office. She finally revealed to Myles that she'd been to see him and asked whether he would come with her, after the secretary had rung to tell her that the tape had been translated. Dr. Dobson welcomed both of them into his office and turned on the tape.

> *'Vlad, what are you doing here? It's past midnight! And you're drunk!'*
>
> *'What do you mean, that you're going to pay? Make me pay? For what? What's my daughter Kristina got to do with it?'*
>
> *'You killed her husband Romas? Shame on you! You are an evil one! Let go of me! Help! Help! Anyone! Help me!'*
>
> *'What do you mean? What did you do to my daughter?'*
>
> *'Nooooo! Don't do this! Let me out! For pity's sake I'm just an old woman! Have mercy!'*
>
> *'Too bad you Prussian bitch! You're going to pay!'*
>
> *'Vlad, please don't set my cottage on fire. No! Help me! Fire! Fire! Someone help me!*

Gaila could say nothing, nothing at all. It was as if she had been pinned to the chair like a butterfly in a display cabinet. If the chair could only sprout wings and whisk her out through the window, into the endless blues skies.

Manly Beach
Sydney, Australia.

Dear Dana,

Thank you for your letter and telling me about my other relatives. We certainly seem to have a lot in common.

I don't know when I'll be able to travel to Lithuania. Maybe in a few years' time when our financial situation improves. Coincidentally, my grandmother Renata died around the same time as her sisters. She lived to be 100!

I think that I will bring the urn with her ashes with me, since she always wanted them scattered in her village. I'll let you know, please keep in touch.

Best wishes from Gaila,
Your cousin in Australia.

After a few years of exchanging emails with Dana, Gaila's plane finally touched down in Vilnius. She then took a connecting flight to Palanga, where she was met by her cousin Dana and her husband Dimas, a gipsy who wore a gold earring in one ear. After spending a night at their apartment, and being stuffed full of cabbage rolls, *kugelis* and a tree-shaped cake called *Šakotis*, she was taken to Palanga where her mother had been born. Dana pointed out the library, where before the war, Grandpa Petras's shops had been. Further along the main street, Dana showed Gaila a grey neglected, two-storey house, that Grandma Renata had been so proud to move into as a bride. Dimas stopped the car and Gaila got out to take a photo. A young couple was working in the front garden, planting flowers.

'What do you want? Why are you snooping around our house?'

'Sorry, but my grandparents lived here before the war.'

'So now you've come to claim it back have you? Fat chance of that!'

'No, just wanted to see what it looked like.'

Dana shrugged her shoulders. 'Don't let them get to you. Now that we're a free country again, everyone's scared stiff that the original owners will want to re-claim their properties.'

'I'm not interested in throwing people out of their homes,' replied Gaila. 'Thanks for bringing me here, mama used to tell me about all the parties that grandma Renata used to have.'

'She certainly was well known here,' replied Dana. 'I think that my grandmother Virginia was a bit jealous of her. Renata and Petras were very well off, whereas Virginia and Marius struggled on his policeman's wage in Ventuva.'

'All right, then. Are we ready to go to Ventuva now? It's not very far away,' said Dimas diplomatically. 'Do you want to see the beach first? It's still nice autumn weather. We call it an old crone's summer.'

Arm in arm, Gaila and Dana walked along the Palanga pier, in the same way their grandmothers did when they were all together during the summer months.

Later, they arrived at Renata's beloved village of Ventuva. It had been raining and as Gaila looked out of the car window, she felt as if time had stood still. Dimas drove the car along the old muddy road full of ruts and she saw the shabby wooden houses on either side. Sad, tumbledown cottages in need of repairs, painted in olive green or mustard. From time to time, they'd see a cow, or a goat. Dogs slept in the autumn sun. Kristina's humble cottage looked the same as in her grandmother's pre-war photos and the water well was still out the back near the barn. Once Dimas stopped the car, the villagers came flooding out of their houses.

'Look, look!' they shouted and waved. 'It's Ella's daughter!'

Old women her mother's age, with colourful, embroidered scarves and carved wooden walking sticks hobbled over to hug Gaila, inviting her into their cottages for endless cups of strong black tea and pieces of apple or plum cake. They showed her the letters and photos that Ella had sent to them over many years. Gaila was overwhelmed to see her own wedding photos among them. She didn't realise that her mother had been such a prolific writer, but obviously she'd kept in touch with her village playmates. Chickens and dogs followed her all over the tiny village. Old men pointed out the Venta River where Darius had fished for pike and the forest where Ventuva's partisans had hidden during World War Two. These people certainly knew their village's history. They told her all about the Singing Revolution, back in 1989 and how they'd linked arms with their Latvian neighbours across the river and sang their hearts out for independence. How they'd held hands with the Estonians too. Gaila thanked them and went to pick some flowers from behind the cottage to put on her great grandparents' graves. Then she went to the edge of the Venta River and scattered Renata's ashes from its banks, just as she had always longed for during the last years of her life.

'You have a special gift,' she'd told Gaila many times. 'But you must travel to Samogitia to unlock it.'

'Look!' exclaimed Dana. ' Just look at all these lovely presents that Renata sent Virginia and Julia over the years! They're still in their original boxes, untouched.'

'But why didn't they wear these clothes? They're all moth eaten now.'

'They kept hoping that the Soviets would let Virginia travel to be with their sister in Australia and then she'd need all these nice clothes over there. Renata even sent the money for her airfare.'

'How come she never came to Australia?' asked Gaila.

'The Soviets wouldn't let her, because of her husband Marius. Did you know he was one of the partisans around here? A freedom fighter. He got caught and was exiled to Siberia. The Soviets considered the whole family guilty back then.'

'That's so sad that they were never able to be together again. But my grandparents weren't very well off. Grandma was always complaining that Grandpa Petras was always short of money. You know, whenever I'd phone Grandma Renata, she would always begin her conversation with, 'Did I ever tell you about the time I jumped on my bike and pedalled like mad to warn the Forest Brothers that the Russians were coming?' She brought me up.'

'My grandma Virginia brought me up too, how about that? She told me lots about our family history. My parents lived in Latvia, but they wanted me to come here. Now tell me. How's my godmother Ella? Is she well?'

Gaila couldn't look into this kind-hearted woman's face and tell her that her Ella had taken an overdose of painkillers, rather than move into an aged care facility. How could she tell her that her grandfather Petras had loved another woman called Agata, and had somehow fathered two sons, whom he loved more than his own daughter? How the lawyer had advised her and Paul that her grandfather's will was still legal, because Grandma Renata hadn't made a new one after Petras died of prostate cancer. How she and Paul could have challenged the will in court, but that the court costs would have been so high they would have eaten up most of their savings.

Instead she said, 'I'm sorry to tell you this Dana, but my mother has passed away.'

'That's sad Gaila, my condolences. And your father? Is he still alive?'

'My father is in an aged care facility in Western Australia, that's thousands of kilometres away from where we live in Sydney. He's 90. My brother Max visits him.' She did not want to reveal that her father had dumped his parents into a shoddy aged care facility in Sydney before he left to live in Kalgoorlie, telling his brother Vygis that he could look after them. Or that Rasa and Bronius had died within three months of each other and that Al didn't even bother to fly back for their funerals.

'How is it that your father lives so far away from you?'

'It's a long story Dana. Have you got a few weeks to hear about it all? Let's just say, that my father was never satisfied with what he had. When his money and luck ran out, he rang up Max and told him that he was flying over to live with him.'

'Oh Gaila! Our poor parents, what traumatic lives they have led! Just think about it! Wars, famine, exile, deportation. You name it, they've had to live through it. I am really sorry that I never got to meet my grandfather. My mother still lives in Latvia. She remarried and is in Riga now. Marius was a really brave man, according to Grandma Virginia. Why don't we go across to that little café and have a coffee? We can talk some more.'

'Sure, that would be wonderful. I'm dying for a hot drink.'

Gaila sipped the strong black coffee. She hesitated before she spoke.

'Um, Dana, do you believe a person could have lived before, like in another era?'

'Why not? Our great grandmother Kristina used to tell Grandma Virginia that the ancient gods lived amongst them. Apparently she used to be a healer and had visions.'

'Ah well, I actually went to see a hypnotherapist.' Gaila told her cousin the story of how she'd been hypnotized and had spoken in a little girl's terrified voice in another language.

'I finally had to talk to a few of the really old people in the Lithuanian community after I'd written down some of the words phonetically. I sort of asked them casually what the words meant.

Those who originally came from Samogitia recognised the dialect straight away.'

'How about that! I can speak the dialect. Then what happened?'

'Well, the hypnotherapist had to be really careful you know. He wrote to the president of our community, when I told him that I'd managed to get some words identified. He asked the president if there was anyone willing to translate a tape he had, but it had to be strictly confidential.'

'Don't keep me in suspense. Come on Gaila, tell me what was on the tape.'

'I know the tape off by heart now.' She took a deep breath and began to recall what was in the tape.

Gaila choked back her sobs. 'And there I was, screaming in a little girl's voice, that the village was on fire!'

'Oh Gaila, Gaila! How dreadful!' said Dana with tears in her eyes. 'And you've had these nightmares, reliving all this? People didn't know how that fire started in Ventuva, just that my great-great grandmother Elena died when her house caught on fire. The authorities assumed that she and many others died, trying to put out the fire as it spread to their houses. It's all there in the village records. That Vlad was certainly an evil one!'

'So, do you think that I really could have been a little girl, living back in those days?'

'Maybe, stranger things have been known to happen,' replied Dana.

Gaila was emotionally exhausted at having to live through the tragedy again.

'Do you think I should ask the hypnotherapist to hypnotise me again and erase that horrible memory?'

'I don't know, you'll have to ask him. You obviously need to do something to stop those nightmares you've been having. Perhaps you really were a little village girl who witnessed what that horrible man Vlad did to our great-grandmother Elena.'

'You're right Dana. How could I possibly know what caused the Great Fire of Ventuva? Um, there's something else I want to ask you. Can you take a look at this little book that my daughter found amongst Ella's things. Is it a recipe book?'

Dana turned the yellowed pages carefully. 'Yes some of it is, but it seems that there are some old remedies for various illnesses here as well. If you like, I can translate the recipes for you from Samogitian into standard Lithuanian.'

'Really? Could you? That would be really helpful. Thank you!'

'I'd be happy to do it. I'll email them to you when I've finished.'

When it was nearly time for Gaila to return to the airport, Dana told her that she had something to give to her. Back they went into Kristina's cottage. Carefully, Dana unlocked a drawer in an ancient sideboard and handed her cousin an old wooden jewellery box, with carved tulips on both sides. Wrapped in a threadbare linen handkerchief, Gaila saw a few pieces of broken amber jewellery. Amongst them, was the same circular amber pendant she'd noticed her great grandmother Kristina wearing, in one of the faded black and white photos that she'd found in Ella's album. At the bottom of the box, was a yellowed card with a sprig of dried rue on the front.

In a shaky, spidery script, Kristina had written these words, *'I leave this pendant to my great granddaughter Gaila. Take this circle of amber and repeat this magic chant three times. Forever it will protect you and those dear to you.'*

Gaila began to read softly to herself, *'Turn circle turn, turn to the East. Turn circle turn, turn to the West. Turn circle turn, turn to the North. Turn circle turn, turn to the South.'*

FAMILY TREES

KRISTINA

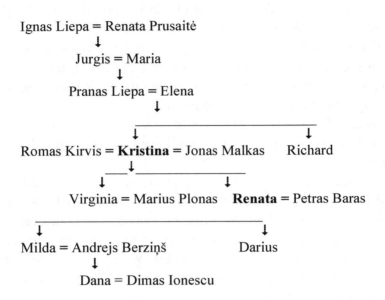

Ignas Liepa = Renata Prusaitė
  ↓
  Jurgis = Maria
   ↓
  Pranas Liepa = Elena
    ↓

Romas Kirvis = **Kristina** = Jonas Malkas Richard
    ↓

Virginia = Marius Plonas **Renata** = Petras Baras

Milda = Andrejs Berziņš Darius
 ↓
Dana = Dimas Ionescu

ROMAS

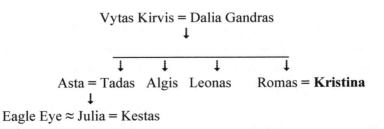

Vytas Kirvis = Dalia Gandras
    ↓

Asta = Tadas Algis Leonas Romas = **Kristina**
 ↓
Eagle Eye ≈ Julia = Kestas

RENATA

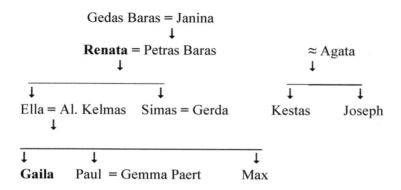

Gedas Baras = Janina
↓
Renata = Petras Baras ≈ Agata
↓ ↓

Ella = Al. Kelmas   Simas = Gerda   Kestas   Joseph
↓

Gaila   Paul = Gemma Paert   Max

GAILA

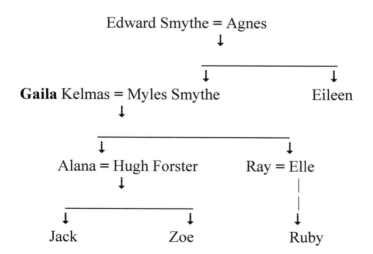

Edward Smythe = Agnes
↓

Gaila Kelmas = Myles Smythe   Eileen
↓

Alana = Hugh Forster   Ray = Elle
↓

Jack   Zoe   Ruby

Notations: ↓ descent   = married   ≈ affair

RECIPE SECTION

Kristina and her daughters would have mixed all their ingredients by hand and cooked on a wood stove. If you use a food processor or a Thermomix, the preparation time for these dishes will be much quicker. With a fan forced oven, set your temperature 10- 20 degrees lower that the temperatures in the recipes, depending on your oven. Icing sugar is also known as powdered sugar. Vanilla or almond essence is also known as vanilla/almond extract. The flour described in these recipes is ordinary plain/all-purpose flour unless self-raising flour is mentioned. Margarine can be substituted for butter if you wish. Different regions in Lithuania have different names for many well-known dishes. There are also quite a few dishes common to Lithuania, Latvia and Estonia. I have included the ones mentioned in the novel. It's useful to watch a video on YouTube first, if you have never attempted these dishes. There are numerous websites as well for these dishes and many others.

TABLE OF MEASUREMENTS

CUPS	FLUID OZ.	TABLESPOONS	TEASPOONS
1	8	16	48
¾	6	12	36
⅔	5⅓	10½	32
½	4	8	24
⅓	2⅔	5.3	16
¼	2	4	12
⅛	1	2	6

POTATO DUMPLINGS

Cepelinai, Didžkukuliai, Kleckai, Cepeliņi, Karfacze

This recipe takes about 70 minutes. Use the smallest holes of your grater or use a food processor or you can buy electric potato graters online. If you've never made *cepelinai* before, here's a video:

https://www.youtube.com/watch?v=MFgygJKtE8E

Ingredients for dumplings:

8 large Idaho or old/starchy potatoes, peeled and finely grated; 2 large Idaho or old/starchy potatoes, peeled, boiled and mashed; 1 medium onion, peeled and finely grated; 1 teaspoon salt; ⅓ cup of potato flour; 1 egg, and 1 crushed Vitamin C tablet or the juice of 1 lemon (to avoid darkening of grated potato)

Ingredients for filling:

1 pound (500 gm.) ground pork (or use a mixture of ⅓ pork, ⅓ beef, ⅓ veal); 1 medium finely diced onion; 1 teaspoon salt; ¼ teaspoon pepper and 1 large beaten egg

Ingredients for sauce:

½ pound (250 gm.) diced bacon; 1 large diced onion; 1 cup of sour cream; fresh mushrooms (optional) with salt & pepper to taste.

In a large bowl, mix all the meat ingredients thoroughly. Refrigerate until ready to use. Add the lemon juice to the grated potatoes so they don't turn dark. Place the grated potatoes in a cheesecloth/muslin cloth/a cotton tea towel and twist over a large bowl to get rid of the excess water. Pour off the water, reserving the potato starch at the bottom of the bowl. Unwrap the cloth and place potatoes in bowl with the potato starch that was reserved. Add the mashed potatoes, grated onion and salt. Mix in the beaten egg and extra potato flour.

Put a large saucepan of water on to boil. Add the salt. Form the *cepelinai*, by taking about 1 cup of dumpling mixture and pat it flat in the palm of the hand. Place ¼ cup or more of meat mixture in the centre and, using slightly dampened hands, fold the potato mixture around the meat into a football/zeppelin shape, sealing well. Continue until both mixtures are used up. You can make smaller *cepelinai* if you prefer. Make sure your hands are damp as you form each *cepelinas*, so it is smooth.

Lower dumplings carefully into salted, boiling water to which 1 tablespoon of cornstarch has been added, to prevent dumplings from falling apart. Make sure the water returns to the boil and continues boiling for approximately 25 minutes. Remove dumplings, with a slotted spoon and place on a heated platter.

While the dumplings are boiling gently, make the sauce. Fry the bacon and onion until tender. Drain and combine with sour cream, salt and pepper. Thin with 1-2 tablespoons milk if necessary. Pour the sauce over the *cepelinai* or serve it in a separate dish at the table. Left over *cepelinai* can be cut in half and fried the next day, or reheated whole in the microwave.

ROAST DUCK

Depending on its size, a duck takes approximately 20-25 mins per 500 gm./1lb. to cook.

Defrost duck in fridge over 1-2 days if it is frozen. You can cook the duck in a large oven bag, on a rotisserie or on top of a rack in a shallow roasting pan. First, preheat the oven to 425F/220C/200 fan-forced.

Wash the duck inside and out having removed all the innards, excess fat and the tail end. Pat dry with kitchen paper. Prick the skin all over with a fork, but don't pierce the meat. Pull out any left -over quills with tweezers. Stuff the cavity with apple quarters and prunes. Cut off wing tips with a knife or kitchen scissors. Tie together the duck's legs and wings with white kitchen string. Set duck on its back on a rack in a big shallow roasting pan and roast in the centre of the oven. After 15 mins, lower heat to 350F/180C/160ff. Turn duck over every 45mins. Remove any fat that may have accumulated at bottom of the pan. To check if cooked, pierce a thigh with the tip of a sharp knife, if the juice is yellow, it is ready, if it's pink, roast for another 5-10 minutes. If you have a meat thermometer, it should register at 175F/165C at the thickest part of a duck leg. Remove duck from oven to rest for 10 minutes before carving.

To serve: Carve the duck and arrange on the platter with the cooked apple and prunes. Serve with your favourite gravy sauce.

COTTAGE CHEESE DUMPLINGS

Sūrnikai, Varškēčiai, Varškētukai

Serves 4 - 6 people.

Ingredients:

1½ lb. (750 gm.) cottage cheese
4 egg yolks
½ tsp. salt
5 oz. (150 gm.) plain flour.
For the sauce:
4 oz. (120 gm.) melted butter
1 cup of dried breadcrumbs.

Method:

Drain the cottage cheese by placing it in a colander, cover with a tea towel and weight it with a heavy dish. Let it drain for 2 - 3 hours. If you buy very firm cottage cheese, you can omit this process. Rub the cottage cheese through a large sieve into a big mixing bowl. Beat in the egg yolks one by one, and gradually mix in the flour and salt. Shape this dough into several, long thin sausage shaped cylinders on a floured board. Using a flat knife, flatten the top of each roll and then make a criss-cross pattern along the length and let it rest for 30 minutes in a cool spot or in the fridge. With a sharp knife, cut the dough into diamond shapes. Boil water in a large pot and gently drop in the dumplings. In the meantime, fry the butter and add the dried breadcrumbs, set aside. The dumplings are ready when they rise to the surface. Remove them carefully with a slotted spoon and arrange them on a warm serving plate. Pour over the sauce.

Alternatively, you can shape the dough into small round balls and then flatten them to look like meat patties. Melt butter/margarine in frypan, fry the *sūrnikai* for 3 - 5 minutes on either side till they are golden brown. Transfer each batch onto a warm plate and put into the oven on a low heat. Serve hot with sour cream or with jam and cream as a dessert.

RYE BREAD

Ruginė Duona, Rudzu Maize.

Ingredients:

¼ oz. dry yeast
1 tsp. sugar
1 egg
1 cup warm milk
1½ tsp. salt
1 cup rye flour
2½ cups bleached all-purpose plain flour
1 tblsp. caraway seeds (optional).
Also use 1tsp. vegetable oil and one large egg, to glaze the top of the loaf.

Method:

Combine yeast, sugar, melted butter, egg and milk into the bowl of an electric mixer, using the dough hook. Beat at low speed for 1 minute. Add salt, rye flour, plain flour & caraway seeds, and beat for another 1 minute until the flour is incorporated. Then beat at medium speed until the mixture forms a ball, leaves the side of the bowl.

Remove dough from the bowl and by hand, form into a smooth ball. Lightly oil a big bowl & place the dough inside, cover with plastic cling-wrap and set aside in a warm place. After about 1 hour it would have doubled in size.

Preheat the oven to 350F / 180C or 160C (fan-forced), lightly grease a 9" x 5½" baking tin.

Remove the risen dough and invert onto a lightly floured surface, then gently knead, erasing any seams. Cover once again with cling wrap and set aside for another hour until it redoubles in size.

Then brush the egg wash over the top of the dough. Bake for about 45 mins, until lightly brown. Tap the crust. If it sounds hollow, the bread is ready. Remove from the oven & invert onto a cooling rack for the bread to cool.

GRATED POTATO BAKE

Kugelis: serves 2

If you have never made *kugelis* before, it is recommended that you watch a video beforehand. Note that in this video, all measures are imperial, not metric. You can use a cake tin, oven proof dish or even a muffin tin to bake *kugelis*. If you are vegetarian, substitute 1 tablespoon of oil for the bacon. You can also use lactose free milk/cream to make the *kugelis* and for the cream sauce.

https://www.youtube.com/watch?v=p9mFb03H1oo

Ingredients:

1 tablespoon butter
2 lb. (1 kg.) old potatoes
¼ lb. (125 gm.) diced bacon
1 medium onion, finely diced
1 beaten egg
30 ml. or 3 oz. cup warmed milk
juice of 1 lemon or 1 crushed Vitamin C tablet to stop potatoes from going grey, and some salt & pepper to taste

Method:

Preheat oven to 425°F/220C/200C fan-forced. Grease an oven proof baking dish. Grate the potatoes on the smallest holes of a big grater, and save the water/potato starch in a separate dish. The mixture should look a bit like apple sauce. You can buy an electric potato grater over the internet or do it in a food processor using the smallest hole grater component.

Fry diced bacon until it's crisp, then add chopped onion to the 2 tablespoons of bacon fat. Cook until onion is soft and brown. Remove from heat and set aside.

Combine beaten eggs and milk and season with salt and pepper. Place grated potatoes in centre of clean tea towel. Close towel around potato and twist the towel to ring out water into a bowl. Repeat until all the water's been squeezed out. Transfer the drained potato mix to a big mixing bowl. Save the drained water and let the potato starch sink to the bottom. In the mixing bowl, add the egg/milk mixture to the drained potato mix. Add chopped bacon and onions, as well as the fat, to the potato mixture and, using a wooden spoon, mix until all ingredients are well combined. Add the starch and the squeezed-out the water from the squeezed out potatoes. Pour the kugelis mixture into a greased baking pan or an oven proof dish, lightly sprayed with oil.

Place in preheated oven and bake on 425F / 220C or 200C fan-forced, for 15 minutes. Turn down heat to 350F / 180C or 160 fan-forced and bake for an hour until the top becomes brown and is beginning to come away from the edge of the baking dish. Serve with sour cream/sour cream and fried mushrooms and chives. Left over *kugelis* can be fried the next day or reheated in the micro-wave. If you freeze *kugelis*, it has a tendency to crumble when defrosted & reheated.

COLD BEETROOT SOUP

Šaltibarščiai, Aukstā zupa, Külm Peedisupp

Ingredients:

4 cups of buttermilk
2 cups of cooked and peeled and cooked beetroot (with the cooking liquid)
1 cup sour cream
¼ cup finely chopped fresh chives
¼ cup finely chopped fresh dill
4 hard-boiled eggs cut into quarters
2 peeled, seeded, and diced cucumbers, with salt & pepper to taste.

Method:

Freeze the cooked beetroot for about two hours and then grate them. Use rubber gloves to avoid staining hands. Otherwise you can use a can of diced beetroot.

Pour the sour cream and buttermilk in another bowl; add in the beetroot (with the cooking liquid) and cucumbers. Refrigerate the mixture till it is chilled. Season the chilled soup with salt and pepper as per your taste. Place the eggs in the soup and garnish it with the chopped chives. Serve with boiled potatoes garnished with dill. If you haven't got any fresh chives or dill, you can use dried ones.

POTATO SALAD

Vinegretas, Mišrainė

Ingredients:

4 large boiled potatoes with the skin on
2 medium sized cooked beetroots with skin on (optional)
2 large diced dill cucumbers
2 hard-boiled eggs
1 handful of fresh, finely chopped dill
1 to 1¼ cups sour cream, with salt & pepper to taste.

Method:

When the potatoes have cooled, peel them, then dice and place in a large bowl. Using rubber gloves, peel the beetroot, dice and add to the potatoes. If you are in a hurry you can use a small can of drained, diced beetroot. Chop and add the dill cucumbers. Dice and add the eggs. Chop and add the dill. Mix everything gently together with sour cream; start with one cup and add more if desired. Salt and pepper to taste. Some people add beans or cooked diced carrots and peas to the potatoes. There are many regional variations of this recipe.

MEAT IN ASPIC

Košeliena, Šaltiena

Ingredients:

1 bay leaf
1 carrot, peeled cleaned and cut into 4 pieces
1 chicken breast with the bone retained
1 pinch of coarse salt
1 onion peeled, but left whole
6 - 10 peppercorns and 1 pig's foot, halved or quartered.

Method:

Fill a large pot with cold water and bring it to the boil. Add the meat, let it come to a boil again and let it boil vigorously for three to four minutes. Pour into a colander and rinse with cold water. Refrigerate the chicken.

Place the pork and all remaining ingredients in a saucepan or slow cooker and cover with cold water. Cook for 6 - 8 hours. The pig's foot should be quite tender, and you should be able to cut through it with a spoon. Add the chicken and continue to cook for another three hours Remove the meat. Remove the skin and bones from chicken, shred the meat and put it in a large bowl. Remove the bones from the pig's foot - there are many small ones - and julienne or finely dice the meat and skin. Mix together with the chicken. Remove and discard the vegetables and bay leaf. If a skin has formed, skim and discard. Divide the meat among three or four shallow bowls. Ladle the remaining broth over the meat until it is covered. Cover with plastic and put in the refrigerator. Scrape off the fat that has risen to the top of the dish. Skim the fat off the remaining broth. Ladle additional broth over the dish to create an aspic layer. To serve, cut into squares or wedges and serve with horseradish or a lemon wedge. Horseradish cream (mayonnaise-based dressing) is also good with this. You can make this is one large dish, just make sure that it's shallow, no more than about 5 cm. / 2 in. deep.

POTATO SAUSAGES

Vėdarai

This recipe will take about 2 hours.

Ingredients:

Ask your butcher for enough pigs' intestines to make 2lb. (1 kg.) of sausages. Rinse the intestines three times and set aside.

This mixture makes 2 lb./1 kg.

12 medium peeled potatoes, finely grated
1 large finely chopped onion.
3 tablespoons butter or 3 strips chopped bacon
2 large eggs.
½ teaspoon marjoram, salt and pepper
a few tblsp. plain/all-purpose flour, if necessary.

Ingredients:

½ lb. (250 gm.) finely diced bacon
1 large chopped onion
1 cup sour cream
salt & pepper to taste
and if necessary, 1 to 2 tablespoons milk.

Method:

Sauté 1 large finely chopped onion in 3 tablespoons butter or omit the butter and sauté the onion in 3 strips chopped bacon. Let it come to room temperature. In a large bowl, combine 12 medium finely grated potatoes, onion with or without bacon, 2 large eggs, ½ teaspoon marjoram, if using, salt and pepper to taste. If mixture is too loose, add a few tablespoons of flour. Stuff the mixture into the cleaned pigs' intestines. Prick the casing in several spots so it doesn't explode while cooking. Boil in salted water for about 1 hour or boil 45 minutes and then brown in a 350F/180C oven in a greased pan for 15 minutes.

Using another method, you can also place the uncooked potato sausage in a greased baking dish with ¼ cup water and bake in the oven for about 1 hour or until golden brown on 350F/180C. Whilst sausages are cooking, make the bacon and cream sauce.

Sour cream sauce

Fry the diced bacon and 1 large chopped onion until tender. Drain off all fat and combine bacon-onion mixture with sour cream and pepper. Thin with 1 to 2 tablespoons milk, if necessary.

SAVOURY PASTRIES

Kibinai

Ingredients:

3½ cups plain/all-purpose flour
1 cup lard or shortening
6 tbsp. butter
½ lb. (250 gm.) minced beef
½ lb. (250 gm.) minced pork
1 large finely diced onion
3 cloves garlic chopped finely, salt & pepper to taste
1 cup icy cold water, and 1 beaten egg for glazing.

Method:

In a large bowl, combine the flour, lard and salt with a knife. Add cold water to form a dough.

Shape it into a ball, wrap it in cling wrap and refrigerate it for a few hours.

Then in a bowl, combine the meat, onions, garlic and seasoning.

Divide the dough into six balls. Roll them out, place a little bit of butter in the centre of each ball, then put about one spoon of filling in the centre. Fold over and join the edges of the dough to make a semicircle. Use fingers or crimp the edges of the semicircle with a fork to seal in the stuffing.

Bake the *kibinai* on a greased tray, or lined with baking paper, in a preheated oven for forty-five minutes to an hour at 350°F / 180C.

To get the gold color, brush them with beaten egg, 10 to 15 minutes once they are cooked.

MEAT DUMPLINGS

Koldūnai

Ingredients:

3 cups of plain flour
5 eggs
1½ lb. (750 gm.) minced beef or pork
1 large diced onion
3 cloves chopped garlic
1 tbsp. water with salt & pepper, to taste.

Method:

In one large bowl, combine two eggs, the meat, salt, pepper, onion, and garlic.

In a second bowl, put in the flour, three eggs, and water, to make a dough.

Divide the dough into three parts and roll it out till it is about ⅛ of an inch thick.

Using a biscuit cutter or a glass, cut out 3 inch (7.5 cm.) diameter discs of dough. Place one tablespoon of the meat mixture in the centre and join the edges of the dough to make a semicircle. Pinch the edges with damp fingers to seal in the mixture. In a large saucepan, add about six cups of water and pinch of salt to it and bring it to a boil. Drop the dumplings in very gently, and let the water continue to boil. Turn down heat. The *koldūnai* are done after they float to the top and have been simmering for 5-10 minutes. Remove 0ne and cut it in half to taste if the meat is cooked. Remove the dumplings and drizzle with some sour cream and garnish with finely chopped parsley. Or you can serve them with diced fried bacon and fried mushrooms in a sour cream sauce if you prefer If you are in a hurry, you can use the oval Chinese *gow-gee* dumpling wrappers from the supermarket or a Chinese store and use the meat recipe above. They are much faster to cook.

POTATO PANCAKES

Bulviniai blynai, Kartupeļu Pankūkas, Kartulikotletid

Ingredients:

4 large peeled and grated potatoes
1egg
1 tblsp. plain flour
1 tblsp. vegetable or olive oil & salt, to taste.

Method:

Add all the ingredients in a bowl and mix well. Heat the oil in a nonstick frying pan. Spoon the potato mixture into the hot oil. Fry until golden brown, flip then fry the other side. Serve hot with sour cream.

CABBAGE ROLLS

Balandėliai, Kāpostu tīteņi , kapsarull

Ingredients:
1 big whole cabbage
1 lb. (500 gm.) minced beef
1cup beef stock
¼ cup uncooked rice
1 large diced onion
2 large carrots cut into thin rings
1-3 cloves chopped garlic
1egg
2 tblsp. tomato puree
1tsp dried marjoram
salt & pepper to taste, and 1 dried bay leaf.

Method:

Run a sharp knife around the central core of a big cabbage, and remove the core. Place the cabbage in a big pot of boiling water with its stump side down, and let it boil for seven to eight minutes. Remove and drain the cabbage, let it cool and separate out the leaves on a clean dry tea towel. You can also cook the leaves separately in the microwave till soft.

In a bowl, mix the meat with the uncooked rice, egg, marjoram, salt, and pepper.

Place a big spoonful of the meat mixture in a cabbage leaf, then roll and fold into a parcel shape. Secure with one or two toothpicks or with cotton thread wrapped around the parcel. Make as many packages as you can with the mixture. Place the rest of the cabbage at the bottom of a big ovenproof dish and layer these little packages on top of them. Pour in the tomato purée and the beef stock onto the cabbage rolls and add the bay leaf. Scatter the carrot rings on the top. Cover with a lid or foil. Cook in a pre-heated oven on 180C / 350F for about forty-five minutes to an hour. You can also cook them in a slow cooker or a big frying pan with a lid. Season according to taste. Transfer to a hot serving dish if necessary. Remove the cotton thread and tooth picks before serving. Serve with boiled potatoes.

BACON BUNS

Lašinėčiai, Pīrāgi, Pirukad

Ingredients:

1lb (500gm) plain/all purpose flour
1 cup milk
4 teaspoons fresh yeast
4 tablespoons butter
2 teaspoons sugar
salt and 1 beaten egg for the glaze.

Ingredients for Filling:

½ lb. (250 gm.) finely diced bacon
1 finely chopped onion
1 tablespoon butter
½ teaspoon ground allspice
¼ teaspoon ground cinnamon and ¼ tsp. ground cloves & a pinch
of salt.

Method:

Mix the yeast with sugar, dissolve in warm milk. Add half of the
flour, mix well and let rise for 1 hour. Then add remaining flour,
melted butter, salt and knead well. Set in warm spot to rise for
another hour. To make the filling, fry the onion in butter, then add
the bacon and spices to the frypan. Mix it all together and gently
heat, but do not over-fry it.

Roll out the dough to ½ inch (1.3 cm.) thickness, cut out 2½ inch
(6 cm.) rounds, or just take a pinch of dough from the whole piece.

Place 1 teaspoon of the filling inside the dough, fold over and seal the edges. Place them on the baking tray and let rise for 30 minutes. Brush tops with beaten egg and bake in a preheated oven at 350F / 180C, until lightly browned for about 30 minutes. Eat hot or cold. Can be frozen and defrosted for later.

AIR DRIED SAUSAGES

Skilandis

Ingredients:

2 lb. (1kg.) ground/minced pork
2 cloves crushed garlic
1tsp pennycress seed
1tsp. mustard seed
1tsp marjoram
1tsp MSG (optional)
1tsp. nitrate of potash, 1tsp freshly ground black pepper and 1tsp. salt.
Pork casings from the butcher. Ask for quantity required.

Method:

Combine the pork and crushed garlic and distribute the garlic evenly throughout the pork. In a small bowl, mix the dry ingredients together. Sprinkle this dry blend over the pork mixture and combine thoroughly.

Stuff this mixture into the casings. Remove any air pockets by forcing them to the open end of the sausage before knotting it shut. Hang the sausages in an area where it is around 60°F/13C with good air circulation to dry for one week. You can drape mesh over the sausages to keep stray insects from reaching it. Drying time will vary with humidity levels and air circulation. After the sausages feel dry to the touch, you can cook them. In a big stockpot, bring water to the boil, add the sausages, and then simmer for one hour. Serve with potatoes and sauerkraut.

SAUERKRAUT

Kopūstai

Ingredients:

1 cabbage
2 cups sauerkraut
1 big onion
3 slices bacon
1 soup spoon of caraway seeds
1tblsp raw brown sugar
1 grated carrot, 4 black peppercorns & bay leaves, and salt & pepper to taste.

Method:

Dice the onions and bacon and sauté in a large pot, on medium heat until the onions are a golden colour. Shred the cabbage and add to the pot with the grated carrot and cover. Lower the heat to medium low and cook until the cabbage starts to get limp (about 20 minutes.) Add the sauerkraut, peppercorns and bay leaves. If you like vinegar, add sauerkraut without rinsing, otherwise rinse it. Stir often. Let simmer for at least an hour and a half, stirring often. Add 1 tblsp. raw brown sugar. The longer you cook it, the better the flavours mix. You can also do this in a slow cooker. Check the taste and add some salt if needed. Don't let the sauerkraut go dry. Add more water if needed. It should be juicy.

WHOLE SAUSAGE

Skilandis, Kinziukas

Traditional Lithuanian sausage. It is made in a pig's stomach stuffed with minced meat, which is cold-smoked and cured for a long time. This recipe will be enough for 6 servings.

Ingredients:

10 kg. (20 lb.) pork
400gm (4/5 lb) salt
10 gm. (⅓ oz.) sugar
10 gm. (⅓ oz.) ground pepper
1 clove garlic
1 pig's stomach from the butcher.
A quantity of lard if the pork is very lean.

Method:

Chop the meat into small pieces, then mix in some chopped lard (if the pork is too lean). Add salt, seasonings and mix thoroughly. Stuff the well-cleaned pork's stomach tightly with the mixture. Squeeze out excess air to avoid air bubbles. Sew up the stuffed stomach with cotton thread and then compress it between two saucers using string. Compress and let set for 3-5 days, then smoke-dry. When the casing fogs up with smoke, tighten the saucers around the sausage. A smaller sized *skilandis* is ready in a week, a bigger one takes longer. *Skilandis* can be eaten raw or cooked. When boiling it in water, it is advisable to wrap the cut piece of *skilandis* into a linen cloth/tea towel so it won't break apart.

LATVIAN GREY PEAS WITH
<u>BACON AND ONIONS</u>

Pelēkie zirņi

Ingredients:

1 cup dried grey peas (available online)1 medium onion, finely diced
¼ lb (125gm) of speck or bacon finely diced, with salt & pepper to taste.

Method:

Soak peas overnight in lots of water. Rinse and drain Pour into a pot and cover with plenty of water. Add a pinch of salt. Bring to boil, reduce to a simmer and cover. Cook for 2 hours or so, until peas are tender. When peas are nearly done, fry up onion and bacon together with some salt and pepper until everything is nicely browned. Spoon the bacon and onions over the bowl of peas. Serves 2.

LATVIAN TWO LAYERED VEGETABLE TARTS

Sklandrausis

Ingredients:

Dough

1 kg. (2 lb.) rye flour
0.5 litre (2 cups) water
2 tblsp. oil
2 tblsp. sour milk
200 gm. (1 cup) wholemeal flour (for dough rolling).

Filling No. 1

1 kg/2lb potatoes
150 gm. (1 cup) framer's cheese or ricotta
300 ml. (½ pint) boiled milk
5 eggs
200 ml. (⅔ cup) sour cream
100 gm. (1 cup) sugar
½ tsp salt and ½ tsp. caraway seeds.

Filling No. 2

1.5 kg. (3 lb.) carrots
5 eggs
300 ml. (½ pint) sour cream
150 gm. (1 cup) caraway seeds
½ tsp salt and ½ tblsp wholemeal flour.

Method:

Tart dough preparation:

Mix all the dough ingredients, and let the dough rest. Then roll out the dough until it is 1.5-2mm (⅛ inch) thick. Cut out circles of 10-12cm (4 inches) in diameter, allowing 1-1.5cm for the border or the tart. Place the tart cases in a greased muffin tin.

Filling no.1: for the bottom layer of the vegetable tart.

Finely grate half of the peeled potatoes. Wring out the excess liquid in a clean cloth. Add caraway seeds, some salt and boiling milk. Cook other half of the unpeeled potatoes. After potatoes are done, peel and mash. Mix with the farmer's cheese or riccotta and the other ingredients. Fill the tart cases with the potato mixture until half full.

Filling no. 2: for top layer of vegetable tart.

Partially cook the whole carrots. When cool, grate half of them roughly and the other half finely. Mix with the rest of ingredients. Put this carrot mixture on top of the first potato filling. Top tarts with caraway seeds. Bake in oven on 200C/400F 10-15 minutes or until done. Whilst still hot, scatter tops of tarts with sugar or with honey or butter.

DILL CUCUMBERS

Marinuoti Agurkai

Ingredients:

2 lb. (1 kg.) small washed cucumbers
10 big sprigs dill; 1 cup white vinegar
2 tblsp. salt
2 tsp. sugar
2 tsp. black peppercorns
2 tsp. caraway seeds
two big 2 pint (1.2 litre) jars with lids that will hold 4-5 cups of liquid.

Method:

Divide cucumbers and dill between the jars. Bring vinegar, salt, sugar, peppercorns, caraway seeds and 2 cups water to a boil in a saucepan, stirring to dissolve salt and sugar. Pour hot brine into jars, dividing evenly, and cover. Let cool, then chill.

DESSERTS

LAZY CAKE

Tinginys

This is known as 'Hedgehog slice' in Australia. No baking needed!

Ingredients:

7 ounces / 220 gm. hard biscuits like Arnott's coffee biscuits
3 oz. / 100 g unsalted butter
1 can (14 ounces / 400 gm.) sweetened condensed milk
5 tblsp cocoa powder
¼ cup / 60 ml milk
¼ tsp salt & a handful of dried fruits and chopped nuts (optional).

Method:

Break the biscuits into small pieces into a mixing bowl. Set aside. Mix the cocoa powder and milk until the mixture is smooth without lumps.

Melt the butter in a saucepan, pour in the condensed milk, add the cocoa mixed in milk and slowly bring to a boil while stirring. Turn off the heat and let cool for 10 minutes. Pour the mixture onto broken biscuits pieces and mix to coat. Mix in any dried fruits or nuts.

Place the mass on a sheet of baking paper, fold the paper over and press firmly to form a cake shape. You can also put the mixture into a square or oval dish lined with baking paper. Place in a refrigerator. Let set for several hours, then slice and serve.

NAPOLEON TORTE

Tortas Napoleonas

This cake needs to be made at least 2 days in advance and you will need a lot of bench space.

Ingredients for the dough:

4 cups all purpose/plain flour
1lb. (500 gm.) salted butter
1 pint (2½ cups) sour cream.

Ingredients for the Filling:

250 ml. (1 cup) milk
1 vanilla bean, split or a tsp of vanilla essence
¾ cup cornflour
½ cup custard powder
220 gm. (1 cup) caster/powdered sugar
750 ml. (3 cups) thickened/heavy cream
50 gm. (just under ¼ of a cup) unsalted butter, and 3 egg yolks.

Method:

Preheat oven to 350F / 180C or 160C fan forced. Sift flour onto pastry board. In a food processor or with two knives, gradually cut softened butter into flour until crumbly. Blend in sour cream. Divide dough into 11 or 12 egg round balls.

Refrigerate overnight in covered bowl. Before baking, let dough stand at room temperature about 15 minutes. Roll each ball so it is wafer thin, placed between 2 sheets of baking paper, or laid on a very lightly floured board.

Place onto a pizza tray lined with baking paper. Prick all over with a fork. Bake each layer for 5 to 10 minutes or until a light golden colour. Cool. Set aside. Make the filling. Stack cake layers atop each other and with a round plate on top, using a very sharp knife, trim the sides, saving trimmings for crumbs to go on top layer. Arrange the layers together with filling, with the top layer spread with the filling. Crumble the left over trimmings and sprinkle all over the cake and refrigerate overnight. Before serving, let cake stand for half an hour at room temperature.

To make the Filling:

Place milk in a pan over medium heat. Scrape in vanilla seeds and add bean too. Warm gently, then set aside for 10 minutes. Place corn flour, custard powder and caster sugar in a pan. Strain milk, (discard vanilla bean) into pan with cornflour and whisk until smooth. Add cream, then return to heat, stirring constantly, over low heat until the mixture thickens and boils. Add butter, stirring well to combine, then remove from heat and whisk in egg yolks, one at a time, until smooth. Set aside to cool.

Assembly

Stack pastry layers on top of each other and with a round plate on top, using a very sharp knife, trim the sides, saving trimmings for crumbs to go on top layer. Arrange the layers together with filling. You can add pureed apples or apricots in some of the layers or jam. Spread the top layer with the filling. Crumble the left over trimmings and sprinkle all over the cake and refrigerate overnight. Before serving, let cake stand for half an hour at room temperature.

NAPOLEON TORTE (QUICK VERSION)

Tortas Napoleonas

Make 24 hours in advance so that the filling can meld with the pastry layers.

Ingredients for pastry layers:

A packet of 5 butter puff pastry sheets

Filling:

200 gm. butter at room temperature
1 tin condensed milk & a few spoonfuls of jam.

Method:

Preheat oven to 360F / 185C or 165fan-forced.

Cut the sheets of puff pastry into 1cm width strips, prick all over and place on trays covered with baking paper. Bake until they are a pale brown colour. Cool pastry strips on a cooling rack. Set aside 3 strips to crumble and put on top of the torte.

In a big bowl, using electric beaters, beat the butter until fluffy and then add the condensed milk slowly, whilst continuing to beat the mixture. Make sure to mix well.

Arrange 5 pastry strips on the bottom of the serving plate, next to each other and spread on about a spoonful of the filling. Continue layers and filling till the last layer. You will have about 4 layers. On the top layer spread the jam of your choice and the last of the filling. Crumble the leftover layer crumbs on the top and the sides.

Place toothpicks on top of cake and cover with foil. Refrigerate overnight so that the filling melds with the pastry layers.

Alternative filling for *Tortas Napoleonas*:

100 gm. / 3 ½ oz. packet of instant vanilla pudding mix, ¾ cup whole full cream milk

1 cup (250 ml) of thickened or heavy cream, 1 teaspoon vanilla essence and some jam.

Method:

Mix the milk and cream in a big mixing bowl. Add the vanilla essence. Sprinkle the pudding mix over the top. Using electric beaters, beat all the ingredients together until thick. Place in refrigerator until you're ready to fill the pastry layers. Place the first layer in a serving dish. Spread it with the custard filling. Spread the last layer with jam and top it with filling and around the sides. If you run out of filling, whip up some left over cream and spread on the sides. Sprinkle the left over crumbs on the top layer and the sides. Place some toothpicks on the cake and wrap around 2 layers of foil, shiny side against the cake. Refrigerate for 24 hours. Take out for at least ½ hour before serving.

TWIGS

Krustai, Žagarėliai

Ingredients:

1 lb. (500 gm.) plain/all purpose flour with a pinch of salt
½ cup butter
6 egg yolks
2 whole eggs
2 tablespoons sugar
1 cup sour cream and 30 ml (1 oz.) rum
1 tsp. vanilla essence
icing sugar for dusting and oil for deep frying

Method for making *Krustai*:

Blend the egg yolks and 2 whole eggs with sugar until thick. Sift flour into eggs. Add sour cream, vanilla and rum. Mix well. Hit the dough with a rolling pin, folding dough inward, until the dough shows blisters. Let dough rest in the refrigerator for a couple of hours. Roll out the dough very thinly, then cut into strips, 10 cm/3 inches long and 2 cm/1 ½ inches wide. Cut a slit in the centre, and pull one end through the slit. Heat the oil in deep pot or a deep fryer. To keep the oil from foaming, add 2 pieces of raw potato. When the dough is placed into hot oil and rises to surface fast, this means that oil is at the right temperature. Fry until golden brown on both sides. Drain *krustai* on paper towels or brown paper and dust with icing sugar while still hot.

DONUTS

Spurgos

Ingredients:

2 lb. (1 kg.) plain/all purpose flour
2 cups milk
3 oz. (90 gm.) fresh yeast
8 egg yolks
1 cup sugar
30ml (1 oz.) rum
1 teaspoon salt
2 tsp. vanilla extract
2 tblsp. sugar
icing sugar for dusting and oil for deep frying & strawberry jam for the filling.

Method:

Make dough with warm milk and one third of the flour, add blended yeast with sugar, mixing well. Cover and let rise for ½ hour. Beat egg yolks with salt, add to risen dough, mixing well. Add the melted butter, rum, vanilla and remaining flour. Mix well. Knead dough until it loses its shine. Cover dough and let rise for 1 hour. Take walnut size pieces of dough and form round donuts, let rise. Heat oil, drop donuts and fry on both sides until golden brown, about 8 minutes for each side. Drain donuts on paper towels or brown paper, insert strawberry jam using a steel piping tube. Dust with icing sugar while still warm.

HONEY CAKE

Meduolis

Ingredients:

1 lb. (500 gm.) honey
1 lb. (500 gm.) plain/all purpose flour
3 eggs separated
1 cup sour cream
½ cup melted butter
½ cup sugar
1 tsp. baking soda
1 tblsp. ground cinnamon and 1 tblsp. ground cloves.

Method:

Pour the honey into a saucepan and cook gently on low heat for about 10 minutes, stirring all the time, then cool. In a separate bowl, cream the egg yolks with sugar and add to the honey, stirring well, then add the cinnamon and cloves. Mix baking soda into the sour cream and flour. Beat well. Melt butter gently and add it to the sour cream beaten with soda and flour. In another bowl, beat egg whites to stiff peaks. Mix all ingredients well and gently fold in the beaten egg whites. Pour the mixture into baking tin lined with baking paper. Bake cake in a preheated oven at 325F / 160C, for about 30 - 45 minutes. Cool cake in baking pan before turning out. Split in half and add whipped cream or just dust with icing/powdered sugar.

POPPY SEED CAKE

Aguonų Pyragas

Ingredients:

1 packet of active dry yeast
2 cups warm milk
8 cups plain/all-purpose flour
¾ cup sugar
1 tsp. salt
5 eggs
4 oz. (125gm) melted butter.

Filling

1lb. (500 gm.) poppy seeds ground in a spice or coffee grinder
1 cup sugar
6 oz. softened butter (approx. 187gm.)
1 cup hot milk & 1 grated lemon rind.

Method:

Grind the poppy seeds in a coffee bean/spice grinder, then combine all filling ingredients. Beat well and set aside. In a small heatproof bowl, dissolve yeast in ½ cup of the warm milk. In an electric mixer or a large bowl, combine flour, sugar, salt and eggs. Add remaining 1 ½ cups warm milk, butter and yeast mixture. With the paddle attachment, or by hand, beat until smooth. Dough will be sticky at this point. Scrape dough into a clean, greased bowl. Sprinkle the top with a little flour and cover. Let stand in a warm place for 1 hour or until double in size. Punch down dough and turn out onto a floured surface. Divide dough in half and shape each half into a rectangle. Spread half of the filling you made on each rectangle of dough and roll up like a sponge roll. Turn ends under so filling will not leak out.

Place the 2 rolls on a baking dish lined with baking paper, cover and let rise again until double in size.

Pre-heat oven to 350F / 180C. Brush tops of rolls with additional melted butter. Bake 45 to 60 minutes or until rolls are golden brown. Remove from oven and cool. Dust rolls with confectioners' sugar, if desired.

EASTER CAKE

Bapka

This is a yeast-free version of a *Babka* cake for those who have an intolerance to yeast.

Ingredients:

Margarine for greasing cake tin
3 tablespoons fine breadcrumbs
⅓ lb. (166 gm.) plain/all purpose flour
¼ lb (125 gm.) potato flour
2 teaspoons baking powder
½ lb (250 gm.) butter or margarine
½ lb. (250 gm.) icing/powdered sugar, sifted
1 teaspoon vanilla sugar
4 large eggs, separated
3 - 4 tablespoons sour cream
1 tablespoon almond extract
½ lemon, zested and juiced and 20 gm. raisins.

Method:

Grease a ring cake tin with margarine, then sprinkle evenly with the breadcrumbs and set aside. Preheat oven to 350F / 180 C.

Sift the plain flour and baking powder. Stir in the potato flour. Set aside.

In a big bowl, cream the butter till light and fluffy. Whisk in icing sugar, vanilla sugar, egg yolks, sour cream, almond extract, lemon zest and juice. Beat till combined. Add in the dry mixture and stir till well incorporated, then fold in the raisins.

In a clean bowl, beat the egg whites to stiff peaks. Gradually add the egg whites to the cake mixture, gently folding in till evenly incorporated. Spoon the mixture into the prepared tin.

Bake for 30 to 40 minutes, or until a skewer inserted in the centre of the cake comes out clean. Cool slightly before inverting the cake onto a serving plate, and dust with icing sugar if desired.

GYPSY CAKE

Čigonas

Ingredients:

2 lb. (1 kg.) equal parts dried fruit (prunes, apricots, figs, dates, raisins), all but the raisins are chopped into small pieces
½ cup light rum (optional)
5 large eggs, separated
1 cup sugar
2 tblsp. plain/all purpose flour, and 1 tblsp. cornstarch.

Method:

Place fruit in a large heatproof bowl and Cover with boiling water. Let sit 2 minutes and drain. Stir in rum, if using, and set aside to cool.

Heat oven to 325F/170C. Line the bottom of a 10-inch spring-form pan with baking paper and lightly spray it and the sides of pan with olive oil spray. In a large bowl, beat egg yolks with sugar until light and fluffy. Thoroughly mix in the fruit.

In a separate medium bowl, whip egg whites until stiff but not too dry. Stir ⅓ of the egg whites into the fruit mixture to lighten it. Then carefully fold in remaining ⅔ whites trying not to deflate them. In a small bowl, whisk together flour and cornstarch. Sift over the batter and fold it in carefully but thoroughly.

Pour mixture into prepared pan and bake 30 minutes to 1 hour, depending on your oven. Begin testing with a wooden skewer after 30 minutes. When ready, only a few crumbs will cling to the skewer. The cake should be golden and set. Do not overbake. Turn oven off and let cool completely in the oven with the door ajar. Dust with icing sugar before serving with whipped cream.

EASTER CREAM CHEESE DESSERT

Paska

Makes 12 serves. No baking needed.

Ingredients:

4 lb. (2 kg.) cottage cheese (farmer's cheese)
1½ lb. (750 gm.) unsalted butter
1 lb. (500 gm.) vanilla caster sugar (enclose vanilla pod with the sugar in tin for a few days before making)
6 eggs separated
1 lb. (500 gm.) raisins
¼ lb. (125 gm.) sultanas
¼ lb (125 gm.) chopped glacé cherries.
Extra glacé fruits and blanched almonds to decorate

Method:

Blend the cream cheese and butter in a food processor, transfer to a big bowl.

Pour vanilla sugar into a bowl. Separate the eggs and add the egg yolks to the vanilla sugar, beat until white. Stir in the raisins, sultanas and cherries. Add this to the cream cheese mixture, mixing all thoroughly together. Beat the egg whites to stiff peaks and fold into the mixture. Pour the mixture into a muslin bag or small pillowcase tied at the top and place into a big container like a clean flowerpot or a moulded dish with a hole, which will allow any surplus moisture to drain off. Place a heavy object on the top. Put into the fridge for 24 hours. Unmould and decorate with almonds and glace cherries. Serve with extra whipped cream.

MUSHROOM BISCUITS

Meduoliai Grybukai

Ingredients:

1 lb. (500 gm.) plain/all pupose flour
2 egg yolks
1 whole egg
3 tblsp. butter
1 cup honey
1 cup sugar
1 teaspoon baking soda
2 tablespoons sour cream
2 teaspoons seasonings.

Icing for Mushroom Biscuits

1 cup icing/powdered sugar
1 egg white
juice of ½ lemon
1 teaspoon cocoa powder.

Method:

Heat the sugar in a saucepan until it's dark brown. Make dough using all the other ingredients. The dough should be quite hard. Let it rest in a cool spot. Divide your dough in half. From one half, make the mushroom caps the size of a walnut, with an indentation on one side. Place the caps with the hole down on the baking tray lined with baking paper. Make the mushroom stems from other half of dough. Roll out pieces about 4 cm. (1¼ inches) long, the width of your index finger. Place them next to the caps and bake in a preheated oven at 325F / 170C, for about 25 - 30 minutes. To make the icing, beat the egg white with icing sugar and lemon juice. When the caps and stems are done, glue the stems into caps with some of the white icing. Ice the stems with the more of the white icing. Add cocoa powder to the remaining icing, mix well and then ice the mushroom caps. Place your iced mushrooms in a cool spot for the icing to dry completely

CHRISTMAS EVE BISCUITS

Kūčiukai

These biscuits are baked for Christmas Eve, when they are served as a dessert with poppy seed milk.

Ingredients:

1 lb. (500 gm.) plain/all purpose flour
1 cup milk
4 tablespoons vegetable oil
4 tsp. fresh yeast
2 tblsp. scalded poppy seeds
¼ cup sugar

Method:

Blend the yeast with sugar and dissolve in warm milk. Add half of the flour to the yeast and mix well. Dust the top of batter with flour, let rise in warm spot for 1 hour. Beat dough, add remaining flour, oil and scalded poppy seeds. Mix well and knead until your dough is not sticky, about 30 minutes. Let rise in a warm spot for 1 hour. Roll dough into 1cm (½ inch) thick rolls and cut into the same lengths. Place these pieces on a baking tray lined with baking paper and bake in a pre-heated oven at 350F / 180C, until golden brown.

MATRON OF HONOUR
WEDDING CAKE

Karvojus

Ingredients:

3 lb. (1.5 kg.) plain/all purpose flour
1½ cups milk
4 tablespoons fresh yeast
10 egg yolks
2 cups butter
2 cups sugar
3 cups raisins
3 teaspoons vanilla extract
a pinch of salt.

Icing

3 egg whites and 3 cups of icing sugar

Method:

Warm the milk and add the yeast blended with 1 cup sugar and ⅓ of the flour. Blend well and let it rise in a warm spot. Beat the egg yolks with the remaining sugar and vanilla until pale yellow and add to the risen yeast dough, blending well. Add the melted and cooled butter and the remaining flour and pinch of salt. Knead the dough until small blisters form. Add raisins, incorporating well into the dough. Cover the dough, set in a warm spot and let it rise for 1-2 hours. Take ¾ of the dough, form a round shape, and place on baking tray with baking paper. Let it rise. With the remaining dough, make a braid and place it around the round dough shape.

On the top, in the centre, make circles by pressing an oven proof glass or cookie cutter into your dough and stick as many wooden skewers as you can, into the top. Bake in a preheated oven at 400F / 200C, for about 1½ hours. When the cake is cool, remove the skewers and in their place you can insert ornamental birds or stars. You can decorate the cake with icing or dust the cake with icing sugar and just before serving, fill the remaining holes with stems of rue and other flowers.

TWISTED WEDDING CAKE

Vestuvinė Riestė

Ingredients:

1 kg. (2 lb.) flour
90 gm. (3 oz.) fresh yeast
1 cup milk
5 egg yolks
1½ cups sugar;1 ½ cups butter
2 cups raisins
2 teaspoons vanilla essence and a pinch of salt.
Icing
3 egg whites
3 cups icing sugar and the juice of 1 lemon

Method:

Warm the milk, add the yeast blended with ½ cup sugar. Mix well. Add ⅓ of the flour to the yeast and blend well, letting it rise in a warm spot. Beat the egg yolks with remaining sugar and vanilla until a pale yellow, then add to the yeast mixture, mixing well. Cool the melted butter a little then mix it into the yeast mixture. Add remaining flour and salt and knead until small blisters form. Add the raisins and mix into the dough. Cover dough, letting it rise in warm spot for 2 hours. Form a figure 8 with the dough, and place on a tray lined with baking paper. To keep the figure 8 during the next rising, insert 2 metal glasses or cups into the two figure 8 holes. Let the dough rise for ½ hour, then bake in a preheated oven at 350F / 180C, for about 1 hour. Remove metal cups or glasses. Cool on the tray, remove onto serving platter and spread the icing thickly on top. Decorate with fresh flowers, rue or berries. You can also place two bottles of wine, inside the figure eight, decorated with ribbons and flowers.

LATVIAN RYE BREAD DESSERT

Rupjmaizes Kārtojums

Ingredients:

10 slices of coarse, day old, rye bread, broken into small pieces
4 tblsp. sugar
1 tblsp. sugar
½ tsp. vanilla essence
1 container marscarpone cheese
3 tblsp. thick cream
1 jar of good quality raspberry jam.

Method:

Mix the rye bread pieces with sugar and cinnamon in a bowl. In a medium sized bowl, combine the marscarpone cheese and cream and mix till smooth. In a big glass bowl or parfait glasses, alternate layers of the bread mixture with the strawberry jam and marscarpone and cream mixture. Refrigerate until ready to serve.

DRINKS

LITHUANIAN BREAD BEER

Gira, Kvasas

Ingredients:

2.5 gallons (9.5 litres) cold water
1 lb. (500 gm.) of classic black, dark or rye bread
1 handful of raisins
4 cups of sugar
1.5 tblsp. dry yeast
3 large or 6 smaller plastic soft drink bottles with screw top lids

Instructions:

Allow 3 days for making this beer.

Fill a big soup pot with 2.5 gallons/9.5 litres of water (or divide it into 2-3 pots) and bring to boil.

Toast the bread slices **twice** on the darkest toaster setting outside your house or place on trays in an oven preheated to 200F / 100C and dry it out for about 1 hour. If you prefer a light colour beer, toast it once.

When water starts to boil, remove the pot from heat. Add a handful of raisins and the pieces of toasted bread to the pot. Chop into bits if necessary. Cover pot with the lid and let it stay overnight or at least 8 hours.

The next day, carefully remove toasted bread with a slotted spoon and discard it. You now have your beer mixture left. In a medium bowl, mix together 4 cups of sugar and 1.5 tblsp. of yeast, add them to the beer mixture and stir well. Cover with plastic wrap or lid and leave the mixture on a bench for another 6 hours, stirring every couple hours. Discard floating raisins by scooping them up with a large slotted spoon. Using a funnel with a strainer or a piece of cheese cloth/muslin over the top, pour the beer into bottles. Put on the lids, but not too tightly and leave the beer in the fridge overnight. You can drink the beer on the third day. The longer you leave it, the higher the alcohol content.

HONEY LIQUEUR

Krupnikas

Ingredients:

8 whole cloves
3 cinnamon sticks
10 cardamom pods, cracked
½ whole nutmeg, cracked
5 allspice berries
1½ tsp. black peppercorns
1 tsp. fennel seed
3 inch (7- 8 cm) piece of ginger root, cut into 4 pieces
2 inch (5 cm) piece of turmeric, cut into 4 pieces
1 orange peel
½ a lemon peel
1 vanilla bean, split and scraped
1½ lb. (750 gm.) honey
1 quart/litre water
750 ml Everclear or Spirytus grain alcohol, or vodka.

Method:

Crack cardamom and nutmeg. Boil them together with the other spices in the water in a big covered pot until the liquid reduces to about 2 cups. In another big saucepan, gently bring honey to boil, skim off any foam. Add the spices liquid to the honey. Remove pot from heat and place on a bench. Slowly pour the alcohol, making sure it is nowhere near a flame. Put the pot back on a very low heat. Heat gently for 15 mins. Cool the liqueur in the same pot overnight. The next day, pour the *krupnikas* into sterile glass bottles with a funnel and over a muslin cloth.

Seal and let the *krupnikas* settle for at least two weeks. Serve at room temperature.

CPSIA information can be obtained
at www.ICGtesting.com
Printed in the USA
BVHW042121291219
568071BV00017BA/366/P

9 780995 386808